PRAISE FOR DONALD TYSON

Necronomicon

"Tyson isn't the first writer to attempt a full 'translation' of the forbidden text, but his may be the most comprehensive."

—*Publishers Weekly*

"Descriptions of the lost city of R'lyeh, the ruins of Babylon, and other, stranger places blend with tales of monsters and demons, lies and truths. Occult nonfiction author Tyson remains true to Lovecraft's spirit in this tribute to a master of horror." —*Library Journal*

"Tyson sets about 'expositing the ways of the dead.'... Here, Lovecraft's skin-crawling nonexistent tome is lifted from the mists of fantasy and loathsomely fleshed out by Tyson, famed dealer in magic and spells and scribe of much nonfiction on magic and the occult... Scholarly horror, marvelously illustrated." —*Kirkus*

"This exhaustively researched volume reproduces and connects the details of the mythology originally created by the eldritch author."

—*Fangoria*

The Dream World of H. P. Lovecraft

"*The Dream World of H. P. Lovecraft* is a thought-provoking and intellectually stimulating book. Its fusion of sound biographical knowledge and critical insight makes it a must-read for Lovecraftians."

—S. T. Joshi, leading authority on H. P. Lovecraft

Familiar Spirits

"Clear, concise ritual instruction, comprehensive tables of correspondences, combined with fascinating historical research and ease of use." —Qetesh, Goat and Candle

"This is a serious book for serious practitioners only and is recommended." —*The Cauldron*, Wales

T0352346

"For the witch or magician interested in branching out, this book must reside on your formulas shelf." —SpiritQuill.com

"Donald Tyson has done a superb job in revealing his own method for calling forth familiar spirits. This book is wonderfully written... no secrets have been withheld. A fascinating tutorial."

—*The Beltane Papers*

THE DEMONOLOGY
OF KING JAMES I

ABOUT THE AUTHOR

Donald Tyson is a resident of Nova Scotia, Canada. After graduating university, he developed an interest in the tarot, which led him to study all branches of the Western esoteric tradition. His first book, *The New Magus*, was published in 1988. He has written about such varied subjects as the runes, crystal and mirror scrying, astral travel, spirit evocation, spirit familiars, the theory of magic, the Kabbalah, and the *Necronomicon*. He designed the popular *Necronomicon Tarot* card deck, illustrated by Anne Stokes, and is the inventor of rune dice. In his spare time he enjoys hiking, kayaking, and woodworking.

DONALD TYSON

THE DEMONOLOGY

OF KING JAMES I

Llewellyn Publications
Woodbury, Minnesota

The Demonology of King James I: Includes the Original Text of Daemonologie and News from Scotland © 2011 by Donald Tyson. All rights reserved. No part of this book may be used or reproduced in any manner whatsoever, including Internet usage, without written permission from Llewellyn Publications, except in the case of brief quotations embodied in critical articles and reviews.

First Edition
Eleventh Printing, 2024

Book design by Donna Burch
Cover art © Dover Publishing
Cover design by Kevin R. Brown
Editing by Tom Bilstad

For a complete list of illustration sources, see page 328.

Llewellyn is a registered trademark of Llewellyn Worldwide Ltd.

Library of Congress Cataloging-in-Publication Data
The Library of Congress has already cataloged an earlier printing under LCCN: 2011281484

Llewellyn Worldwide does not participate in, endorse, or have any authority or responsibility concerning private business transactions between our authors and the public.

All mail addressed to the author is forwarded but the publisher cannot, unless specifically instructed by the author, give out an address or phone number.

Any Internet references contained in this work are current at publication time, but the publisher cannot guarantee that a specific location will continue to be maintained. Please refer to the publisher's website for links to authors' websites and other sources.

Llewellyn Publications
A Division of Llewellyn Worldwide Ltd.
2143 Wooddale Drive
Woodbury, MN 55125-2989
www.llewellyn.com

Printed in the United States of America

OTHER BOOKS BY DONALD TYSON

The Messenger
(Llewellyn, January 1990)

Ritual Magic: What It Is & How To Do It
(Llewellyn, January 1992)

Three Books of Occult Philosophy
(Llewellyn, January 1992)

Scrying For Beginners
(Llewellyn, February 1997)

Enochian Magic for Beginners: The Original System of Angel Magic
(Llewellyn, September 2002)

Familiar Spirits: A Practical Guide for Witches & Magicians
(Llewellyn, January 2004)

The Power of the Word: The Secret Code of Creation
(Llewellyn, March 2004)

1-2-3 Tarot: Answers In An Instant
(Llewellyn, October 2004)

Necronomicon: The Wanderings of Alhazred
(Llewellyn, December 2004)

Alhazred: Author of the Necronomicon
(Llewellyn, July 2006)

Portable Magic: Tarot Is the Only Tool You Need
(Llewellyn, October 2006)

Soul Flight: Astral Projection and the Magical Universe
(Llewellyn, March 2007)

Grimoire of the Necronomicon
(Llewellyn, August 2008)

Runic Astrology
(Llewellyn, July 2009)

The Fourth Book of Occult Philosophy
(Llewellyn, November 2009)

The 13 Gates of the Necronomicon
(Llewellyn, July 2010)

CONTENTS

NEWS FROM SCOTLAND

ILLUSTRATION CAPTIONS

Figure 1: Original title page of *Daemonologie*, 1597, reproduced in the Bodley Head reprint. page xv

Figure 2: Turning the riddle, or sieve, from the *Opera omnia* of Cornelius Agrippa, sixteenth century. It is difficult to judge from the illustration, but it may be that the oracle was given when the sieve slipped down between the blades of the shears, causing it to rotate slightly. page 77

Figure 3: Knot magic was believed to be a favorite method of witches. A sorcerer stands on a headland and sells two sailors favorable winds bound up in three knots. In the background another ship has been driven into the rocks by adverse winds and has foundered. From Olaus Magnus' *Historia de gentibus septentrionalibus*, 1555. page 78

Figure 4: A complex magic circle from Reginald Scot's *Discoverie of Witchcraft*, 1584. Below it is the descriptive text: "This is the circle for the master to sit in, and his fellowe or fellowes, at the first calling, sit backe to backe, when he calleth the spirit; and for the fairies make this circle with chalke on the ground, as is said before." page 87

Figure 5: Four familiar demons perform tasks for witches. In the center, one sweeps out a stable; left, another digs for treasure with a pointed rod; top, a third draws four witches through the clouds in a wagon; right, the fourth creates a wind to propel a ship. From Olaus Magnus' *Historia de gentibus septentrionalibus*, 1555. page 93

Figure 6: Satan impresses his mark into the forehead of a young male witch, from Francesco Maria Guazzo's *Compendium Maleficarum*, 1626. page 113

Figure 7: Witches kiss the Devil's buttocks, from Francesco Maria Guazzo's *Compendium Maleficarum*, 1626. page 119

Figure 15: This is one of two woodcuts in the Bodley Head reprint of an early edition of *News From Scotland* that was not designed specifically for the work. It may have been included to suggest how the North Berwick witches were chastised with a rod before King James and the chief magistrate.   page 191

Figure 16: The initial of two woodcuts included in the first edition of *News From Scotland*, designed to illustrate the material in the text. In the Bodley Head reprint of a slightly different 1592 edition of the tract, this woodcut is reproduced twice—just after the title page, and again in the body of the work. Clockwise from the left, it depicts the Devil of the North Berwick witches preaching from an outdoor pulpit to an audience of female witches while John Fian sits at a table recording his words with pen and paper; a ship foundering in a storm at sea; four female witches brewing a potion in an iron kettle with a long-handled ladle, a peddler lying upon his side; and finally, the same peddler lying in a similar posture in a wine cellar in Bordeaux, France.   page 197

Figure 17: The second of two woodcuts made specifically for the first edition of *News From Scotland* depicts the activities of John Fian. Clockwise from the upper right, we see Fian attempting to remove the bewitchment from an amorous cow; Fian riding on an illuminated black horse behind a man clothed in a black cape and hat; the church at North Berwick; and a gallows. The cow refers to the story attributed to Fian that was borrowed from the *Golden Ass* of Appuleius. As for the illuminated horse, part of the charges read against Fian at his trial were that when he was riding past Tranent on horseback with another man in the middle of the night, he "by his devilish craft, raised up four candles upon the horse's two legs, and another candle upon the staff which the man had in his hand; and gave such light, as if it had been daylight; like as, the said candles returned with the said man, upon his homecoming; and caused him to fall dead at his entry within the house." The gallows, which appears to have been inserted into the woodcut, shows that the artist was an Englishman, since witches were burned in Scotland, not hanged.   page 200

Figure 18: This is the second of two woodcuts in the 1924 Bodley Head reprint of a 1592 edition of *News From Scotland* that was not created specifically for the tract. It is located at the end of the work, after the text, and appears to show a man being led to prison between a jailor with keys hanging at his waist and a nun who grasps the man by the ear.   page 203

Figure 19: Wedges are driven into the boots to shatter the bones in the shins and ankles of the unfortunate man being tortured. At the right, a standing inquisitor asks questions while one seated at a desk records the man's confession. Although this is not a particularly good illustration of the boots themselves, it does show the type that were used in Scotland during the North Berwick affair. A woodcut from the late sixteenth century.   page 218

Figure 20: Title page to the first edition of *News From Scotland*, published in 1592.   page 284

DAEMONOLO-
GIE, IN FORME
of a Dialogue,

Diuided into three Bookes.

EDINBVRGH

Printed by Robert Walde-graue

Printer to the Kings Majeſtie. An. 1597.

Cum Priuilegio Regis.

Figure 1

DEMONOLOGY,
In the Form
of a Dialogue,
Divided into Three Books.
Edinburgh
Printed by Robert Waldegrave
Printer to the King's Majesty, anno 1597.
With Royal Privlege.

INTRODUCTION
James and the Witches

THE ONCE AND FUTURE KING

James Stuart was born on June 19, 1566, at Edinburgh, from the union of Mary, Queen of Scots, with her second husband, Henry Stewart Lord Darnley. When his mother was forced to abdicate her throne by Queen Elizabeth, James was proclaimed King James the Sixth of Scotland on July 24, 1567. For the first twelve years of his life he was not permitted to participate in state affairs, but was kept for his own security in Sterling Castle, safe from the constantly bickering Scottish factions.

Physically he was weak and sickly, a misfortune of health that played a significant part in his tendency in later life to achieve his purposes by manipulation and deceit rather than the bold exercise of power. For the first six or seven years of his life he was unable to stand up or walk without aid. As a young man he developed a love for horseback riding, but it was necessary that he be tied on to his horse due to the weakness in his legs, and once when he fell into a body of water while out riding he nearly drowned because he was unable to help himself. Throughout his life he preferred to walk leaning on the shoulder of an attendant.

Weakness of body was in part compensated for by keenness of intellect. When Sir Henry Killigrew saw the boy in 1574 he was impressed by the skill of eight-year-old James in translating Latin and

French texts. From an early age he was trained by his guardians in the Protestant faith, and developed an aversion for Catholicism, although this did not prevent him from sending a letter to the pope in 1584, hinting that he might be persuaded to change his faith if it forwarded his political goals. James was always ready to imply friendship and favor, provided there was no actual necessity of ever giving them.

There seems little doubt that James was a coward. He fought against this tendency throughout his life, but it was his nature and he could never overcome it. In 1582 he was kidnapped by a faction of Scottish nobles during the Raid of Ruthven. Although he was then old enough to shave, he was so terrified of his captors that he cried like a child. Sir Thomas Lyon, one of the men keeping him hostage, gruffly told the young king it were better "bairns [children] should greet [cry] than bearded men." James parted from his captors in 1583 and began to rule his kingdom, but always remained timid. The Marquis de Fontenay, French ambassador to the Scottish court during the early part of his reign, spoke of James as cowed by the violence around him. When in 1587 his mother was executed by order of Elizabeth, he made little effort to prevent it.

His personal appearance and manners were not attractive. He had a tendency to bluster and make promises he had no intention of ever fulfilling. He talked too much in a very thick Scottish accent, and was pedantic and put on airs of scholarship that he did not merit. In dress he was slovenly and unclean. His physical caresses and frequent gifts to male favorites in his court gave rise to gossip that he was homosexual. All these tendencies were strongly despised by the English people when he ascended to the throne of England in 1603 at the death of Elizabeth, but they swallowed their distaste and welcomed him in a practical spirit, as the only alternative to bitter civil war.

In 1589 James married Anne, second daughter of Frederick the Second, king of Denmark. This union between the Protestant monarch and the Protestant princess greatly alarmed the Catholic factions in England and Scotland, who saw their hope for a restoration of the papacy slipping away. Until this marriage, James had done his best to maintain a cordial relationship with both the Vatican and the royal family of Spain, but this choice of a bride left no question about his religious leanings. Perhaps the only romantic and courageous action James ever took was to sail out to meet Anne after her ship was driven by storm into the port of Oslo in Norway. It was there that James enjoyed his first night of connubial bliss with his fifteen-year-old bride.

The trials of the North Berwick witches (who received this title because they were supposed to congregate in the kirk, or church, at North Berwick near Edinburgh in the dead of night to meet with the Devil and concoct their plots) took place mainly between the years 1590 and 1592, although the fallout of the affair dragged on for years. It marked a major turning point in the thinking of the young king. The charges against the accused included numerous attempts by magic on his life, and even one effort to kill the queen while she was on her voyage from Denmark to England. Previously James had only faced plots by the rebellious Scottish nobles that endangered his life by physical means, but now he found himself and his new bride threatened by the supernatural.

James keenly interested himself in the trials, and was a direct participant in much of the questioning. He mentioned in his Tolbooth speech of 1591 (see Appendix C) that the proceedings against the accused witches occupied him for a full nine months, and it would not be excessive to say that he was the prime mover in the whole affair. Undoubtedly he observed the torture of the accused, and heard the confessions wrung from their own agonized mouths. He was gratified to learn from Agnes Sampson that the Devil considered him to be his chief opponent, and it was for this reason that Satan hated him and wished to bring about his death. She testified that when the witches asked Satan why he hated the king so much, the Devil replied: "By reason the king is the greatest enemie hee hath in the world."

By this extraordinary statement the Devil cast James into the role of an avenging knight of the Christian faith. James was fond of making reference to the warrior mounted upon a white horse (Revelation 19:11–16) who is prophesied to descend to Earth to punish the wicked in the latter days, which James believed to already have arrived. As an intensely religious man, and as the leader of his nation in matters military, spiritual, and judicial, it would have been difficult for James to decline the role of Satan's chief adversary. He accepted it as a challenge and spent the better part of the next four decades trying to do it honor.

Since this mythic figure upon his white horse is so central to the view James held of his own crusade against witchcraft, it is worth quoting the relevant verses from the King James Bible version of the text:

> And I saw heaven opened, and behold a white horse; and he that sat upon him was called Faithful and True; and in righteousness he doth judge and make war.
>
> His eyes were as a flame of fire, and on his head were many crowns; and he had a name written that no man knew but he himself:
>
> And he was clothed with a vesture dipped in blood: and his name is called The Word of God.
>
> And the armies which were in heaven followed him upon white horses, clothed in fine linen, white and clean.
>
> And out of his mouth goeth a sharp sword, that with it he should smite the nations: and he shall rule them with a rod of iron: and he treadeth the winepress of the fierceness and wrath of Almighty God.

Can there be any doubt that James saw in the brave knight on the white horse with "many crowns" a reflection of himself? Or that the sharp sword that proceeds from his mouth was for James the book *Demonology* and the 1604 Witchcraft Statute of England? He viewed himself as a general in the army of Christ, "clothed in fine linen, white and clean." It must have struck James as significant, in light of this biblical passage, that the accused North Berwick witches sought to bring about his death by procuring a piece of linen that he had soiled, so as to use his bodily excretions in their magic against him.

James was a strong believer in the supernatural and the power of magic, but he ascribed all working of magic to the Devil. He did not recognize what Cornelius Agrippa called "natural magic," or what was sometimes termed "white magic," as a lawful activity. The efficacy of herbs and stones was either an inherent part of their composition, and so a matter of medicine and science, or it was infused into them by the power of Satan in order to deceive those who used them for healing or other purposes. For James, there was no such thing as occult forces that could be used for benevolent purposes. On the one hand there was the power of God, which had ceased to produce prophecies or miracles since the time of Christ, and on the other hand there was the power of Satan, which waxed stronger in the modern age than at any other time in history due to the imminence of the end of the world, and was responsible for all marvelous effects that were other than natural.

The supernatural must have terrified him at least as much as the political intimidations used by his Scottish nobles. In an effort to know his spiritual enemies as well as he knew his temporal foes, he made an extensive study of the available literature on the subjects of magic, witchcraft, and demons. It is tempting to assume that his reading was wider than it was deep. Summers wrote disparagingly about the degree of learning he displayed in his treatise on witchcraft: "In many passages King James has borrowed from the Continental demonologists, whom he read with more diligence than acumen. For all his zeal and dexterous learning one feels that there is something just a little superficial in his grasp of the more scholarly writers and theologians" (Summers, *Geography of Witchcraft*, page 224).

In the king's defense, he had been present during the actual questioning of the accused North Berwick witches, and had heard their testimony, so James' knowledge of the subject was not entirely theoretical, as was the knowledge of his critic Summers. In any case, James was hardly about to instruct his readers in the finer points of practical necromancy and witchcraft, regardless of how much theoretical knowledge he might himself possess. The purpose of his book, which arose as a direct visceral reaction to the North Berwick trials and the supposed plots against his life by magic, was to increase the persecution of witches in Scotland and England. Everything in the work is tailored to achieve this end.

Shortly after assuming the English throne in 1603, James ordered a new edition of his book published in London so that he could extend his crusade against witchcraft into England. A Dutch translation was published in 1604, and Latin editions came off the presses in Hanover in 1604 and 1607. A year after his coronation, James succeeded in getting the 1563 witchcraft statute that had been enforced during most of the long reign of Elizabeth abolished, and a new statute erected in its place that contains harsher and broader punishments for witches and practitioners of magic. So keen was James on this matter that his reinterpretation of the witchcraft laws went to the House of Lords for consideration only eight days after the first sitting of parliament of his reign as the English king, and passed on first reading.

The main difference between the law of Elizabeth and that of James concerned what should be the focus of the punishment. Under Elizabeth, those who practiced witchcraft and sorcery were subject to the most severe punishment only if they were found to have used these arts to commit murder or other injuries. It was the crimes in which witchcraft had been employed that were the primary object of punishment, not the practice of witchcraft itself, which was of secondary concern. James wanted the practice of any form of magic punished severely, regardless of whether it was used to commit injuries to others, because he held all such practice to be trafficking with the Devil, whom he believed to be the source of the efficacy for all magic.

Under the law of Elizabeth, anyone who bewitched another without causing his death was subject to a penalty of one year in prison; the law of James made the same crime punishable by hanging. Minor infractions, such as using divination to locate stolen property, making love potions, or damaging property such as laming a cow or causing hail to flatten a crop in the field were still punishable by a year in prison and a term in the pillory, as they had been under the old law. James caused it to become a felony to invoke any evil spirit, or to have any dealings with an evil spirit. This meant that to keep a familiar spirit in the form of a cat, dog, rabbit, or other pet was punishable by death. The Devil was thought to mark those with whom he made a pact. To be found to have a witch mark anywhere on the body was also enough evidence of consultation with an evil spirit to be punishable by death, hence the vigorous questioning by the courts about familiars, and the intensity of the search for the witch mark.

The statute of James made it a crime punishable by hanging to:

1) invoke, consult, covenant with, entertain, employ, feed, or reward any evil spirit for any purpose

2) take any dead body, or any part of a dead body, for use in any witchcraft, sorcery, charm, or enchantment

3) practice any form of witchcraft, enchantment, charm, or sorcery in which any person is killed, destroyed, wasted, consumed, pined, or lamed in the body, or any part of the body

4) aid, abet, or counsel others in any of the above acts

The statute also made it a crime punishable by one year in prison to use witchcraft, enchantment, charms, or sorcery to:

1) locate any treasure of gold or silver in the earth or other hiding places

2) locate any lost or stolen goods or things

3) intend to provoke any person to unlawful love

4) destroy, waste, or impair any chattel or goods of another person

5) attempt without success to hurt or destroy any person in the body

All of the offences punishable by a year in prison on the first offence were felonies on the second commission, and punishable by hanging.

On the matter of capital punishment for witchcraft, in England it was hanging, the same as for other more common felonies such as murder. In Scotland, witchcraft was punished by burning, but the custom was to strangle the condemned witch at the stake before lighting the fire, and in this way to lessen the suffering of the witch. This was done as an act of mercy when the witch confessed to her supposed crimes, and did not recant the confession once the torture used to extract the confession had been halted. If the witch retracted the confession, the mercy of strangulation might be withdrawn and she might be burned alive, though this barbarity was uncommon.

In practice, the English courts carried on much as they had before the passage of the witch statute of James in meting out the death penalty. It was usually only given to those who had been convicted of causing the death of another person with witchcraft or necromancy. For example, even though it was a capital offence under the new law to dig up a corpse for use in magic, no one was ever put to death for this crime. There were exceptions. In 1645 seven women were hanged at Chelmsford for entertaining evil spirits, which is to say, for keeping familiars. What the law did accomplish was the more frequent and vigorous prosecution of accusations of witchcraft in

England, and later in America. The Salem witch trials were carried out under the statute of James, which was not abolished until 1736.

During the early part of his reign as English monarch, James was as rabid in his prosecution of witchcraft as he had been while living in Scotland, but as the years passed, his fervor began to wane. He was able to prove to his satisfaction that several of those who had accused others of witchcraft had been lying.

In 1605 James paid three hundred pounds to the Reverend Samuel Harsnett to question a fourteen-year-old girl, Anne Gunter, who had accused three woman in Abingdon of witchcraft. The girl admitted under the sharp questioning of Harsnett that she had only been pretending to fall into fits, and had falsely accused the women.

While traveling north in 1618, James stopped at Leicester when six women were due to be hanged as witches on the evidence of a twelve-year-old boy, John Smith, who claimed that his convulsions were caused by their bewitchment of him. Nine other women had already been executed on the lad's testimony. James examined the boy and determined to his satisfaction that his fits were nothing but fraud. The women were freed, and Chief Justice Sir Edward Coke, who had presided over their trial, was disgraced.

In 1621 James questioned yet another youthful accuser, a girl of the town of Westham in Essex (now a part of greater London) named Katherine Malpas, who pretended to be subject to fits of demonic possession, and accused two women of bewitching her. Since James had personally witnessed cases of possession, he was difficult to fool. A woman was made to confess that she had taught the girl to simulate the fits so that she could charge money of those who came to watch her convulsions.

This and similar evidence of deception both enraged James and shook his confidence in his beliefs. It is asserted by some historians that James went so far in his later years as to completely repudiate the reality of witchcraft. Robbins quoted Thomas Fuller as asserting in his *Church History of Britain* that James "grew first diffident of, and then flatly to deny, the workings of witches and devils as but falsehoods and delusions" (Robbins, *Encyclopedia of Witchcraft and Demonology*, page 279). This seems unlikely in view of the strength of these convictions, particularly since the intensity of his religious faith never wavered. Whether his own attitude changed or not, during his last nine years as king it is recorded that only five convicted witches were executed.

Viewed as a whole, the prosecution of witches under his rule, though more vigorous than it had been during the reign of Elizabeth, was not so severe as might appear from the tenor of his book and his statute. Montague Summers observed that there are only fifty cases of witches having been executed in England during the entire reign of King James. Summers wrote: "It would appear that the popular ideas concerning the holocausts in the reign of James the I are anything but historically exact, and instead of shuddering at the large numbers who perished, we may well be surprised that the executions in England were so few" (*Geography of Witchcraft*, page 132).

Only fifty executions in England, yet many more women were tried, and even those who did not suffer imprisonment as a result of a guilty verdict had to face the humiliation of having their bodies shaved of all hair and a search made of their private parts for the witch mark, the censure and condemnation of their family, friends, and neighbors, and worst of all the protracted ordeal of torture used on them in an effort to extract a confession. It is probable that the number of executions would have been much higher had James been able to freely work his will during the early part of his reign, but his personal crusade against witchcraft was in part inhibited by the conservative nature of English common law, which is slow to change its way of doing things, and perhaps also by the common sense of many of the judges.

One more incident must be related of James before we leave his life and proceed to a closer examination of the North Berwick affair.

Margaret Murray related in *God of the Witches* that as James lay on his deathbed, an attempt was made in his bedchamber by his attendants to lessen his pain by transferring it into the body of an animal. A young pig was for this purpose dressed in the clothing of a human baby. One of the ladies of the court played the part of its mother, and the Duchess of Buckingham assumed the role of midwife. A gentleman who was dressed in the robes of a bishop read the service of baptism, while the Duke of Buckingham and other nobles played the part of the pig's godfathers. The pig was baptized, and then chased out of the room.

It may be assumed that James was in a very bad state at that point, perhaps not even conscious of his surroundings. Yet if he did retain any of his mental faculties, what must he have thought of the performance of what was clearly a blasphemous ritual of witchcraft for his personal benefit? Was he inwardly horrified by what his concerned attendants were doing in their effort to lessen his suffering, or was he hypocritical enough to justify it in some way in his own mind, even though it was opposed to everything he had ever written or said concerning witchcraft? History has not recorded his last thoughts, only the incredible irony of the performance of a magic ritual over the deathbed of a man who all his life was steadfast in his loathing and rejection of anything remotely connected with the art of magic.

THE NORTH BERWICK WITCHES

The incidents that formed the basis for the North Berwick witch trials, which are partially detailed in the tract *News From Scotland*, may have been instigated, insofar as they have any factual basis, by the determination of James to wed Anne of Denmark. Among the charges against the witches is that they tried to sink the ship carrying James to Denmark to meet with his future bride, and also the ship bringing Anne to England. Two of the items filed against John Fian, one of the supposed leaders of the plot, read as follows:

(7) ITEM, for the raising of winds at the King's passing to Denmark, and for the sending of a letter to Marian Linkup in Leith, to that effect, bidding her to meet him and the rest on the sea within five days; where Satan delivering a cat out of his hand to Robert Grierson, and gave the word to "Cast the same in the sea, *hola!*" And thereafter, being mounted in a ship and drunk like unto others, where Satan said, "You shall sink the ship;" like as they thought that did.

(8) ITEM, for assembling himself with Satan, at the King's returning from Denmark, where Satan promised to raise a mist, and cast the King's Majesty in England: and for performing thereof, he took a thing like to a soot-ball, which appeared to the said John like a wisp, and cast the same in the sea; which caused a vapor and a reek to rise.

A charge against Agnes Sampson accused her of sending a letter to another witch ordering her to "warne the rest of the sisteris, to raise the wind this day, att eleavin houris, to stay the Quenis cuming in Scotland."

At the same time that women and men were being accused in Scotland of trying to prevent the union of James and Anne, similar accusations were being made in Denmark. The spy of Lord Burghley in Copenhagen wrote to him in a letter dated July 23, 1590, that the admiral Peter Munk in Denmark "hathe caused five or six witches to be taken in Coupnahaven, upon suspicion that by their witchecraft they had staied the Queen of Scottes voiage into Scotland, and sought to have staied likewise the King's retorne." A woman named Anna Koldings was interrogated, and under the fear of greater tortures was compelled to give the names of five other women, one of them being the wife of the burgomaster of Copenhagen. Eventually all were induced to confess to raising a storm to sink Anne's ship, and of having sent demons to climb the keel of the vessel and pull it under the waves.

It is a curious coincidence that the same storm that held back Queen Anne from initially sailing to Scotland also sank a ferry traveling between Burntisland and Leith with Lady Mary Melville of Garvock aboard. Burntisland is just west of Kinghorn on the opposite side of the Firth of Forth from Edinburgh. Lady Mary was the wife of Sir Andrew Melville, the master of the household affairs of King James, and was traveling to meet Anne upon her arrival in Scotland. Concerning this tragedy of September, 1589, Sir James Melville wrote in his *Memoirs*, "She, being willing to mak diligence, wald not stay for the storm, to sail the ferry; when the vehement storm drave a ship upon the said boat, and drownit the gentlewoman and all the persons except twa."

Why this sudden furor to prevent the king from bringing his new bride back to Scotland? Margaret Murray, Montague Summers, and others have speculated that the purported attempts by the accused witches to kill James and Anne were motivated by the royal ambitions of Francis Stewart, the Earl of Bothwell. His title descended through his mother Jane Hepburn, who was the sister of the former Earl of Bothwell that had married Mary, Queen of Scots, but his claim to the throne was from his father, Lord John Stewart, the illegitimate son of James the Fifth of Scotland. For so long as James remained without an heir, Bothwell could make a plausible claim for the Scottish crown at his death, but once James married and had children, that claim was void.

There is some evidence to support this theory of Bothwell's involvement with the North Berwick witches. In her confession, Agnes Sampson revealed that she had constructed a wax image of James, saying: "This is King James the sext, ordonit to be consumed at the instance of a noble man Francis Erle Bodowell." Murray and Summers both believed that Bothwell played the part of the Devil at the sabbat meetings of the witches, and it is true that in later years during his exile in Italy, Bothwell kept the reputation of being a powerful magician.

This fanciful theory depends on a rather startling presupposition—that prior to the exposure of the plots of the witches, Bothwell was the active head of a large coven of witches accustomed to meet at the North Berwick Kirk and elsewhere in the dead of night, where he dressed up in costume and played the part of Satan. If such nocturnal meetings took place, they must have been executed with a mastery of stealth and guile since this considerable undertaking of manpower and resources passed unnoticed in the small, closely knit communities near the church, where the members of the coven lived.

James despised Bothwell for his pretensions to the succession. In a speech to the Scottish parliament in 1592 he denounced Bothwell and said of him that he was "but a bastard and could claim no title to the crown" (Margaret Murray, *Witch-cult in Western Europe*, page 56). Murray pointed out that this was not accurate—Bothwell's father was a bastard, but Bothwell himself had been born of a legal marriage; and in any case, Bothwell's father had been granted a letter of legitimacy by Mary, Queen of Scots.

Though he felt contempt for this upstart, James was deathly afraid of him. When Bothwell came to Holyrood Castle in July of 1593 seeking a pardon from the king for the crimes he stood accused of, he was admitted directly and without warning into the king's bedchamber by a lady of the court, where he caught James in the middle of dressing. The terrified James tried to run and hide in his wife's bedchamber, but the men who accompanied Bothwell blocked his path of escape and locked the door to prevent him from leaving before Bothwell had his say. James asked them their purpose: "Came they to seek his life? Let them take it—they would not get his soul" (Murray, *Witch-cult in Western Europe*, page 59). If James considered Bothwell as the leader of the witches who conspired to bring about his death and a powerful necromancer in league with Satan against him, little wonder the sudden apparition of Bothwell in his bedchamber gave James a nasty turn.

The whole business of the North Berwick witches started innocently enough with the uncanny healing abilities of a maidservant named Gilly Duncan. Although she had never been a healer before, she began to go to those who were sick or infirm to try to help them. Her neighbors took notice of this admirable charity when her efforts suddenly began to succeed with astonishing frequency. Rather than praise Duncan for her good works and count themselves fortunate to know her, they began to murmur behind her back that she must be accomplishing the miraculous cures with means that were other than natural.

Duncan had the misfortune to work for David Seaton, the deputy-bailiff of the town. He decided to question his maid as to where she had acquired the skill to work such amazing cures, and why she was in the habit lately of stealing out of his house to sleep elsewhere every other night. It is impossible not to speculate about the personal motives that prompted Seaton to question Duncan. Did he have some affection for her that was not returned, and did he take this excuse to ferret out information about his imagined rival? Or was Seaton upset with her because he thought her night wanderings were bringing scandal upon his household?

Whatever his original suspicions, her stubborn silence enraged him. He had her held down and applied a set of thumbscrews to her fingers in an effort to compel her to speak. When she still did not answer to his satisfaction, he bound her head and wrung it with a rope, a popular form of torture in the sixteenth century. Duncan still refused to say what Seaton wanted her to say, so he decided to probe her for a witch mark, which was considered to be a sure sign of a witch. A witch mark is a small mole or other skin blemish insensitive to pain that is supposedly impressed on to the body of a witch at the time of her initiation into the craft by Satan himself. The way of locating it was to take a long, thick needle and thrust it deeply and successively into all moles, scars, or other marks on the skin, presumably with the unfortunate individual blindfolded, until one was located that did not produce a shriek of pain. He found what he was looking for in the front of her throat, and this apparent evidence broke her will and induced her to confess that she was a witch, and that all her cures had been the work of Satan.

Duncan was cast into prison, where she shortly began to name the names of her supposed accomplices in witchcraft. They were not all of low station in life. Agnes Sampson, the key figure among the women accused who was known locally as the Wise Wife of Nether-Keith, was a mature, educated woman said to be grave in her manner and settled in her answers to her inquisitors. Effie Mc-Calyan was the daughter of Lord Cliftonhall, and a woman of some social stature. John Fian was a schoolmaster. Barbara Napier was described as a woman of good family. These four appear to have been the leaders in the affair, or at least were nominated as its leaders by James and the magistrates, and were not in a position to decline the elevation.

As more individuals were implicated and questioned, two threads emerged. One was the standard fantastic tale of malicious acts of magic worked at the behest of the Devil against ordinary townsfolk in the region around Edinburgh. The other was the plot to assassinate James and his wife. It is impossible to know how much truth is contained in either thread of the confessions. Although the interrogations of the accused have provided boundless matter for speculation, it will probably never be definitively proven either that there was any witchcraft going on or that there was ever a witch plot to kill James. Since the confessions were extracted under torture, or threat of torture, not a word of them can be trusted.

It may be useful to gain some notion of how local was the affair of the North Berwick witches. Most of the communities involved were on the same side of the Firth of Forth as Edinburgh and were within walking distance of each other. The town of Tranent where the unfortunate Gilly Duncan was tortured by her master was about eight or nine miles from Edinburgh. Leith was only a mile or two away. Saltpans, where John Fian taught school, also sometimes called Saltpreston, was where Prestonpans is today, and some five or six miles from the city. The notorious North Berwick Kirk occupied a headland around twenty miles from Edinburgh. All these places are on the southern shore of the Firth of Forth. Kinghorn and Burntisland, from where the ferryboat sailed that was supposed to have been sunk by the witches, with a loss of sixty lives, are both located opposite Leith across the Firth. The whole affair might be said to have occurred in the backyard of the king, which may be one reason he took so active an interest.

The heart of the testimony concerned a sabbat meeting that took place in 1590 on Halloween at around midnight at the North Berwick Kirk. Here the witches, drunk and merry after riding down the Firth on their sieves and dancing on the green outside the church to the sound of a Jew's harp played by Gilly Duncan, entered the church to convene with the Devil, who stood in the pulpit dressed in a black hat and black gown, surrounded by burning black candles. In Melville's *Memoirs* he is described as terrible in appearance, with a nose like the beak of an eagle, great burning eyes, hairy hands and legs, with claws upon his hands and feet like those of a griffon.

In a low voice the Devil called the roll, naming each witch by his or her witch name, with the exception of one named Robert Grierson, who was quite annoyed when the Devil addressed him by his real name, since it had been agreed that they use only nicknames, his being "Rob the Rower." The Devil asked the witches what evil they had worked in his name, and after hearing their deeds, they discussed their efforts to bewitch a wax image of King James to bring about his death. The Devil instructed them to dig up four corpses, two outside the church in the graveyard and two that had been buried inside the building in vaults. From the corpses they removed the joints of the fingers, toes, and knees, and divided the parts up between them. The Devil told them to let the joints dry, then powder them and use the powder in works of evil magic. At one point during the evening they all kissed the Devil's bared buttocks as a homage to him. His skin was described as being cold and as hard as iron.

The account of this Halloween meeting, contained in the somewhat disordered confessions of the accused, has provided the prototype for countless subsequent descriptions of the witches' sabbat. Many of its elements are mentioned in earlier confessions of those accused of witchcraft in different European nations, but the North Berwick Kirk sabbat is perhaps the most complete and well-rounded of the descriptions.

The judicial proceedings began in 1590 and extended for three years to the trial of the Earl of Bothwell in August 1593. There is some evidence that they dragged on even longer than this. In all some seventy persons were implicated. Margaret Murray wrote that thirty-nine persons were involved in the affair, a number she perceived as significant because it is three times thirteen, and thirteen is sometimes supposed to be the number of members in a witch coven. Murray also wrote that only four were ever tried (*Witch-cult in Western Europe*, page 50). Neither of these numbers is accurate. There were various gradations of involvement. Not all those accused were arrested, and not all those arrested were convicted. The exact numbers of persons arrested in the affair remain unknown, but the initial round of arrests took place in the months of November and December in 1590, and the trials began in 1591.

The execution of justice was capricious. A few of the accused fled to England, and the king instructed the same David Seaton who had started the whole affair to follow after them and recapture them. At least one woman was identified and imprisoned in England, causing James to go to great lengths to have her extradited to Scotland, where she was tortured and gave the names of more supposed accomplices. John Fian also escaped for a brief time, and tried to hide himself near his home in Saltpans, but was recaptured and was executed on Castle Hill in Edinburgh in January 1591, after the most terrible tortures that James could conceive to use upon him.

Fian was killed in the usual way, by strangulation at the stake, immediately before his body was burned. John Grierson, who had his name spoken aloud at the Halloween sabbat, died in prison. Agnes Sampson, who undoubtedly was a witch in the more conventional sense of one who predicts the future and makes magic charms, was strangled and then burned to ashes on Castle Hill.

Barbara Napier may or may not have been a witch, but she certainly led a charmed life. When her stake was prepared for her execution on May 11, 1591, and the townspeople had assembled to watch her be strangled and burned, her friends made the claim that she was pregnant, and her execution was delayed until this could be demonstrated to be either true or false. Her jury had refused to find her guilty of treason against the king, on grounds of insufficient evidence, which enraged James and led him to declare her verdict an "assize of error." He called for a new trial against her, and started legal proceedings against the jury members themselves. His strident address to the jury has been preserved, and is known as his Tolbooth speech, because it occurred at the Tolbooth building in Edinburgh where the law courts were located (see Appendix C). There is no record of Barbara Napier ever having been executed, so it may be that after the elapse of time the wrath of the king cooled, or her friends were able to provide reasons for him to mitigate his persecution of this woman.

When Effie McCalyan discovered that her six lawyers were no help in her defense, she also tried the pregnancy ploy, but with less success than Barbara Napier. McCalyan was due to be burned alive on June 19, 1591, but when she declared that she was with child, her execution was delayed. She could not have been very convincing, since she was executed on June 25, only a week after making her plea. There may have been a last-minute mitigation in the severity of her punishment, since contemporary records show that McCalyan was not burned alive, but was strangled first in the usual manner for executing witches. Just before being strangled, McCalyan made a statement to the spectators declaring that she was innocent of all the crimes charged against her.

There can be little doubt, in view of the persecution of Bothwell by James, that the king firmly believed Bothwell to be the leader in the North Berwick affair. On April 17, 1591, Bothwell confronted the king and his council and demanded to know what James intended to charge him with. Robert Bowes wrote of the meeting to Lord Burghley, "The King answered, with practice to have taken his life. Bothwell asked if he would lay any other matter than that only. The King said it sufficed, and willed him to clear himself thereof." In May of 1591 the king began to actively work to have Bothwell tried for witchcraft and high treason. On May 9, Bothwell was held in Edinburgh Castle for "conspyringe the King's death by sorcerye." On June 25 a proclamation was issued against Bothwell accusing him of "consultatioun with nygromancris, witcheis, and utheris wickit and ungodlie prsonis, bayth without and within this cuntre for bereving of his Hienes lyff."

The king was unable to muster enough support to have Bothwell, who was a powerful man, put on trial, so he sent Bothwell out of Scotland. In June he wrote to John Maitland: "Sen theire can na present tryall be hadd of the Erl Bothuell, I thinke best he praepaire him self to depairt uithin threttie or fourtie dayes, his absence to be na neirairhande nor Germanie or Italie." His fear of Bothwell's power of magic probably played a part in this decision, although it may also have had political motives.

In the spring of 1592 Bothwell sent a letter to the ministry defending himself against the rumors and charges gathering over his head like a thundercloud, but the king was not to be denied. The next year, in August, Bothwell was finally tried. Most of the evidence against him came from the accusations of a minor courtier and would-be necromancer named Richard Graham. When the defense was able to demonstrate that Graham had never accused Bothwell of anything until after threatened with torture and execution for witchcraft, and that he was promised his release and continuing protection if he spoke against his master, Graham's testimony was discredited. This, coupled with the testimony of many accused of witchcraft in the North Berwick affair that they knew nothing of Bothwell other than his reputation as a man of noble character, procured Bothwell's acquittal.

The North Berwick affair exerted a profound influence in shaping laws against witchcraft, and the attitudes of the general population of Scotland, England, and New England toward witches and magic, for more than a century. Its influence was not finally lifted until the repeal of the witch statute of James in 1736. It is impossible to understand the character of James the First without knowing how deeply shaken he was by the supposed magical plots on his life at the time of his marriage. His reaction to the alleged statement by the Devil in the North Berwick church that James was his greatest foe was to cast himself into the role of the white knight of God who dispensed the wrath of heaven against the wicked, using as his weapon the power of the word.

SEPARATING TRUTH FROM FICTION

Although it is not possible to know with any exactitude how much of the testimony extracted under torture, or threat of torture, from those accused in the North Berwick affair was true and how much a mere fabrication to forestall further suffering, there is enough information available to construct a plausible scenario explaining the principal motives and main events surrounding the trials.

In 1589 James married Anne of Denmark by proxy. Hence when she sailed to Scotland she was already queen, though the marriage had not been consummated. On the way the Danish fleet encountered a terrible storm that sprang a plank on Anne's own ship, so that it began to take on water. The Danish admiral guiding Anne to her new home, Peter Munk, put in at Oslo, Norway, for repairs. This was the same storm that sank the ferryboat carrying Lady Mary

Melville across the Firth of Forth from Burntisland to Leith to meet with the Queen and present her with jewels and other gifts.

James must have regarded this storm with suspicion even as he made the impetuous decision to sail to Oslo and remain with his new bride over the winter. His voyage was uneventful, and his wedding night successful, but Peter Munk, a superstitious man who had already in his own mind attributed the storm to the malicious magic of witches in Denmark, must have filled the imagination of James with frightening conjectures. He and Anne would have ample opportunity to discuss the prevalence of witchcraft in her homeland on the long and snowy nights that James spent in Denmark with his wife. James himself may have been instrumental in initiating the great witchhunt that took place in Copenhagen in the summer of 1590, although by that time he was back in Edinburgh with Anne.

Their return voyage was hindered by the same sort of unnatural weather that had prevented Anne's initial coming into Scotland. Even though the ships that accompanied James and Anne sailed as a fleet, his ship was the only one that encountered contrary winds. They also ran into dense fog, but with the help of the English navy, they were safely guided into port without tragedy. Whatever suspicions had been aroused in the mind of the King by the first storm, and by the superstitious opinions of Admiral Munk, were confirmed by this foul wind and treacherous mist. Magic was afoot, and was being worked against him specifically to prevent his union with Anne.

Who would have a reason to want him to remain without a wife? Someone who desired that he should not engender a child and successor. It would not have taken James long to narrow the list of candidates. Among the nobility of Scotland, no one held him in lower regard than the heroic warrior of the Border Marches, Francis, Earl of Bothwell. James viewed Bothwell with contempt because of his dubious birth and lack of refinement and learning. He probably also envied Bothwell for his courage. Bothwell, for his part, regarded

James as a sniveling cleric with pretensions of scholarship and an arrogant air of superiority that was unfounded on any virtue in his nature. The two men truly despised each other. It is quite possible that Bothwell had a reputation as a necromancer, whether merited or not, and this would only have served to confirm the suspicions of James.

These suspicions might never have born fruit had not the deputy-bailiff of Tranent, David Seaton, decided to torture his maid about her nocturnal disappearances and her suddenly acquired skill as a healer. It is significant that among those first named by Gilly Duncan in her confession was Agnes Sampson, the renowned midwife and healer known as the Wise Wife of Nether-Keith. Sampson was indeed a witch. This is persuasively indicated by the content of the numerous accusations made against her. However, she was not a witch by the definition of James, who believed that all witches had made a pact with Satan to work evil, and who met with the Devil periodically for carnal unions. She was, as her rustic title indicates, a wise woman, one who employed spoken prayers and natural materials for use in midwifery, healing, divination, and such relatively innocuous activities as the manufacture and sale of love charms.

It is not unreasonable to speculate that Gilly Duncan's sudden skill in healing had been acquired through her friendship with Agnes Sampson. Perhaps on some of the nights Duncan spent away from the residence of her master, she was studying the art of witchcraft from the elder Sampson. She must have been a gifted pupil, to judge by her success in healing her neighbors, but it was inevitable that the appearance of this gift, where none had been noticed to exist before, should give rise to rumors and gossip about her doings at night.

If Gilly Duncan was an apprentice to magic, Agnes Sampson was its mistress. She was the first of the accused in the North Berwick affair to be extensively questioned, and the list of accusations against her is longer and more varied than against any other. The accusations also differ in quality. The majority of the crimes Sampson was charged with involved healing the sick or divining information of a harmless or personal nature on behalf of her clients. These charges have an air of plausibility that is lacking in the wild charges that concern conventions with the Devil and sailing over the sea in sieves. Sampson was a professional witch. She made her living not only as a midwife but as a healer and prognosticator. The testimony surrounding her activities shows that she was a shrewd judge of human nature, able to play upon the superstitions and fears of her clients to force them to pay their bills and to increase the fame of her powers of witchcraft.

James became interested in the Sampson interrogation late in 1590. We can only speculate about what may have attracted his attention to the case. Probably Sampson was asked if she had been responsible for the storms that hindered the union between the King and Queen, which must still have been a topic of conversation only a few months after the second storm. By this point, Sampson's will had been broken. The humiliation of having her entire body shaved and probed with a sharp instrument more like a dagger than a pin, the probing having been concentrated in her genitals and other secret places of the body, must have overwhelmed her natural dignity. Coupled with the ordeal of the witches' bridle she was made to wear to prevent her uttering charms, and the deprival of her sleep, these indignities rendered her willing to say anything at all in the hope of shortening her ordeal.

Sampson was a clever woman and vain about her abilities. When at one point James jumped up in fury and declared that she was a liar, Sampson took him aside and convinced him of her power by telling him secret matters he had whispered to his wife on their wedding night in Oslo. James was astounded, and from then onward had no doubt as to the guilt of the accused. What Sampson did was nothing that would have been beyond the ability of any competent fortuneteller adept in the art of reading facial expressions, and who knew how to present information acquired long ago through ordinary channels as occult revelations. It is even possible that she did indeed possess some degree of psychic ability. Why she did it is obvious—as long as the King thought she was lying, he would continue to have her tortured. Once he believed that she was telling the truth, the torture would stop.

Much of the underlying structure of the events attributed to the accused in the North Berwick affair was supplied by Agnes Sampson, who as a true witch was able to provide details about magic practices, such as the use of joints, or knucklebones, from corpses, and the casting into the sea of a cat to cause a storm. She probably had not employed either of these methods herself, but she would have had knowledge of them. James, having read deeply in the works of the Continental demonologists such as Weyer and the occult writers such as Agrippa, was perfectly capable of supplying any material that was lacking that concerned the association and allegiance of the accused to the Devil.

The confession of Agnes Sampson was the evidence James had been looking for that the storm that had almost taken the life of his wife, and the contrary wind that had delayed his voyage home, were the work of the Devil. As God's anointed upon the Earth, and as the living embodiment of the brave knight of Revelation, mounted upon the white horse, robed in white linen stained with the blood of the wicked, wearing many crowns, who used as his weapon the power of the word, James saw it as not only his duty, but his destiny, to confront Satan and triumph over him. That is why he involved himself personally in the interrogations and tortures of the accused. When he suggested to Sampson that her magic was directed against him, she was eager to agree as a way of stopping her torture.

As Agnes Sampson continued to name names, and more suspected witches were questioned, at some point the focus moved beyond the small rural region around Saltpans and Tranent and enlarged to embrace Edinburgh. In the beginning only those of lower social standing were implicated. However, Sampson in her capacity of midwife and healer had moved in higher circles, and had become acquainted with those of wealth and title. That she ever knew Bothwell is doubtful, but she testified that Bothwell had asked her to divine how long James should reign, and what would happen after his death; and that he had induced her to send her familiar spirit to kill the king, but that it had failed.

One of those arrested of higher social standing was Barbara Napier, a personal friend of the Earl of Bothwell. She wrote to him in April 1591, telling him to stand fast, that his enemies were conspiring against him, so it is clear that Napier was asked leading questions about his involvement in the affair, though she refused to implicate Bothwell. The letter came open during transit, and was read by many, and its contents found their way back to the King, who was left in no doubt concerning a connection between the accused witches and Bothwell.

Near the end of 1590 a courtier of limited importance named Richard Graham was taken into custody. Graham practiced some form of magic, though it would be the height of charity to call him a necromancer. Bothwell had felt sorry for the man, because Graham had been excommunicated, and had given him shelter. Bothwell only saw him a few times. He testified at his trial in 1593 that once, in an attempt to impress him, Graham had shown him "a sticke with nickes in yt all wrapped about with longe haire eyther of a man or a woman, and said yt was an enchanted stick." This may have been a rune staff, and the nicks carved into its sides may have been runes, though it is impossible to know either the details of the stick's appearance or its intended function. Another time Graham tried to sell Bothwell a ring with a familiar spirit inside it. Bothwell paid scant attention to Graham, his stick, or his ring. Graham simply was not important enough to occupy the attention of the Earl.

When he was taken in the North Berwick affair, having been implicated by the confession of those already arrested, Graham was confronted with a simple choice. He could accuse Bothwell of being the leader of the witches, and the instigator of their magical attacks against the King, whereupon he would be released and given physical protection for the rest of his life—which he would need, since Bothwell had a great many friends—or Graham could remain silent and suffer unimaginably agonizing tortures until his execution on Castle Hill. At Bothwell's trial several defense witnesses testified that Graham had told them "tht he must eyther accuse the Erle Bothwell falselye, or els endure such tormentes as no man were able to abyde." Graham's own brother testified that Graham had "protested to him that he was forced to accuse the Erle Bothwell for feare of maymynge with the bootes and other tortures."

It is easy to see why Bothwell was acquitted. Yet these testimonies had no effect on James, who continued to believe that Bothwell was his enemy, had tried to murder him numerous times by magic, and was a great necromancer. James was convinced that the more vigorously he persecuted those he viewed as the servants of the Devil, the less power the Devil would have to harm him or anything that was his. This included not only his wife and household but the entire nation of Scotland. By using the utmost severity against the accused witches, James was defending his realm against the power of Satan.

John Fian, who figures so prominently in the tract *News From Scotland*, seems to have had very little to do with anything. There is no plausible evidence that he knew magic, or had ever practiced magic. He was simply an easy target, a well-known young man who through his work as a teacher came into contact with a large number of local people, and through his strong sexual appetites had carnal knowledge of a great many women, some of whom were married. In the sixteenth century anyone who could read and write, and who had much to do with books written in Latin or Greek, was apt to be suspected by the uneducated people around him of possessing forbidden knowledge.

The only two accused in the affair who can be demonstrated to have had both knowledge and practice of magic are Agnes Sampson and Richard Graham. Sampson's magic, though extensive, was confined mostly to good works. The testimony that she used her arts to cause harm and death, having been extracted by torture, is worthless. Graham was a dabbler trying to impress his betters with his arcane knowledge. Gilly Duncan and Bothwell may or may not have had some slight acquaintance with magic. In my opinion, no significant evidence exists to show that there ever was a plot to kill King James, or that there was any form of organized witchcraft in the North Berwick area. The only devil in the affair wore the crown of Scotland.

DESCRIPTION OF THE CONTENTS
OF *DEMONOLOGY*

Demonology is in the form of a dialogue between two men, Philomathes and Epistemon. They meet and begin to talk about the "strange news" that is the only subject of conversation lately, the doings of witches. Philomathes is a bit skeptical about the reality of witches and witchcraft, but Epistemon, who is obviously the alter ego of King James himself, uses his powers of logical argument and his depth of learning to convince his friend that witchcraft does exist, and that every form it takes is a serious crime because all witchcraft involves dealings with the Devil. Many of his examples are drawn from the Bible.

In Book One of the work, after arguing that there is indeed such a thing as witchcraft, and that its practice is sin, Philomathes divides the arts of magic into two branches, one that he calls magic or necromancy, and the other sorcery or witchcraft. Magicians or necromancers are those who are allured to this sin by a curiosity after obscure and deep learning; sorcerers or witches are motivated by either a thirst for revenge against others or a desire for gain. Epistemon ultimately rejects what he calls the vulgar distinction between these two types of occult practices, although there is much to be said for the brevity and clarity of the popular definitions: "Surely, the difference the vulgar put between them is very merry, and in a manner true; for they say, that the witches are servants only, and slaves to the Devil; but the necromancers are his masters and commanders."

Epistemon divides the occult arts into what he terms the Devil's school and the Devil's rudiments. The first is the study of the magicians and necromancers, who are often men of great learning. It involves complex circles, conjurations, numerous types of spiritual beings, and divine words of power. The second, the rudiments, is the study of the unlearned sorcerers and witches, and involves the manipulation of common words, herbs, and stones for the making of what Epistemon terms "unlawful charms" that operate without natural causes.

Philomathes, the skeptic, objects that many of the practices that fall under these definitions have always been regarded as lawful and harmless, such as the practice of astrology. Epistemon divides astrology proper into two branches, the observation of the natural effects of the heavenly bodies on the seasons and the weather, which he regards as not strictly unlawful when used in moderation, and the use of such observations to foretell the future, which is always unlawful in his opinion, even though such practices are widely condoned. From this unlawful type of astrology spring many other pernicious forms of divination, such as palm reading and numerology, all of which he condemns on the grounds that foretelling the future by the planets and stars is forbidden in the Bible.

The study of necromancy is said not in itself to be an offense, although it is perilous, but the use of magic circles and conjurations is always unlawful, in the opinion of Epistemon, since no one can be a student in a school without being subject to the master of that school, and the master of the school of magic is the Devil. Although the magician may start out using magic circles and words of power to bind the Devil and his servants, Epistemon asserts that he quickly moves toward the making of a pact with Satan. Philomathes is a bit skeptical as to why a magician should give up the circles and other aspects of his art that allow him to rule and control demons, and instead voluntarily subject himself to the Devil's authority by means of a contract. The answer of Epistemon seems a bit weak on this point. He asserts that the conjuration of spirits by means of a magic circle is long and arduous, and that if the magician has omitted or spoiled even one detail in the process, he will immediately be seized by the Devil and carried away to hell, whereas if he enters into a pact with Satan, he can summon familiar spirits easily and safely to do his bidding for the term of the contract.

The two enter into a discussion of what the pact with the Devil entails, and what benefits it provides, and of the different types of fallen angels. Epistemon denies that there are elemental spirits on the grounds that the fallen angels did not fall by gradations of weight, to be differentiated into the various elemental layers, but fell all together according to their nature, and wander the world as God's hangmen, ready to execute his wrath upon the wicked. He also denies the complex hierarchies of fallen spirits such as are printed in the grimoires, on the grounds that the order of heaven was broken when these angels fell into hell; and in any case, we cannot know what their hellish hierarchies may be because God would not permit this information to be conveyed by demons. The Devil is not to be trusted. Some of his revelations are true, the better to beguile humanity, but the rest are false.

Concerning the black pact itself, Epistemon states that it is either written out in the magician's own blood or is signified by a mark which the Devil makes somewhere on the body of the magician. Unlike the witch's mark, the magician's mark is not necessarily visible.

Philomathes asks why it is that whereas witches are universally condemned and persecuted, many states not only allow magicians to live untroubled, but rejoice in demonstrations of their skill. He offers two possible justifications: first, that it is the long-held custom, and second, that Moses was himself a magician. Epistemon counters with the argument that an evil custom should never be considered a good law. As to Moses working magic, he doubts that was ever the case, but suggests that if Moses did study or even practice the magic of Egypt, he did so before he was called upon by God. He asserts that magicians should be punished with exactly the same severity as witches.

In Book Two of the work, Philomathes raises three objections to the existence of witchcraft. The first, which has a bearing on the language of the King James version of the Bible, is that many scholars believe that the references to magic in the Bible refer to magicians and necromancers only, not to witches. The second is that those who believe themselves to practice witchcraft are mentally ill and self-deluded. The third objection is that if witches really possessed all the powers that are claimed for them, there would be no godly person left alive on the face of the Earth.

Epistemon agrees that many referred to in the Bible who used magic were necromancers and magicians, but asserts that others were witches, according to the vulgar definition of a witch being one controlled or ruled by the Devil. As to the objection that witches are afflicted with melancholy madness, he argues that they exhibit none of the symptoms of melancholy. The answer to the third objection is that the Devil himself is bridled by God in the amount of harm he can work, so naturally his chosen instruments are similarly limited.

Epistemon defines the term "sorcery," that it signifies the casting of a lot, and divides sorcerers into two types according to their station in life. The rich are motivated to practice sorcery by a desire for revenge against others, while the poor practice it in the hope that it will lead to the acquisition of money or goods.

The Devil comes to the sorcerer or witch while they brood in solitude, either as a disembodied voice or in the form of a man, and he asks them what is troubling them. Then the Devil offers to remove all their difficulties if they follow his advice and do all he requires of them. So much for the first meeting. At the second encounter the Devil persuades the candidate to pledge service to him, then reveals himself to the witch, compels the witch to renounce God, and gives the witch a mark on some hidden part of the body where it will not be easily noticed. The mark remains unhealed and extremely painful until the time of the third meeting, when the Devil heals it as a demonstration of his power. Forever thereafter it remains completely insensible to pain. At the third meeting the Devil also begins to teach the new witch the art of witchcraft.

Philomathes inquires what are the practices of the witch, and Epistemon divides them into two classes: actions pertaining to themselves, and actions pertaining to others. The first consists mainly of meeting in groups to worship Satan. The main form of adoration involves kissing the Devil on the buttocks. Epistemon lists some of the supposed powers of witches employed in getting to these meetings, such as flying through the air, making themselves invisible, transforming into small beasts so that they can find their way through the smallest crack into a sealed house, and causing their souls to leave their bodies while they lie in a trance.

Flying, Epistemon believes, is possible when the Devil carries the witch, but the agency of a great wind could not be used for a longer time than the witches could hold their breath, or they would suffocate. Invisibility is also possible in his view, by the Devil thickening the air to conceal the witch from sight. He offers the opinion that the transformation of witches into small animals to pass through tiny cracks is implausible, but says the Devil can simulate the appearance of this change. He also rejects the concept of the soul leaving the body, since surely this only occurs after death, and it is not in the Devil's power to restore the dead to life.

Philomathes asks what the actions of witches are directed against others. Epistemon answers that witches first gather in churches, and at these gatherings propose their intended evil doings to the Devil, who approves them and also instructs the witches on the methods. His friend interrupts him, asking why there are twenty female witches for every male witch. Epistemon's response is the stock answer of the demonologists—women are inherently weaker than men, and ever since the Serpent deceived Eve, he has been more at home tricking women than men.

The ways of witches for working evil are examined by Epistemon. They are pictures of wax or clay bearing the name of the intended victim that are roasted over a fire, occult poisons that receive their active virtues from the Devil, spells that cause love or hate, the spreading of diseases, the raising of tempests, the inducing of madness, the causing of spirits to haunt persons or houses, and the causing of individuals to become possessed.

Philomathes wonders whether God would permit such misfortunes to befall men and women who believe in him, and Epistemon assures him that witches can afflict both the godly and the wicked. Is it ever lawful to seek out a witch for a cure to a disease that has been caused by witchcraft? Never lawful, Epistemon assures his friend; the only lawful remedy is prayer.

If all men are subject to the evil effects of witchcraft, Philomathes asks how any man can be brave enough to punish them. His friend rather stiffly replies that we should not refrain from virtue merely because the way may be perilous; and in any case, no one is more protected against witchcraft than those who zealously prosecute witches. The magistrate who sits in judgment over a witch is protected from her malice in proportion to the degree of his severity toward her—the more lenient he is, the more he is in danger. On the contrary, if the magistrate applies the just laws of God in a rigorous way to the examination and punishment of witches, God will protect him.

In response to the question, does the Devil visit witches while they languish in prisons, Epistemon says that Satan only visits the unrepentant witch, in order to give false hope, but he never comes to the witch who has repented and rejected him. When he does visit a prison, the Devil comes to apprentice witches in the form they previously agreed that he would adopt when coming to them, but to master witches he comes in any form he pleases or deems best for his purposes, which he can easily do since his body is composed of air.

How can he be felt by witches if his body is of air, Philomathes wonders. Epistemon admits that there is not much on this matter contained in the confessions of witches, but he believes it is done either by the Devil animating and possessing a corpse, or by deluding the witches' sense of touch. As to whether others can see the Devil when he comes to witches in prison, Epistemon says sometimes yes, sometimes no. The talk shifts to why spirits and ghosts were commonly seen when Scotland was Catholic, but are very rare now that it is Protestant; yet at the same time, witches were rare in past times, but are now become common. Epistemon puts it down to the gross ignorance of the papists, which caused God to punish them with night terrors, whereas in the present the error is one of arrogance, punished by God with an abounding of witchcraft.

Book Three opens with a consideration of the four main sorts of spirits: spirits that haunt houses or deserted places, spirits that follow and trouble individuals, spirits that enter into and possess individuals, and the spirits commonly known as fairies. Yet all these four types are really only one type, asserts Epistemon, who take on various shapes and perform various offices to more efficiently plague mankind.

Epistemon explains that the first type received different names from the ancients depending on their works. Those that haunted houses were called *lemures*, or specters, but if they appeared in the form of a dead man to his friends, they were termed "shades of the dead." They haunt deserted places rather than large gatherings because God will not permit the Devil to dishonor the societies of

Christians, and besides, men are more apt to be frightened in lonely places. When they haunt an inhabited house, it is a sure sign that those who live there are ignorant of God's laws, or are wicked.

Philomathes wants to know how such a spirit can enter a house the doors and windows of which are sealed. Epistemon is not entirely convincing in his answer. If the spirit possesses the body of a dead person, it can easily open a door or window without any great noise, he says, but does not explain how the spirit bypasses locks or bolts. Philomathes wonders if God would allow a spirit to desecrate a body. It is no desecration, says Epistemon, because the soul is absent. The Devil can as easily cause the disinterment for his purposes of the body of a godly man as one who is ungodly. What is the best way to banish a spirit from a house? Two ways, says Epistemon, prayer to God and the amending of a life of sin.

In response to Philomathes' query about the spirits that appear to impersonate the newly dead to his friends, Epistemon says they are called "wraiths" in English, and were very common among the pagan nations, where they were believed to be good spirits sent to forewarn them of the death of their friend or teach them the way of his end, but all this was only the deception of the Devil. What about werewolves, asks Philomathes. Are they not a form of this kind of spirit? His learned friend agrees that this was the opinion of the Greeks, but for his own part, he believes them nothing more than men afflicted with a melancholy humor that has unhinged their reason and made them run wild.

The next two types of spirits are those who either trouble men by following them or by possessing their bodies. This only happens to those of the worst sort who are guilty of serious offenses, as a punishment of God; or to the best sort of persons, as a test of their faith. Why should the Devil bother doing God's work for him in this way, Philomathes wonders, and his friend replies that the Devil has two goals: the lives and the souls of those he persecutes in this manner.

Considering the spirits that follow after men, Philomathes observes that there are two sorts, those who trouble the individuals they associate with, and another kind that does them good service and warns them against future dangers. He asks whether the second sort are what is known as guardian angels. Epistemon retorts that the pagan belief that everyone has a good angel and an evil angel is a gross error, but that in Christian times the Devil attempts the same sort of fiction by sending spirits that are known as brownies into houses to do necessary work, in order to make the inhabitants believe that they are good spirits. But what possible reason could the Devil, who is only interested in doing evil, have for sending spirits to do good? Is it not reason enough, demands Epistemon, to deceive the ignorant into believing the Devil to be their friend?

Another type of following spirit is treated, those called incubi or succubi, who have sex with women or men. Philomathes wants to know if they exist, and if there is any difference of sex among spirits. Epistemon replies that this sort of spirit operates either by stealing the sperm of dead men and injecting it into women, which caused many nuns to be burnt, or else by animating a corpse. Either way, the sperm used by the Devil is always icy cold. Epistemon denies that spirits have any inherent sexual differentiation, since the division of the sexes is confined to living things, or that such spirits can engender monsters. The seed of a dead man cannot impregnate, being also dead, and if the seed of a living man is stolen and used, overlooking for the moment the fact that it would cool down and become infertile in transit, the child engendered will be normal, since the seed is normal. However, the Devil can make a woman who is not pregnant get a swollen belly, and appear to be pregnant, and on such occasions the midwife may pretend that she has given birth to something monstrous.

Philomathes raises the interesting question as to why incubi and succubi are more common in northern lands, such as Lapland, Finland, or the islands of Orkney and Shetland. His learned friend sets this down to the greater ignorance of their populations. Do any give their willing consent to the lovemaking of this class of following spirit? Some witches do, Epistemon admits, and they are to be punished and detested, but as for those women who suffer this indignity unwillingly, they are only to be pitied and prayed for.

Philomathes wonders if what is called "the mare" is this type of sexual spirit, but he is answered that the mare is only a kind of natural sickness caused by thick phlegm lying over the heart, and giving the impression that a weight is holding the body down while at the same time sapping the body of its strength to move.

Two matters interest Philomathes concerning the class of possessing spirits: how can the possessed be distinguished from the insane, and how can the priests of the Catholic church, being heretics, cast these spirits out? There are various ways to tell a person possessed from one who is insane, Epistemon tells him. The possessed fear the cross and the name of God, have unnatural strength and agility, and have the power to speak in languages they never learned, which they do in a hollow voice that seems to emanate from the breast rather than the mouth. As for how the priests can cure the possessed, usually the cure is not permanent but only temporary, and when it is permanent, as it sometimes is, the cure proceeds not from any virtue of the priests but from the virtue of Christ, when the priests follow his instructions for exorcism, which are fasting, prayer, and that the action be done in his name.

Progressing to the last class of spirits, the fairies, Epistemon declares that stories about them were much more common under the papists, but that for his part, he does not believe in their existence, except on occasions when they are mere deceptions of the Devil. Philomathes objects that many men have gone to their deaths swearing that they were transported by the fairies into a hill, where they met the fairy queen and received from her a magic stone that they were able to produce in evidence. His friend responds that in the same way the Devil can make men believe that their soul can leave their body, so can he deceive them into thinking they have visited fairyland while they lie senseless in a trance, and can convey a common stone into their hand. And when they see those they know among the fairies, and take this for an omen of the imminent deaths of those persons, it is only another trick of the Devil.

Philomathes wonders if fairies only appear to witches, or can appear to others also? To both, says Epistemon. They come to others either to frighten them or to impersonate a cleaner sort of spirit than they really are, but to witches they serve as a way of persuading gullible magistrates that they ought to be punished with less severity. The first group should be pitied, but those who use these spirits for divination deserve an even more severe punishment than the average witch, because they are less honest.

The two discuss briefly the question of the multitude of names of spirits. Epistemon dismisses this as just another knavery of the Devil, used for the purpose of deception.

As they approach the end of their conversation, they consider the matter of suitable punishment for magicians and witches. Epistemon states flatly that they should be put to death. In what way, he is asked. Commonly it is done by fire, but any form of execution accepted by the laws of the nation will serve as well. Should any sex, age, or rank be exempted from this punishment? None at all, says Epistemon. Not even children, asks Philomathes. Yes, but only because they are not yet capable of reason. All the rest, those who consult, or trust in, or turn a blind eye to, or entertain, or incite to magic are just as guilty as those who practice it, and should be put to death. May the prince or chief magistrate spare the life of one guilty of witchcraft? He may delay the punishment, says Epistemon, if he has good reason for doing so, but must not shirk to apply it in the end.

Philomathes observes that judges ought to beware condemning any unless they are sure the accused is guilty, and his friend agrees that no one should be condemned on the testimony of only one man of poor reputation. How much weight is to be given to the multiple confessions of the guilty in finding against the accused? Epistemon gives his opinion that since in cases of treason defamed persons may act as witnesses, their testimony should also be sufficient in cases of witchcraft, which is treason against God; for who but witches can prove the doings of witches?

What if witches accuse others of having been present at their imaginary conventions, while their physical bodies lie in trance, Philomathes wants to know. In the view of Epistemon, such persons are not a hair the less guilty, since the Devil would never dare to borrow their image to place at the witches' convention without their consent. And consent in these matters is death under the law. Thinking to score debating points with his learned friend, Philomathes quickly answers, then Samuel must have been a witch, since the Devil borrowed his shape to appear before Saul. But his friend is ready for this argument—Samuel was already dead at the time and for this reason could not be slandered by the Devil. God never permits innocent persons to be slandered in this way, says Epistemon, and as proof of this, those who are carried away by the fairies never see the shade of anyone in the fairy court who is not involved in some way with witchcraft. Indeed, those whom witches accuse, even when witchcraft cannot be actually proved against them, always turn out to be of evil life and reputation.

There are two methods for determining a witch, according to Epistemon. One is to find the witch mark and test that it is insensitive to pain. The other is the floating of the accused person on the water. Those who have renounced the sacred water of baptism and refused its benefits are themselves rejected by water, which will not receive them into its depths; indeed, they cannot even shed tears no matter how much you threaten or torture them, despite the fact that women cry dissembling tears like crocodiles at the lightest of occasions.

The two friends, having exhausted their topic, say goodbye to each other. Philomathes offers the hope with his final words that God will purge Scotland of the scourge of witchcraft, which was never before so common as it is now. Epistemon offers his last snippet of erudition by observing that the reasons for it are manifest. On the one hand, the great wickedness of the people has procured this punishment of God; while on the other hand, the approaching end of the world causes Satan to be all the more anxious to work as much evil as he can before his power is ended. And so ends the discourse.

NOTE ON THE ORIGINAL TEXTS

This new edition of *Demonology* by James the Sixth of Scotland, who would later go on to become James the First of England, is designed to make this historically important book on witchcraft and magic fully accessible to the modern reader. The original text was penned during the late Elizabethan Age. Its spelling is archaic, and its paragraphing and sentence construction irrational, rendering a complete comprehension of the material an ordeal. Understanding is further inhibited by the many obsolete Scottish terms that pepper the book. These terms would not have been immediately familiar even to educated individuals in the south of England in the same decade in which the work was written, and to the average reader of today they are incomprehensible.

While modernizing the work, I endeavored wherever possible to retain the words and prose structure used by James. Where it was necessary to substitute a modern equivalent in place of an archaic Scottish word, I tried to not only find the closest synonym but the word that best preserved the sound and connotation of the original. Biblical references that appear as abbreviated marginal glosses in the original have been expanded and inserted into the body of the text in parentheses. In the few instances where words have been interjected into the text to clarify its meaning, they are enclosed in square brackets. Those who wish to compare the modernized version with the original, or who need the original text for purposes of reference or quotation, will find it in Appendix A.

Once the difficulty in comprehending the text itself is surmounted, there is still the problem of the numerous obscure references to magic and witchcraft made by James throughout the work. The explanatory notes that appear at the end of each chapter will help the reader to understand not only what James wrote but what he meant. Woodcuts from the late sixteenth and early seventeenth centuries have been inserted were applicable to further clarify topics mentioned by James.

The modernized text of *Demonology* is based on the 1924 Bodley Head reprint of the original 1597 edition of the work. The Bodley Head reprint also contains the full text of a 1592 edition of the tract *News From Scotland* and reproductions of its woodcuts. The title pages of the original editions of *Demonology* and *News From Scotland* included with the present work, along with the woodcut illustrations of *News From Scotland*, were derived from the Bodley Head edition.

News From Scotland has long accompanied *Demonology*, and for good reason. The events it details were the impulse that triggered the lifelong battle waged by James against witchcraft, and inspired him to write *Demonology*. James regarded witchcraft as a personal threat because he believed that his death had been plotted by the accused men and women involved in the New Berwick witch affair, described in the tract. He looked upon Satan as a personal foe. In the testimonies of these supposed witches, spoken in the presence of the King, the Devil was reported to have identified James as his greatest enemy.

The authorship of *News From Scotland* is not know, but it may have been based on an account of the North Berwick affair written by James Carmichael, the Minister of Haddington. Sir James Melville recorded in his *Memoirs* that Carmichael had written "the history whereof, with their whole depositions." The work itself was written in England rather than Scotland, to judge by the language and other internal evidence. William Wright, the publisher, is unlikely to have been the author, but probably edited the work extensively. Although 1591 appears on the title pages of early editions, that date refers to the execution of John Fian. The work has been dated at 1592, though the document upon which it was based was probably written in the latter half of 1591.

Copies of the first edition are extremely rare—only a handful survive. Two other editions, also undated, were published shortly after the first printing of the work, probably in 1592, with slight variations in the format of the title page. The original contained two woodcuts. One of the other early editions duplicated the first of these illustrations at the start of the work. The 1924 Bodley Head reprint was based on this edition with the duplicate woodcut, and contains two other woodcuts that obviously were not created for the work itself but were added for decorative purposes. The early editions are in black letter, except for the section To the Reader and the concluding section, which are in Roman typeface.

News From Scotland is here treated as a natural companion to *Demonology*. Its text has been similarly modernized, and its matter illuminated by a complete set of notes that provide information about the larger context of the North Berwick witch trials not covered in the tract. The original text appears in Appendix B for purposes of comparison with the modernized version and quotation.

Appendix C is occupied by a modernized version of the full text of the infamous witch act, or witchcraft statute, of 1604, passed by the English parliament shortly after the ascension of James to the throne of England. Also in this appendix is a modernized version of the Tolbooth Speech, which James uttered in 1591 after overturning the acquittal by an Edinburgh jury of one of the accused witches he believed had plotted to kill him with magic. Both documents convey very clearly the attitude of the king toward witchcraft and its legal prosecution.

Modernization of the texts, coupled with the explanatory notes, introductory essay, and additional period illustrations, make these unique documents of the witch persecutions in Scotland fully accessible to all readers, especially to modern Wiccans and pagans, for whom the doings during the reigns of James are not mere historical abstractions but matters of direct interest and concern.

THE PREFACE
to the Reader

The fearful abounding at this time, in this country, of these detestable slaves of the Devil, the witches or enchanters, has moved me (beloved reader) to dispatch in the post, this following treatise of mine, not in any way (as I protest) to serve for a show of my learning and ingenuity, but only (moved by conscience) to press thereby, so far as I can, to resolve the doubting hearts of many both that such assaults of Satan are most certainly practiced, and that the instruments thereof merit most severely to be punished, against the damnable opinions of two principally in our age. Whereof, the one called Scot,[1] an Englishman, is not ashamed in public print to deny that there can be such a thing as witchcraft, and so maintains the old error of the Sadducees in denying spirits. The other called Wierus,[2] a German physician, sets out a public apology for all these craftsfolk,[3] whereby, procuring for their impunity, he plainly betrays himself to have been one of that profession.

And to make this treatise more pleasant and easy, I have put it in the form of a dialogue, which I have divided into three books: the first speaking of magic in general and necromancy in particular, the second of sorcery and witchcraft,[4] the third containing a discourse of all these kinds of spirits and specters that appear and trouble persons, together with a conclusion of the whole work.

My intention in this labor is only to prove two things, as I have already said: the one, that such devilish arts have been and are; the other, what exact trial and severe punishment they merit. And therefore I reason what kind of things are possible to be performed in these arts, and by what natural causes they may be: not that I touch every particular thing of the Devil's power, for they are infinite, but only, to speak scholastically (since this cannot be spoken in our language), I reason upon *genus*, leaving *species* and *differentia* to be comprehended therein.[5]

As, for example, speaking of the power of magicians in the first book, sixth chapter, I say that they can suddenly cause to be brought unto them all kinds of dainty dishes by their familiar spirit, since as a thief he delights to steal, and as a spirit he can subtly and suddenly enough transport the same. Now, under this *genus* may be comprehended all particulars, depending thereupon, such as bringing wine out of a wall (as we have heard of to have been practiced) and such things, which particulars are sufficiently proved by reasons of the general. And similarly, in the second book of witchcraft in particular, the fifth chapter, I say and prove by diverse arguments that witches can, by the power of their Master, cure or cast on diseases. Now, by these same reasons that prove their power by the Devil of diseases in general, is as well proved their power in particular, as of weakening the nature of some men to make them unable for women,[6] and making it to abound in others more than the ordinary course of nature would permit, and such like in all other particular sicknesses.

But one thing I will pray you to observe in all these places where I reason upon the Devil's power, which is the different ends and scopes that God as the first cause, and the Devil as his instrument and second cause, shoots at in all these actions of the Devil (as God's hangman): for where the Devil's intention in them is ever to kill either the soul or the body, or both of them, that he is so permitted to deal with, God by the contrary draws ever out of that evil, glory to himself, either by the wreck of the wicked in his justice, or by the trial of the patient and amendment of the faithful, being wakened up with that rod of correction.

Having thus declared to you then, my full intention in this treatise, you will easily excuse, I doubt not, as well my omitting to declare the whole particular rites and secrets of these unlawful arts, and also their infinite and wonderful practices, as being neither of them pertinent to my purpose, the reason whereof is given in the latter part of the first chapter of the third book.

He who likes to be curious of these things may read, if he will hear of their practices, Bodin's *Demonomania*,[7] collected with greater diligence than written with judgement, together with their confessions, that have been at this time apprehended. If he would know what has been the opinion of the ancients concerning their power, he shall see it well described by Hyperius[8] and Hemmingius,[9] two late German writers, besides innumerable other modern theologians that write at length upon that subject. And if he would know what are the particular rites and curiosities of these black arts (which is both unnecessary and perilous), he will find it in the *Fourth Book*[10] of Cornelius Agrippa, and in Wierus who spoke of it. And so, wishing my pains in this treatise (beloved reader) to be effectual in arming all those that read the same against these above mentioned errors, and recommending my good will to your friendly acceptance, I bid you hearty farewell.

James, Regent

NOTES ON THE PREFACE

Note 1: Reginald Scot, author of *The Discoverie of Witchcraft*, a work first published in 1584. Scot provoked the ire of King James not only because he dared in his book to reveal details of the lore of magic, such as the names and offices of demons, but also because he maintained that those accused of witchcraft were deluded and incapable of committing the crimes of which they stood accused. After James became king of England, he ordered all copies of Scot's book gathered up and burned. Examining the work, it is easy to see what troubled James so greatly. For example, Scot wrote:

> I am also well assured, that if all the old women in the world were witches; and all the priests, conjurers: we should not have a drop of raine, nor a blast of wind the more or the lesse for them. For the Lord hath bound the waters in the clouds, and hath set bounds about the waters, untill the daie and night come to an end: yea it is God that raiseth the winds and stilleth them: and he saith to the raine and snowe; Be upon the earth, and it falleth. The wind of the Lord, and not the wind of witches, shall destroie the treasures of their plesant vessels, and drie up the fountaines, saith Oseas. Let us also learne and confesse with the Prophet David, that we our selves are the causes of our afflictions; and not exclaime upon witches, when we should call upon God for mercie. (Scot, *Discoverie of Witchcraft*, page 2)

Note 2: Johann Weyer, author of *De praestigiis daemonum*, first published in 1563. Weyer, whose last name is sometimes spelled "Wierus," annoyed James in a number of ways—by revealing practical details of ceremonial magic, by defending the reputation of his teacher Cornelius Agrippa, who was widely regarded as a sorcerer, and by denying the powers of witchcraft, as shown by his quotation from the *Decretum* of Gratian:

> This very phenomenon is confirmed by the *Decretum*: "Certain silly women who are devoted to Satan and who have been seduced by demonic illusions believe that they also commit other unspeakable deeds, such as tearing young children away from their mother's milk and roasting and eating them, or entering into homes through chimneys and windows and disturbing the inhabitants in various ways. But all of these things and others like them happen to them only in fantasy. Indeed, when the woman makes a small ditch and pours urine or water into it, and thinks that by moving a finger she is stirring up a storm, the demon acts in collusion with her, disturbing the air in order that

he may keep her bound in service to him." (Weyer, *On Witchcraft* [*De praestigiis daemonum*], pages 91–92)

Note 3: James' use of the term "craft" for witchcraft and "craftsfolk" for witches is worth noting because witchcraft is in modern times often referred to simply as the Craft. Here, he was punning on "craft" in the sense of slyness and deceit.

Note 4: James regarded magic as synonymous with necromancy, and sorcery as synonymous with witchcraft. The best definition of the distinction between these two branches of the occult arts that James can find is what he refers to as "the difference vulgar put betwixt them" (Bk. I, Ch. III): that magicians and necromancers are the Devil's masters, but sorcerers and witches are the Devil's servants. He did not accept this definition, believing as he did that all who work any form of magic will eventually fall under the power of Satan, but he could not present a more concise or meaningful alternative.

If we leave the Devil out of the mix, the distinction is very similar to what we today call high magic and low magic. High magic involves elaborate rituals, circles, pentacles, divine names, and words of power; whereas low magic is more concerned with intuitive healing, scrying, and the occult properties of natural things such as herbs and stones. High magic tends to be somewhat intellectual and abstract, low magic to be immediate and intuitive. High magic has its roots in the wisdom teachings of Egypt and Greece; low magic has arisen largely from the indigenous practices of northern Europeans.

Neither branch of Western occultism can be said to exist in a pure form in modern times, and even four centuries ago, witches probably derived at least some of their methods from the grimoires of high magic, especially when they were led and instructed by educated individuals. Those who could read and write were more likely to study high magic because its methods were available in manuscripts and printed texts; the uneducated were inclined to seek to acquire the folk wisdom of divinations and charms directly, by observing and imitating the practices of their elders. In the sixteenth century, the division between magicians and witches was based largely on social class, since standing in society determined the level of education, or lack of it. As Charles Leland put it, "it was only the aristocracy who consulted Cornelius Agrippa, and could afford *la haute magie*" (Leland, *Gypsy Sorcery and Fortune Telling*, page xxxiii).

Note 5: James was making the point that he has based his argument on general principles that comprehend specific instances.

Note 6: The *Malleus Maleficarum* lists five ways that a man may be rendered unable to copulate by the Devil, enumerated by Peter of Palude: first, by physically preventing a man from approaching a woman; second, by freezing his desire with "secret things of which he best knows the power;" third, by making the woman appear loathsome; fourth, by directly preventing erection of the penis; fifth, by preventing the emission of semen (Kramer and Sprenger, *Malleus Maleficarum*, page 55). Witches were also supposed to have the power to take away the male genitals entirely so that only a smooth patch of skin remained between the legs, though it is argued in the *Malleus Maleficarum* that this is only a type of glamour (ibid., page 58).

Note 7: Jean Bodin (1530–1590) was a professor of law at the University of Toulouse and an active trial judge, as well as a member of the *Parlement de Paris*. He had children tortured to extract confessions, and was reluctant to admit even the possibility that anyone accused of witchcraft might be innocent. His book on witchcraft, *De la demonomanie des sorciers*, more commonly known in English as *Demonomania*, published in 1580, may have offended the puritanical sensibilities of James with its explicit sexual references— for example, Bodin wrote that the Devil sexually seduces girls as young as the age of six. This work opens with Bodin's famous definition of sorcery or witchcraft (the terms were used more or less interchangeably): "A sorcerer is one who by commerce with the Devil has a full intention of attaining his own ends."

Note 8: A. Hyperius (1511–1564), also known as Gerhard of Yprès, was a conciliatory Lutheran and a professor of theology at Marburg. In 1553 he wrote *De Formandis Concionibus*, a work that earned him the honorary title of father of homiletics. His 1556 work *Four Books on the Study of Theology* is said to be the first appearance in print of practical theology.

Note 9: Nicholas Hemmingius, also known as Niels Hemmingsen (1513–1600). A Danish Lutheran who traveled to Wittenberg to study theology. He has been called one of the most learned Protestant theologians of the sixteenth century. He wrote about witchcraft and its use in curing illnesses. His work *De lege naturae apodictica methodus* appeared in 1566. In 1575 his work *Admonitio de superstitionibus magicis vitandis* was published at Copenhagen.

Note 10: Cornelius Agrippa (1446–1535) was both famous and infamous in the time of King James as the author of *Three Books of Occult Philosophy*, first published in its complete form in 1533. This is a practical encyclopedia of all aspects of Western magic. A work known as the *Fourth Book of Occult Philosophy* was often attributed to Agrippa, and bound up with his other works, but it was not written by Agrippa. It falls into the class of the anonymous grimoires, or grammars, of practical magic, and contains some interesting material. It was supposed to have been the key to the true understanding of Agrippa's *Occult Philosophy*, but having studied the work, I can find little basis for this claim.

THE FIRST BOOK

ARGUMENT

The exordium of the whole. The description of magic especially.

CHAPTER I

ARGUMENT:

Proven by the Scripture that these unlawful arts in general have been, and may be, put into practice.

———

PHILOMATHES and EPISTEMON reason the matter.

Philomathes

I am surely very glad to have met you this day, for I am of the opinion that you can better resolve me of something, whereof I stand in great doubt, than any other with whom I could have met.

Epistemon

In what I can, of that you like to speak to me, I will willingly and freely tell my opinion, and if I prove it not sufficiently, I am heartily content that a better reasoning carry it away.

Philomathes

What think you of this strange news[1] which now furnishes the only purpose to all men at their meeting, I mean of these witches?

Epistemon

Surely it is wonderful, and I think so clear and plain confessions in that purpose have never fallen out in any age or country.

Philomathes

No question if they be true, but thereof the doctors doubt.

Epistemon

What part of it doubt you of?

Philomathes

Even of all, for aught I can yet perceive: and namely, that there is such a thing as witchcraft or witches; and I would pray you to resolve me thereof if you may, for I have reasoned with several in that matter and yet could never be satisfied therein.

Epistemon

I shall with good will do the best I can. But I think it the more difficult, since you deny the thing itself in general, for as it is said in the logic schools, *contra negantem principia non est disputandum.*[2] Always for that part, that witchcraft and witches have been, and are, the former part is clearly proved by the Scriptures, and the last by daily experience and confessions.

Philomathes

I know you will produce as evidence Saul's Pythoness,[3] but that, as appears, will not make much for you.

Epistemon

Not only that place [in Scripture], but diverse others. But I marvel why that should not make much for me?

Philomathes

The reasons are these: first, you may consider that Saul, being troubled in spirit and having fasted long before, as the text testifies (I Samuel 28), and being come to a woman that was reputed to have such knowledge, and that to inquire so important news, he having so guilty a conscience for his heinous offences, and especially, for that same unlawful curiosity and horrible defection, that the woman crying out upon the sudden in great admiration for the uncouth sight that she alleged to have seen, discovering him to be the king, though disguised, and denied by him before, it was no wonder, I say, that his senses being thus distracted, he could not perceive her feigning of her voice, he being himself in another chamber and seeing nothing.

Next, what could be, or was, raised? The spirit of Samuel? Profane and against all theology. The Devil in his likeness? As unapparent, that either God would permit him to come in the shape of his saints (for then could never the prophets in those days have been sure what spirit spoke to them in their visions), or then that he could foretell what was to come thereafter; for prophecy proceeds only of God, and the Devil hath no knowledge of things to come.

Epistemon

Yet if you will mark the words of the text, you will find clearly that Saul saw that apparition; for, giving you that Saul was in another chamber at the making of the circles and conjurations needful for that purpose (as none of that craft will permit any others to behold at that time), yet it is evident by the text that how soon that once that unclean spirit was fully risen, she called in upon Saul. For it is said in the text, that Saul knew him to be Samuel, which could not have been by the hearing tell only of an old man with a mantle, since there were many more old men dead in Israel than Samuel, and the common dress of that whole country was mantles.

As to the next, that it was not the spirit of Samuel, I grant, in the proving whereof you need not insist, since all Christians of whatsoever religion[4] agree upon that, and none but either mere ignorants or necromancers or witches doubt thereof. And that the Devil is permitted at some times to put himself in the likeness of the saints, it is plain in the Scriptures, where it is said that Satan can transform himself into an angel of light (II Corinthians 11:14). Neither could that cause any inconvenience with the visions of the prophets, since it is most certain that God will not permit him so to deceive his own, but only such as first willfully deceive themselves by running unto him, whom God then suffers to fall into their own snares, and justly permits them to be deluded with great efficacy of deceit, because they would not believe the truth (as Paul says).

And as to the Devil's foretelling of things to come, it is true that he knows not all things future, but yet that he knows part, the tragic event of this history declares it (which the wit of woman could never have forespoken[5]); not that he hath any prescience which is only proper to God, or yet knows anything by looking upon God, as in a mirror (as the good angels do), he being forever debarred from the favorable presence and countenance of his creator, but only by one of these two means: either, as being worldly wise, and taught by continual experience ever since the creation, he judges by the likelihood of things to come according to the like that has passed before, and the natural causes in respect of the vicissitude of all things worldly; or else, by God's employing of him in a turn, and so foreseen thereof, as appears to have been in this, whereof we find the very like in Micaiah's prophetic discourse to King Ahab (I Kings 22).

But to prove this my first proposition, that there can be such a thing as witchcraft and witches, there are many more places in the Scriptures than this (as I said before). As first, in the law of God it is plainly prohibited (Exodus 22);[6] but certain it is that the law of God speaks nothing in vain, neither doth it lay curses or enjoin punishments upon shadows, condemning that to be ill which is not in essence, or being, as we call it. Secondly, it is plain, where wicked Pharaoh's wise men imitated any number of Moses' miracles (Exodus 7–8) to harden the tyrant's heart thereby. Thirdly, said not Samuel to Saul (I Samuel 15) that disobedience is as the sin of witchcraft?[7] To compare to a thing that were not, it were too too absurd. Fourthly, was not Simon Magus (Acts 8) a man of their craft? And fifthly, what was she that had the spirit of Python? (Acts 16:16) Beside innumerable other places that were irksome to recite.

NOTES ON BOOK I, CHAPTER I

Note 1: The allusion of James to "strange news" may be a punning reference to the tract *News From Scotland*, published in 1592, which describes the doings in the North Berwick witchcraft affair of the year previous.

Note 2: "There is no disputing a negative premise."

Note 3: The Python was an enormous serpentine dragon that guarded the oracle of Gaia at Delphi, on the slope of Mount Parnassus. The god Apollo slew the Python and took over the oracle, making it his own. The oracle was a woman who was known as the Pythoness. She sat above a fissure of rising gases upon a tripod or three-legged seat, her body positioned so that the steam from the fissure rose between her legs and was presumed to enter her womb. Whether as a result of breathing this vapor, or from some natural inclination of her nature, she fell into prophetic trances during which she uttered future events in the form of enigmatic verses. The term "Pythoness" came to be applied generally to any woman who uttered oracular information, and is synonymous with "prophetess." To have a spirit of Pytho, or spirit of Python, is to be possessed by a familiar spirit that speaks oracular information.

Note 4: Catholic or Protestant.

Note 5: "To forespeak" has two meanings, "to prophesy" and "to bewitch." Here, James employs the term in the first sense.

Note 6: In the King James Bible, Exodus 22:18 reads: "Thou shalt not suffer a witch to live." There has been considerable debate among modern Wiccans and pagans as to what the word "witch" actually represents in the original Hebrew text. In the Knox translation of the Bible, which is considered to be one of the most accurate, the verse reads "Sorcerers must not be allowed to live." However, Knox has added the footnote, "In the Hebrew the word is feminine, 'witch.'" The Hebrew word in question is MKShPH, a feminine form of the word MKShP, which Gesenius translates as "enchanter" or "magician." The Hebrew word is based upon KShP, "to use enchantment"—to use magical songs, to mutter. Hence the best translation would seem to be "enchantress."

In Isaiah 8:19 reference is made to "wizards that peep and that mutter." This quaintly worded description concerns the two ways in which those who used magic were supposed to work evil on their neighbors. The first way is through the use of the evil eye, which is sometimes referred to as "overlooking." The second supposed manner of projecting evil was through verses or charms spoken quietly under the breath, which James refers to later in his book as "forespeaking." "To enchant" is to do magic through the use of spoken or sung words.

The Vulgate uses *maleficus* in place of "witch," which is to say, one who does wickedness. It appears in the title of the most notorious of all the books on witch persecution, the *Malleus Maleficarum*, or *Hammer of Witches*. The Latin term *maleficia* was sometimes employed for noxious creatures such as serpents. Since the Latin is only an interpretation of the Hebrew and Greek verses, it is not relevant in attempting to determine what the Hebrew original actually means, but it exerted a profound influence on the interpretation of the verse over the centuries. The word "witch" in the King James Bible has often been presumed, unjustly, to be a mistranslation of the words "poisoner" or "murderer."

King James recognized no distinction between a sorceress and a witch. Both terms held for him a connotation of one who works magic for evil. For him, the translation of MKShPH as "witch" seemed perfectly appropriate, particularly since he believed that female witches outnumbered their male counterparts by a ratio of twenty to one. It is only in the last century that witch and witchcraft have been able to escape from under this shadow of malice in the understanding of a minority of enlightened individuals; however, for the greater portion of the world's population, the term "witch" still signifies an evildoer.

Note 7: In the King James Bible, the word "witchcraft" appearing in I Samuel 15:23 is glossed as "divination."

CHAPTER II

ARGUMENT:

What kind of sin the practitioners of these unlawful arts commit.
The division of these arts. And what are the means that allure
any to practice them.

———

Philomathes

But I think it very strange that God should permit any of mankind (since they bear his own image) to fall into so gross and filthy a defection.

Epistemon

Although man in his creation was made to the image of the Creator (Genesis 1), yet through his fall having lost it, it is but restored again in a part by grace only to the elect; so all the rest, falling away from God, are given over into the hands of the Devil, that enemy, to bear his image,[1] and being once so given over, the greatest and the grossest impiety is the most pleasant and most delightful unto them.

Philomathes

But may it not suffice him to have indirectly the rule, and procure the perdition, of so many souls, by alluring them to vices and to the following of their own appetites, suppose he abuse not so many simple souls in making them directly acknowledge him for their master?

Epistemon

No, surely, for he uses every man, whom of he has the rule, according to their complexion and knowledge, and so whom he finds most simple, he most plainly uncovers himself unto them. For he being the enemy of man's salvation, uses all the means he can to entrap them so far into his snares, as it may be impossible to them thereafter (suppose they would) to rid themselves out of the same.

Philomathes

Then this sin is a sin against the Holy Ghost.

Epistemon

It is in some, but not in all.

Philomathes

How that? Are not all these that run directly to the Devil in one category?

Epistemon

God forbid, for the sin against the Holy Ghost has two branches. The one, a falling back from the whole service of God, and a refusal of all his precepts. The other is the doing of the first with knowledge, knowing that they do wrong against their conscience, and the testimony of the Holy Spirit, having once had a taste of the sweetness of God's mercies (Hebrews 6:10). Now in the first of these two, all sorts of necromancers, enchanters, or witches, are comprehended; but in the last, none but such as err with this knowledge that I have spoken of.

Philomathes

Then it appears that there are more sorts than one that are directly professors of his service, and if so be, I pray you tell me how many, and what are they?

Epistemon

There are principally two sorts, whereunto all the parts of that unhappy art are redacted; whereof, the one is called magic or necromancy, and the other sorcery or witchcraft.

Philomathes

What, I pray you, and how many, are the means whereby the Devil allures persons into any of these snares?

Epistemon

Even by these three passions that are within ourselves: curiosity at great ingenuities; thirst of revenge for some offenses deeply held; or greedy appetite of possessions, caused through great poverty. As to the first of these, curiosity, it is only the enticement of magicians or necromancers; and the other two are the allures of the sorcerers or witches. For that old and crafty Serpent, being a spirit, he easily spies our affections,[2] and so conforms himself thereto to deceive us to our wreak.

NOTES ON BOOK I, CHAPTER II

Note 1: A reference to the mark of the Beast. See Revelation 13:16, where those who worship the image of the first Beast that has seven heads and ten horns (Revelation 13:1) are given a mark upon their foreheads or the palms of their right hands by the second Beast that has two horns like a lamb (Revelation 13:11). This is obviously the basis for the belief that the Devil impressed each witch with a mark as a symbol of his or her acceptance of Satan as master. The shape of the mark is not described, nor is there any reason to necessarily connect the mark with the number of the Beast (Revelation 13:18).

Note 2: James seems to mean that the Devil, being a spirit, is able to hide unseen and watch us to spy out our secret desires. He then uses this knowledge to present to us the prospect of attaining those things we desire, whether they be occult and forbidden learning in the case of magicians and necromancers, or a way to exact revenge and attain wealth in the case of sorcerers and witches. Elsewhere James mentions that the Devil cannot read our thoughts, so he must learn our desires by observing our actions.

CHAPTER III

ARGUMENT:

The significance and etymology of the words magic and necromancy. The difference between necromancy and witchcraft. What are the entrances and beginnings that bring any to the knowledge thereof.

———

Philomathes

I would gladly first hear what thing is it that you call magic or necromancy.

Epistemon

This word magic in the Persian tongue[1] imports as much as to be a contemplator or interpreter of divine and heavenly sciences: which being first used among the Chaldeans, through their ignorance of the true divinity, was esteemed and reputed among them as a principal virtue, and therefore was named unjustly with an honorable style; which name the Greeks imitated, generally importing all these kinds of unlawful arts. And this word necromancy is a Greek word, compounded of *nekron* and *manteia*, which is to say, the prophecy by the dead.[2] This last name is given to this black and unlawful science by the figure synecdoche,[3] because it is a principal part of that art, to serve themselves with dead carcasses in their divinations.

Philomathes

What difference is there between this art and witchcraft?

Epistemon

Surely, the difference vulgar [persons] put between them is very merry, and in a manner true; for they say that the witches are servants only, and slaves, to the Devil, but the necromancers are his masters and commanders.

Philomathes

How can that be true, that any men being specially addicted to his service can be his commanders?

Epistemon

Yes, they may be, but it is only *secundum quid*, for it is not by any power that they can have over him, but *ex pacto*[4] all and only, whereby he obliges himself in some trifles to them, that he may on the other part obtain the fruition of their body and soul, which is the only thing he hunts for.

Philomathes

A very inequitable contract, in truth. But I pray you discourse unto me, what is the effect and secrets of that art?

Epistemon

That is over large a field you give me, yet I shall do good will, the most summarily that I can, to run through the principal points thereof. As there are two sorts of folk that may be enticed to this art, to wit, learned and unlearned, so is there two means which are the first stirrers up and feeders of their curiosity, thereby to make them to give themselves over to the same; which two I call the Devil's school, and his rudiments.

The learned have their curiosity wakened upon, and fed by that which I call his school: this is the astrology judicial.[5] For diverse men, having attained to a great perfection in learning, and yet remained over bare (alas) of the spirit of regeneration and fruits thereof, finding all natural things common, as well to the stupid pedants as unto them, they assay to vindicate unto them a greater name by not only knowing the course of things heavenly, but likewise to claim to the knowledge of things to come thereby. Which, at the first face appearing lawful unto them, in respect the ground thereof seems to proceed of natural causes only, they are so allured thereby, that finding their practice to prove true in sundry things, they study to know the cause thereof; and so mounting from degree to degree upon the slippery and uncertain scale of curiosity, they are at last enticed, that where lawful arts or sciences fail, to satisfy their restless minds, even to seek to that black and unlawful science of magic. Where, finding at the first that such diverse forms of circles and conjurations rightly joined thereunto will raise such diverse forms of spirits, to resolve them of their doubts, and attributing the doing thereof to the power inseparably tied, or inherent, in the circles, and many words of God[6] confusedly wrapped in, they blindly glory of themselves, as if they had by their quickness of ingenuity make a conquest of Pluto's dominion, and were become emperors over the Stygian habitats.[7] Where, in the mean time (miserable wretches) they are become, in very deed, bond slaves to their mortal enemy; and their knowledge, for all that they presume thereof, is nothing increased except in knowing evil, and the horrors of hell for punishment thereof, as Adam's was by the eating of the forbidden tree (Genesis 3).

NOTES ON BOOK I, CHAPTER III

Note 1: "Magic" is a word signifying the art of the magi, a priestly cast of wise men in ancient Persia who may originally have come from a single Median tribe. "Magus" is a Latin word, from the Greek μαγοσ, which in turn is from the Old Persian *magu*.

Note 2: "Necromancy" is from the Greek word *nekromanteia*, a combining of *nekros* ("corpse") and *manteia* ("divination").

Note 3: Synecdoche is a figure of speech in which a part is used to represent the whole, or the whole is used to represent its individual parts. James' meaning is that the art of necromancy is called necromancy, or corpse divination, because one of its principal activities is divination through the use of corpses. The name of the part is applied to the whole.

Note 4: "From the pact." Magicians were supposed by King James and his more credulous contemporaries to acquire their powers by signing a pact with the Devil, who would then send them a familiar demon to serve their needs.

Note 5: James used the term "judicial astrology" for all forms of astrology that seek to interpret the occult or nonphysical influences of the stars and planets upon human affairs. Since the seventeenth century, all astrology is judicial astrology in this broad sense. James was distinguishing judicial astrology from natural astrology, which in the sixteenth century was the observation of the movements of the stars and planets in order to predict natural events such as solar and lunar eclipses, and to establish the dates of the equinoxes, solstices, and holy days such as Easter. We now class natural astrology as a part of astronomy.

Note 6: Divine names play a central role in Western high magic. Drawn from the Old Testament, they embody both the power and the authority of God. The supreme name is יהוה, called by the Greeks "Tetragrammaton," a word that means "name of four letters" (*tetra*: "four," *gramma*: "letter"). In the grimoires this is either found in the original Hebrew, or is written as "Tetragrammaton." More rarely it occurs in the form "Jehovah." Other divine names from the Bible are Adonai, Elohim, Shaddai, and Eheieh. During the Renaissance the previously secret teachings of the system of Jewish mysticism and magic known as the Kabbalah became known to Europeans, and began to be employed by magicians. Cornelius Agrippa wrote extensively about the uses of the Hebrew names of God in the third book of his *Occult Philosophy*.

In addition to divine and angelic names drawn from the Bible and the Kabbalah, Western magic also makes use of what are known as barbarous words of power. These are unrecognizable words or names held to convey occult energies, even though their meanings have been forgotten. Many of the grimoires contain barbarous words in their invocations. Barbarous words found their way into the grimoires from Egypt and Greece through the teachings of the Gnostics, and also by a simple process of corruption in which names were misspelled and misread repeatedly, until their meanings were lost. Many barbarous words of power were originally the names of pagan gods.

Note 7: The river Styx encircles the Greek underworld, which is ruled by Hades (Pluto to the Romans), hence Stygian habitats are the regions of hell.

CHAPTER IV

ARGUMENT:
The description of the rudiments and school, which are the entrances to the art of magic. And especially the differences between astronomy and astrology. Division of astrology into diverse parts.

———

Philomathes

But I pray you likewise, forget not to tell what are the Devil's rudiments.

Epistemon

His rudiments, I call first in general, all that which is called vulgarly the virtue of word, herb, and stone, which is used by unlawful charms, without natural causes. As likewise all kind of practices, freits,[1] or other extraordinary actions which cannot abide the true touch of natural reason.

Philomathes

I would have you to make that plainer by some particular examples, for your proposition is very general.

Epistemon

I mean either by such kind of charms as commonly daft wives use for healing of forespoken[2] goats, for preserving them from evil eyes,[3] by knitting rune-trees,[4] or various kinds of herbs, to the hair or tails of the goats; by curing the worm, by stemming of blood,[5] by healing of horse-crooks, by turning of the riddle,[6] or doing of such like innumerable things by words, without applying anything meet to the part offended, as mediciners do; or else by stopping married folks to have naturally to do with [each] other (by knitting so many knots[7] upon a point at the time of their marriage), and suchlike things, which men use to practice in their merriness.

For since unlearned men (being naturally curious, and lacking the true knowledge of God) find these practices to prove true, as some of them will do, by the power of the Devil for deceiving men, and not by any inherent virtue in these vain words and freits; and being desirous to win a reputation to themselves in suchlike turns, they either (if they be of the shamefaced sort) seek to be taught by some that are experienced in that art (not knowing it to be evil at the first), or else being of the grosser sort, run directly to the Devil for ambition or desire of gain, and plainly contract with him thereupon.

Philomathes

But I think these means which you call the school and rudiments of the Devil are things lawful, and have been approved for such in all times and ages: as especially, this science of astrology, which is one of the special members of the mathematics.

Epistemon

There are two things which the learned have observed from the beginning, in the science of the heavenly creatures, the planets, stars, and such like. The one is their course and ordinary motions, which for that cause is called *astronomia*, which word is a compound of *nomos* and *astron*, that is to say, the law of the stars;[8] and this art indeed is one of the members of the mathematics and not only lawful but most necessary and commendable. The other is called *astrologia*, being compounded of *astron* and *logos*, which is to say, the word and preaching of the stars,[9] which is divided into two parts: the first by knowing thereby the powers of simples, and sicknesses, the course of the seasons and the weather, being ruled by their influence, which part depending upon the former, although it be not of itself a part of mathematics, yet it is not unlawful, being moderately used, though not so necessary and commendable as the former; the second part is to trust so much to their influences, as thereby to foretell what commonwealths shall flourish or decay, what persons shall be fortunate or unfortunate, what side shall win in any battle, what man shall obtain victory at singular combat, what way and of what age shall men die, what horse shall win at match running, and diverse suchlike incredible things, wherein Cardanus,[10] Cornelius Agrippa, and diverse others have more curiously than profitably written at large.

Of this root last spoken of spring innumerable branches, such as the knowledge by the nativities,[11] the chiromancy,[12] geomancy,[13] hydromancy,[14] arithmancy,[15] physiognomy,[16] and a thousand others, which were much practiced and held in great reverence by the pagans of old. And this last part of astrology whereof I have spoken, which is the root of their branches, was called by them *pars fortunae*. This part now is utterly unlawful to be trusted in, or practiced amongst Christians, as leaning to no ground of natural reason, and it is this part which I called before the Devil's school.

Philomathes

But yet many of the learned are of the contrary opinion.

Epistemon

I grant, yet I could give my reasons to fortify and maintain my opinion, if to enter into this disputation it would not draw me quite off the ground of our discourse, besides the misspending of the whole day thereupon. One word only I will answer to them, and that in the Scriptures (which must be an infallible ground to all true Christians), that in the prophet Jeremiah (Jeremiah 10) it is plainly forbidden to believe or harken unto them that prophesy and forespeak by the course of the planets and stars.

NOTES ON BOOK 1, CHAPTER IV

Note 1: A freit is an omen, augury, charm, or magical practice, especially done with a religious significance. The word has no modern equivalent. It comes from the Old Norse *frett*, meaning "inquiry" or "augury."

Note 2: In this place, James uses the term "forespoken" to mean "bewitched." A forespoken goat is one that has had a curse muttered over it.

Note 3: Since the time of the ancient Greeks, witches were supposed to possess the power of the evil eye. It was thought that merely with their glance they could cause misfortune or even death. The effect of the evil eye was more potent when it was cast slantwise, out of the corner of the eye, by the witch, and when it met the gaze of the victim. It was also thought to be more virulent when the eye of the witch was bloodshot.

Note 4: By rune-tree (or in the original, "roun-tree"), James probably meant a small wooden wand incised with magic symbols, which may or may not have been actual runes.

Note 5: Spoken charms for stopping the flow of blood from a wound were common, as was the application of the bloodstone to the injured part. Bloodstone is a type of rock with red flecks in it that resemble spots of blood, and because of this association it was thought to have the power of staunching open wounds.

Note 6: A riddle is a type of coarse-screened sieve used to separate chaff from grain. Turning the riddle was a form of divination that resembled somewhat the use of the dowsing wand. Two individuals would support by the handles on the tips of their middle fingers a large pair of shears. Between the opened blades of the shears a sieve was held in such a way that it was free to revolve under variations of pressure on its sides. The sieve moved in the same way that the planchette of the Ouija board moves, through

minute and unconscious forces exerted by the hands of the par-
ticipants. Grillot de Givry gives an explanation of the method
by Pietro d'Abano, drawn from Agrippa's *Opera omnia* (*Collected
Works*):

> [T]he sieve is suspended by tongs or pincers which are sup-
> ported by the middle fingers of two assistants. So may be dis-
> covered, by the help of the demons, those who have commit-
> ted a crime or theft or inflicted some wound. The conjuration
> consists of six words—understood neither by those who speak
> them nor by others—which are Dies, Mies, Juschet, Benedoefet,
> Dowima, and Enitemaus; once these are uttered they compel
> the demon to cause the sieve, suspended by its pincers, to turn
> the moment the name of the guilty person is pronounced (for
> all the suspected persons must be named), and thus the culprit
> is instantly known. (de Givry, *Witchcraft, Magic and Alchemy*,
> page 300)

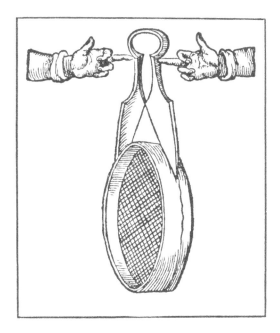

Figure 2

Note 7: Knot magic is a form of magic believed to be especially favored by witches. An intention was spoken through a loop of thread as the thread was drawn tight into a knot. The belief was that the knot captured and held the intention so that it would not fade away, but would endure and fulfill itself. Knot magic involved tying significant numbers of knots, such as three, or seven, or nine, and using specific colored threads, for different purposes.

Figure 3

Note 8: The word "astronomy" is from the Greek *astronomia* (*astron*: "star," *nomos*: "law").

Note 9: The word "astrology" is from the Greek *astrologia* (*astron*: "star," *logia*: "to speak").

Note 10: Girolamo Cardano (1501–1576) was an Italian mathematician, astrologer, and physician. He was educated at the universities of Pavia and Padua, where he received a degree in medicine, but was excluded from the College of Physicians in Milan due to his illegitimate birth. He attained celebrity as both a mathematician and as an astrologer through his published writings, and in 1547

was appointed professor of medicine at Pavia. In 1551 he traveled
to Scotland to act as the medical advisor to Archbishop Hamilton
of St. Andrews, who he successfully treated for asthma. He cast
the horoscopes of important figures of the day such as Edward VI
of England and Martin Luther. So antagonistic were his feelings
about Luther, Cardano deliberately changed the time of Luther's
birth in order to make his horoscope unfavorable. In later life
Cardano's fortunes declined. He was arrested for heresy in Italy,
a charge that was dropped at the intercession of his friends, but he
was prohibited from teaching or publishing thereafter. He is best
remembered for his autobiography *De Vita Propria*.

Note 11: A nativity is the birth chart or horoscope used in astrology
to examine and prognosticate the life of an individual.

Note 12: Divination by reading the lines in the palm of the hand.

Note 13: Geomancy is a method of divination by means of sixteen
geomantic figures. Each figure is made up of four rows, each row
containing either one dot or two dots. They are somewhat similar to the figures of the Chinese method of divination known as
the I Ching, save that the I Ching hexagrams consist of six rows,
not four, and each row is composed of either a broken or solid
line, rather than two or one dots. Selection of the geomantic
figures to be included in a divination is accomplished by poking
random number of holes in lines along the ground with a stick,
then counting the number of holes in each line to see whether it
is even or odd. An even number produces a row in a geomantic
figure with two dots, an odd number a row with one dot. Sixteen
horizontal lines of holes are poked one above the other in the
ground, and when reduced to even or odd summation, yield four
geomantic figures to take part in the divination. It is this method
of deriving the figures from holes poked in the ground that is responsible for the name "geomancy," which means "earth divination" (*geo*: "earth," *manteia*: "divination"). There are other forms

of geomancy, but it is likely that James refers to divination by the sixteen geomantic figures, which were quite popular in his time.

Note 14: Hydromancy is divination by water. The method James probably had in mind was that thought to have been used by Nostradamus, which involves gazing into a basin of water in order to see visions, in a way similar to crystal gazing.

Note 15: Arithmancy is what we would today call numerology—divination by interpreting numerical values associated with the letters in a person's name.

Note 16: Physiognomy is divination by interpreting the lines and other features in the face, and is similar in its general principles to palmistry.

CHAPTER V

ARGUMENT:
*How far the using of charms is lawful or unlawful. The description
of the forms of circles and conjurations. And what causes the
magicians themselves to weary thereof.*

———

Philomathes

Well, you have said far enough in that argument. But how prove you
now that these charms or unnatural practices are unlawful? For so
many honest and merry men and women have publicly practiced
some of them, that I think if you would accuse them all of witchcraft, you would affirm more than you will be believed in.

Epistemon

I see if you had taken good attention (to the nature of that word,
whereby I name it) you would not have been in this doubt, nor mis-
take me, so far as you have done. For although, as none can be scholars in a school and not be subject to the master thereof, so none
can study and put in practice (for the study alone, and knowledge, is
more perilous than offensive; and it is the practice only that makes
the greatness of the offence) the circles and art of magic, without
committing a horrible defection from God.[1] And yet, as they that
read and learn their rudiments are not the more subject to any
school master, if it please not their parents to put them to the school
thereafter, so they who ignorantly prove these practices, which I call
the Devil's rudiments, unknowing them to be baits cast out by him

for trapping such as God will permit to fall into his hands, this kind of folk I say, no doubt, are to be judged the best of, in respect they use no invocation nor help of him (by their knowledge at least) in these turns, and so have never entered themselves into Satan's service. Yet to speak truly for my own part (I speak but for myself), I desire not to make so near riding, for in my opinion our enemy is over-crafty, and we over-weak (except the greater grace of God) to assay such hazards where he presses to trap us.

Philomathes

You have reason indeed, for as the common proverb says: They that sup kettle with the Devil have need of long spoons. But now I pray you, go forward in the describing of this art of magic.

Epistemon

After they be come once unto this perfection in evil, in having any knowledge (whether learned or unlearned) of this black art, they then begin to be weary of the raising of their Master by conjured circles, being both so difficult and perilous, and so come plainly to contract with him, wherein is specially contained forms and effects.

Philomathes

But I pray you before ever you go further, discourse [with] me somewhat of their circles and conjurations, and what should be the cause of their wearying thereof, for it should seem that that form should be less fearful yet, than the direct haunting and society with that foul and unclean spirit.

Epistemon

I think you take me to be a witch myself, or at the least would fain swear yourself apprentice to that craft. All ways, as I may, I shall shortly satisfy you in that kind of conjurations which are contained in such books which I call the Devil's school. There are four principal parts: the persons of the conjurers, the action of conjuration, the words and rites used to that effect, and the spirits that are conjured.

You must first remember to lay the ground, that I told you before; which is, that it is no power inherent in the circles, or in the holiness of the names of God blasphemously used, nor in whatsoever rites or ceremonies at that time used, that either can raise any infernal spirit or yet limit him perforce within or without these circles. For it is he only, the father of all lies, who having first of all prescribed that form of doing, feigning himself to be commanded and restrained thereby, will be loath to pass the bounds of these injunctions; as well thereby to make them glory in the empiring over him (as I said before), as likewise to make himself so to be trusted in these little things, that he may have the better commodity thereafter, to deceive them in the end with a trick once and for all, I mean the everlasting perdition of their soul and body.

Then, laying this ground, as I have said, these conjurations must have few or more in number of the persons, conjurers (always passing the singular number)[2] according to the quality of the circle, and form of apparition. Two principal things cannot well in that errand be wanted: holy water (whereby the Devil mocks the Papists) and some present of a living thing unto him.[3] There are likewise certain seasons, days, and hours, that they observe in this purpose.[4] These things being all ready, and prepared, circles are made triangular, quadrangular, round, double, or single, according to the form of apparition that they crave.[5] But to speak of the diverse forms of the circles, of the innumerable characters and crosses that are within and without, and throughout the same, of the diverse forms of apparitions that that crafty spirit deludes them with, and of all such particulars in that action, I remit it to overmany that have busied their heads in describing of the same, as being but curious, and altogether unprofitable.

And this far only I touch, that when the conjured spirit appears, which will not be until after many circumstances, long prayers, and much muttering and murmuring of the conjurors, like a Papist priest dispatching a hunting Mass; how soon, I say, he appears, if

they have missed one iota of all their rites, or if any of their feet
once slide over the circle through terror of his fearful apparition, he
pays himself at that time in his own hand, of that due debt which
they own him; and otherwise would have delayed longer to have
paid him.[6] I mean he carries them with him body and soul. If this be
not now a just cause to make them weary of these forms of conjuration, I leave it to you to judge upon; considering the longness of
the labor, the precise keeping of days and hours (as I have said), the
terribleness of apparition, and the present peril that they stand in, in
missing the least circumstance or freit that they ought to observe.
And on the other part, the Devil is glad to move them to a plain and
square dealing with him, as I said before.

NOTES ON BOOK I, CHAPTER V

Note 1: This is an important point. Someone like Cornelius Agrippa
or John Dee could publicly proclaim themselves well versed in the
techniques of necromancy or natural magic, and could even publish books on the subject, without placing themselves at risk of
legal prosecution, provided they could prove that they had never
put their knowledge into practice. A danger always existed for
those who studied magic that their friends or neighbors would
accuse them of actually working it.

When John Dee was accused of being a magician during the
reign of James the First, he was eager to force a trial so that he
could prove his innocence and regain his reputation. On June 5,
1604, just four days before the witchcraft statute of James was
passed into law by the English Parliament, Dee sent James a petition in which he demanded that the king should "cause your
Highnesse said servant to be tryed and cleared of that horrible
and damnable, and to him most grievous and dammageable
sclaunder, generally, and for these many yeares last past, in this
kingdom raysed and continued, by report and Print against him,

namely that he is or hath bin a conjurer or caller or invocator of divels" (Smith, *John Dee: 1527–1608*, page 293).

In 1592 Dee had been called in print "the conjuror of the Queen's Privy Council." This still rankled with Dee, but presumably more recent gossip had impelled his petition to James. Dee's audacity is quite breathtaking, since his own records of the communications he had years before conducted with a hierarchy of spirits identifying themselves as the angels who had instructed Enoch in a system of heavenly magic were evidence enough to have had him hanged a thousands times. However, Dee's handwritten transcripts of the angelic communications were kept carefully hidden by Dee, and did not come to light until after his death.

Dee's petition was ignored. It may be that James saw nothing to be gained by putting on public trial one of the favorites of Queen Elizabeth. Dee lived out the last years of his life widely regarded as a magician, which, indeed, he was, and thoroughly detested by James, who remained convinced that the gossip about Dee was true. James refused to give Dee any financial aid when he was in dire need, and there is no question that he would have liked nothing better than to have watched Dee hanged as a witch. Perhaps he respected Dee's legal knowledge and oratorical skills enough to suspect that an accusation of witchcraft might fail against him, or perhaps Dee had a friend or two left. In any event, no formal accusation was ever made against him.

Note 2: It is sometimes specified in the grimoires that the magician should have an assistant or assistants, though there is no obvious reason for this directive.

Note 3: James meant the blood sacrifice of a beast. Animal sacrifice is mentioned in some of the grimoires, either directly or indirectly. For example, in the most celebrated of all the grimoires, the *Key of Solomon*, the directions concerning animal sacrifice read:

In many operations it is necessary to make some sort of sacrifice unto the Demons, and in various ways. Sometimes white animals are sacrificed to the good Spirits, and black to the evil. Such sacrifices consist of the blood and sometimes of the flesh.

They who sacrifice animals, or whatsoever kind they be, should select those which are virgin, as being more agreeable unto the Spirits, and rendering them more obedient.

When blood is to be sacrificed it should be drawn also from virgin quadrupeds or birds, but before offering the oblation, say:

May this Sacrifice which we find it proper to offer unto ye, noble and lofty Beings, be agreeable and pleasing unto your desires; be ye ready to obey us, and ye shall receive greater ones. (Mathers, *The Key of Solomon the King*, page 119).

Note 4: This was known as the observation of times, and was expressly forbidden in the Old Testament. In Leviticus is written: "Ye shall not eat any thing with the blood; neither shall ye use enchantment, nor observe times" (Leviticus 19:26). In Deuteronomy we read: "There shall not be found among you any one that maketh his son or his daughter to pass through the fire, or that useth divination, or an observer of times, or an enchanter, or a witch. . . . For these nations, which thou shalt possess, harkened unto observers of times, and unto diviners: but as for thee, the Lord thy God has not suffered thee to do so" (Deuteronomy 18:10, 14). Operations in ritual magic were believed only to be effective when done under auspicious aspects of the stars and planets, and in the hours dedicated to spirits helpful to the work. It was generally held that if rituals were performed at the wrong time, they would fail.

Figure 4

Note 5: Evil spirits considered dangerous to deal with were called
forth to visible appearance into a triangle, while the magician and
his assistants stood within the protective circle, or circles. Beside
a picture of such a triangle, the text of the *Goetia* reads: "This is
the Form of the Magical Triangle, into the which Solomon did
command the Evil Spirits. It is to be made at 2 feet distance from
the Magical Circle and it is 3 feet across. Note that this triangle is
to be placed toward that quarter whereunto the Spirit belongeth.
And the base of the triangle is to be nearest unto the Circle, the
apex pointing in the direction of the quarter of the Spirit. Observe thou also the Moon in thy working" (Mathers, *Goetia*, pages
71–72). The image in Mathers' book shows an equilateral triangle
with a circle inside it, the letters of the angelic name Michael written in its three points ("Mi-cha-el"). Outside and along its base is

written the word of power "Primeumaton," outside and along its left side the word "Anaphaxeton," and outside and along its right side the word "Tetragrammaton."

Although the triangle of evocation lies flat on the floor, it is to be conceived as upright upon the air, and as actively revolving so that it creates a vortex shaped like an inverted tornado. The spirit is induced to come into being within the triangle through the point at the apex of this vortex. These matters were not spelled out in the texts of the grimoires, but were details transmitted from teacher to student, as indeed they still are today. The reference in the *Goetia* to observing the Moon in the working is an example of the observation of times. The waning phase of the Moon is most appropriate for the evocation of evil spirits.

Note 6: The fanciful tale is told of the student of Cornelius Agrippa who, one day when his master was away from home, took out Agrippa's book of conjuration and summoned a demon. The demon demanded of the student why he had been summoned, and when the terrified youth was too overcome with dread to respond, the demon immediately killed him. Upon returning home, Agrippa was confronted with his corpse, which the magician was forced to spirit away by magic lest he be implicated in the student's death. It need hardly be added that this story has not one shred of truth in it. However, it does illustrate the belief that to step outside the magic circle during evocation, or to make an error in the words spoken or procedures enacted, was to risk death at the hands of the thing called. This belief is still held by many practitioners of high magic in modern times.

CHAPTER VI

ARGUMENT:

*The Devil's contract with the magicians. The division thereof in two
parts. What the difference is between God's miracles and the Devil's.*

―――

Philomathes

Indeed there is cause enough, but rather to leave him at all, than to
run more plainly to him, if they were wise he dealt with. But go forward now I pray you to these turns, until they become once deacons
in this craft.

Epistemon

From the time that they once plainly begin to contract with him, the
effect of their contract consists of two things; in forms and effects, as
I began to tell already, were it not you interrupted me (for although
the contract be mutual, I speak first of that part wherein the Devil
obliges himself to them). By forms, I mean in what shape or fashion
he shall come unto them, when they call upon him. And by effects,
I understand, in what special sorts of services he binds himself to be
subject unto them.

The quality of these forms and effects is less or greater, according to the skill and art of the magician.[1] For as to the forms, to some
of the baser sort of them he obliges himself to appear at their calling upon him, by such a proper name which he shows unto them,[2]
either in the likeness of a dog, a cat, an ape, or suchlike other beast;
or else to answer by a voice only. The effects are to answer to such

demands, as concerns curing of diseases, their own particular house-work, or such other base things as they require of him.

But to the most curious sort, in the forms he will oblige himself to enter in a dead body, and there out of, to give such answers of the event of battles, of matters concerning the estate of common-wealths, and such like other great questions;[3] yea, to some he will be a continual attender, in the form of a page;[4] he will permit himself to be conjured, for the space of so many years, either in a table[5] or a ring,[6] or suchlike thing, which they may easily carry about with them. He gives them power to sell such wares to others, whereof some will be dearer, and some better cheaper, according to the lying or true speaking of the spirit that is conjured therein.

Not but that in very deed, all devils must be liars, but so they abuse the simplicity of these wretches, that become their scholars, that they make them believe that at the fall of Lucifer, some spir-its fell in the air, some in the fire, some in the water, some in the land; in which elements they still remain.[7] Whereupon they build, that such as fell in the fire, or in the air, are truer than they who fell in the water or in the land; which is all but mere gossips, and forged by the author of all deceit. For they fell not by weight, as a solid substance, to stick in any one part; but the principal part of their fall, consisting in quality, by the falling from the grace of God wherein they were created, they continued still thereafter, and shall do until the latter day, in wandering through the world, as God's hangmen, to execute such turns as he employs them in. And when any of them are not occupied in that, return they must to their prison in hell (as it is plain in the miracle that Christ wrought at Gennesaret (Matthew 8)), therein at the latter day to be all enclosed forever.

And as they deceive their scholars in this, so do they in imprint-ing in them the opinion that there are so many princes, dukes, and kings among them, every one commanding fewer or more legions, and empiring in diverse arts, and quarters of the earth.[8] For though that I will not deny that there be a form of order among the angels in heaven, and consequently, was among them before their fall, yet either that they brook the same since then, or that God will permit us to know by damned devils such heavenly mysteries of his, which he would not reveal to us neither by Scripture nor prophets, I think no Christian will once think it. But to the contrary, of all such mysteries as he hath closed up with his seal of secrecy, it becomes us to be contented with a humble ignorance, they being things not necessary for our salvation.

But to return to the purpose, as these forms wherein Satan obliges himself to the greatest of the magicians are wonderful curious, so are the effects correspondent unto the same. For he will oblige himself to teach them arts and sciences, which he may easily do, being so learned a knave as he is; to carry them news from any part of the world, which the agility of a spirit may easily perform; to reveal to them the secrets of any persons, so being they be once spoken: for the thought, none knows but God, except so far as you may guess by their countenance, as one who is doubtlessly learned enough in the physiognomy. Yea, he will make his scholars to creep in credit with princes, by foretelling them many great things, part true, part false, for if all were false he would lose credit at all hands; but always doubtsome, as his oracles were. For no man doubts but he is a thief, and his agility (as I spoke before) makes him to come [with] such speed.

Likewise, he will guard his scholars with fair armies of horsemen and footmen in appearance, castles and forts: which are all but impressions in the air, easily gathered by a spirit drawing so near to that substance himself. As in like manner he will learn them many jugglery[9] tricks at cards, dice, and suchlike, to deceive men's senses thereby; and in such innumerable false practices, which are proven by overmany in this age, as they who are acquainted with that Italian called Scoto, yet living, can report. And yet are all these things but deluding of the senses, and nowise true in substance, as were the false miracles wrought by King Pharaoh's magicians, for counterfeiting Moses's. For this is the difference between God's miracles and the Devil's: God is a creator, what he makes appear in miracle, it is so in effect, as Moses's rod being cast down, was no doubt turned into a natural serpent; whereas the Devil (as God's ape) counterfeiting that by his magicians, made their wands to appear so, only to men's outward senses, as shown in effect by their being devoured by the other. For it is no wonder that the Devil may delude our senses, since we see by common proof, that simple jugglers will make a hundred things seem both to our eyes and ears otherwise than they are.

Now as to the magician's part of the contract, it is in a word that thing which, I said before, the Devil hunts for in all men.

Philomathes

Surely you have said much to me in this art, if all that you have said be as true as wonderful.

Epistemon

For the truth in these actions, it will be easily confirmed to any that pleases to take pains upon the reading of diverse authentic histories, and the inquiring of daily experiences. And as for the truth of their possibility, that they may be, and in what manner, I trust I have alleged nothing whereunto I have not joined such probable reasons, as I leave to your discretion, to weigh and consider. One word only I omitted, concerning the form of making of this contract, which is either written with the magician's own blood,[10] or else being agreed upon (in terms) his school master touches him in some part, though peradventure no mark remains, as it does with all witches.[11]

NOTES TO BOOK I, CHAPTER VI

Note 1: Spirits of greater power and authority assume shapes that are more refined and complex, whereas spirits of lesser power take on the shapes of simpler and lower forms of life. For example, in the *Fourth Book of Occult Philosophy* the particular forms of the spirits of Saturday are listed as a bearded king riding on a dragon, an old man with a beard, an old woman leaning on a staff, a hog, a dragon, an owl, a black garment, a hook or sickle, and a juniper tree (*Fourth Book of Occult Philosophy*, page 43). The more skilled the magician, the more potent the spirits he is able to summon and employ, and the more refined and complete their manifestation.

Francis Barrett commented in a footnote concerning the forms of the spirits of Saturday: "Those spirits who appear in a kingly form have a much higher dignity than them who take an inferior shape; and those who appear in a human shape, exceed in authority and power them that come as animals; and again, these latter surpass in dignity them who appear as trees or instruments, and the like: so that you are to judge of the power, government, and authority of spirits by their assuming a more noble and dignified apparition" (Barrett, *The Magus*, Bk II, Part III, page 127).

Figure 5

Note 2: The first act of a magician after making contact with a spirit is to demand of the spirit its true name, by which it may be summoned and controlled. Lower spirits are reluctant to divulge their names, but may be compelled to do so by the authority of the names of God or the names of the angels that rule over them. This is why the purity of the magician is so often stressed in the grimoires. In order to use a name of God or a name of an angel to command a lower spirit that has been evoked, it is necessary for the magician to invoke that aspect of God, or that angel, into himself, so that he becomes the vessel of God or the angel. Only then can he speak with the power and authority of the holy name to command the lower spirit to reveal its true identity. Once the name of the lower spirit is known, it can be effectively used to command the spirit to appear and do whatever work the magician requires of it.

Note 3: This is the primary activity of necromancy. John Dee's crystal scryer, the alchemist Edward Kelley, is reputed to have exhumed the corpse of a pauper from his grave in the churchyard of Walton-le-Dale, near Preston in Lancashire, with the help of a friend named Peter Waring. This was done at the request of a young man of wealth and social position, who wished Kelley to animate the corpse with necromantic magic and compel it to reveal the young man's term of life and future prospects. The success or failure of the effort has not been recorded, but in my opinion the story itself is very likely true. This instance of graverobbing took place before Kelley entered into Dee's employ, and it is probable that Dee never knew anything about it. Contrary to some reports, Dee was not present at the time, since he and Kelley had yet to meet. Dee met Kelley in the spring of 1582. Kelley's experiment in necromancy may have occurred around 1580. Under the witchcraft statute of Elizabeth in force at the time, he would not have been subject to the death penalty for his crime, only a year in prison for a first offense, but under the statute of 1604 brought in by James he would theoretically have faced hanging, although in actuality no one was ever executed in England solely for digging up a corpse and using it in works of magic.

Note 4: The Devil was supposed to appoint a demon to act as a familiar to a magician with whom he had signed a pact. The most famous example is that of Mephistopheles, the familiar serving demon of the magician Faust. The relationship between Faust and his familiar is examined in the play *The Tragical History of Doctor Faustus* by Christopher Marlowe, and the play *Faust* by Johann Wolfgang von Goethe.

Note 5: The summoning of spirits into tables played a key part in the spiritualist movement of the nineteenth century. Spirits of the dead were supposed to enter into the table around which the medium and her clients were seated, then to respond to questions either with a series of raps from within the table, or by moving, lifting, or tipping the table so that its legs banged alternately against the floor.

Note 6: Magicians commonly possessed rings containing familiar spirits. For example, the Greek sage Apollonius of Tyana was presented as a gift a set of seven rings containing spirits by the leader of the Brahmans of India. His biographer Philostratus wrote: "And Damis says that Iarchas gave seven rings to Apollonius named after the seven stars, and that Apollonius wore each of these in turn on the day of the week which bore its name" (Philostratus, *Life of Apollonius*, Bk III, Ch. XLI). A ring has the advantage of being always on the person of the magician, allowing instant access to the familiar spirit when its services may be required.

Note 7: James refers to the elemental spirits of Paracelsus, the Salamanders of Fire, the Sylphs of Air, the Undines of Water, and the Gnomes of Earth. Since the elements Fire and Air tend to rise upward, their spirits might be considered more spiritual, but since Water and Earth tend to fall downward, their spirits might be viewed as more earthy. The notion that spirits are divided into the elements is quite old. It occurs in the *Key of Solomon*, but in a less orderly form than that established by Paracelsus:

> For when thou shalt have conjured any Spirits in any art or experiment, they will not come when the air is troubled or agitated by winds, seeing that Spirits have neither flesh nor bones, and are created of different substances.
>
> Some are created from Water.
>
> Others from Wind, unto which they are like.
>
> Some from Earth.
>
> Some from Clouds.
>
> Others from Solar Vapours.
>
> Others from the keenness and strength of Fire; and when they are invoked or summoned, they come always with great noise, and with the terrible nature of fire. (Mathers, *Key of Solomon the King*, page 82).

Note 8: The seventy-two infernal demons of the *Goetia* are each given a rank and a certain number of legions of spirits under their command. For example, the demon Foras is called a mighty President, and said to rule twenty-nine legions of spirits; Asmoday is said to be a great King, and to rule seventy-two legions. These seventy-two demons are in turn ruled by four demon kings, each presiding over one of the four quarters of the world: Amaymon rules the east, Corson the west, Zimimay the north, Göap the south (Mathers, *The Goetia*, page 67).

Note 9: Jugglery was what we would today call stage magic, or slight of hand.

Note 10: Written pacts signed by magicians and various demons actually exist. For example, one of the contracts found in the possession of Urbain Grandier, the priest of Loudoun, was written in blood, presumably his own, and reads in French:

> My Lord and Master, I own you for my God; I promise to serve you while I live, and from this hour I renounce all other

gods and Jesus Christ and Mary and all the Saints of Heaven and the Catholic, Apostolic, and Roman Church, and all the goodwill thereof and the prayers which might be made for me. I promise to adore you and do you homage at least three times a day and to do the most evil that I can and to lead into evil as many persons as shall be possible to me, and heartily I renounce the Chrism, Baptism, and all the merits of Jesus Christ; and, in case I should desire to change, I give you my body and soul, and my life as holding it from you, having dedicated it for ever without any will to repent. Signed Urbain Grandier in his blood. (de Givry, *Witchcraft, Magic and Alchemy*, pages 118–119).

Grandier was accused by the nuns at the Ursuline convent at Loudun of causing them to become possessed by demons. He was tortured by Capuchin monks, but refused to confess, and was burned alive on August 18, 1634, "together with all compacts and magical apparatus used by him" (Robbins, *Encyclopedia of Witchcraft and Demonology*, page 315). Apparently some of his demonic contracts escaped the fire. Another document of Urbain Grandier is written in mirror script, and shows the highly distinctive signatures of six demons: Lucifer, Beelzebub, Satan, Elimi, Leviathan, and Astaroth. Each signature is completely different in style from all the others. Leviathan used a particularly heavy hand with his pen, which is perhaps to be expected (Seligmann, *The History of Magic*, page 242).

Note 11: Because the mark of the pact supposed to be impressed on magicians was not visible, they were not subject to pricking, as were witches.

CHAPTER VII

The reason why the art of magic is unlawful.
What punishment it merits, and who may be accounted
guilty of that crime.

―――――

Philomathes

Surely you have made this art to appear very monstrous and detestable. But what, I pray you, shall be said to such as maintain this art to be lawful, for as evil as you have made it?

Epistemon

I say they savor of the pan themselves, or at least little better; and yet I would be glad to hear their reasons.

Philomathes

There are two principally, that ever I heard used, beside that which is founded upon the common proverb (that the necromancers command the Devil, which you have already refuted). The one is grounded upon a received custom, the other upon an authority which some think infallible. Upon custom, we see that diverse Christian princes and magistrates, severe punishers of witches, will not only overlook magicians living within their dominions, but even sometimes delight to see them prove some of their practices. The other reason is, that Moses being brought up (as it is expressly said in the Scriptures) in all the sciences of the Egyptians,[1] whereof no doubt this was one of the principals, and he not withstanding of this art, pleasing God, as he did, consequently that art professed by so godly a man could not be unlawful.

Epistemon

As to the first of your reasons, grounded upon custom, I say, an evil custom can never be accepted for a good law, for the over-great ignorance of the word in some princes and magistrates, and the contempt thereof in others, moves them to sin heavily against their office in that point. As to the other reason, which seems to be of greater weight, if it were formed in a syllogism, it behooves to be in many terms and full of fallacies (to speak in terms of logic).

For first, that that general proposition affirming Moses to be taught in all the sciences of the Egyptians, should [give cause to] conclude that he was taught in magic, I see no necessity. For we must understand that the spirit of God there, speaking of sciences, understands them that are lawful; for except they be lawful, they are but abusively called sciences, and are but ignorances indeed: *nam homo pictus, non est homo.*[2]

Secondly, giving that he had been taught in it, there is great difference between knowledge and practicing of a thing (as I said before), for God knows all things, being always good; and of our sin and our infirmity proceeds our ignorance.

Thirdly, giving that he had both studied and practiced the same (which is no less than monstrous to be believed by any Christian), yet we know well enough that before that ever the spirit of God began to call Moses, he was fled out of Egypt, being forty years of age, due to the slaughter of an Egyptian; and in his good father Jethro's land, first called at the fiery bush, having remained there another forty years in exile: so that suppose he had been the wickedest man in the world before, he then became a changed and regenerate man, and very little of the old Moses remained in him. Abraham was an idolater in Ur of the Chaldeans before he was called, and Paul, being called Saul, was a most sharp persecutor of the saints of God, before that name was changed.

Philomathes
What punishment then think you merits these magicians and necromancers?

Epistemon
The like, no doubt, that sorcerers and witches merit; and rather so much greater, as their error proceeds of the greater knowledge, and so draws nearer to the sin against the Holy Ghost.[3] And as I say of them, so say I the like of all such as consult, enquire, entertain, and oversee them, which is seen by the miserable ends of many that ask counsel of them: for the Devil has never better tidings to tell of any, than he told to Saul; neither is it lawful to use so unlawful instruments, were it never for so good a purpose, for that axiom in theology is most certain and infallible: *nunquam faciendum est malum ut bonum inde eveniat*[4] [marginal gloss: *Ast 3.*].

NOTES TO BOOK I, CHAPTER VII

Note 1: Acts 7:22, which reads, "And Moses was learned in all the wisdom of the Egyptians, and was mighty in words and in deeds."

Note 2: "For man embellished is not man."

Note 3: The point made by James is that magicians and necromancers, being better educated than sorcerers and witches, are more likely to commit the second branch of the sin against the Holy Ghost defined in Chapter II: a falling back from the whole service of God and a refusal of all his precepts, with full knowledge that it is a sin.

Note 4: "Evil is never to be done so that therefrom good will happen." This popular saying had its origin in Romans 3:8.

THE SECOND BOOK

ARGUMENT:

The description of sorcery and witchcraft in particular.

CHAPTER I

ARGUMENT:

Proved by the Scripture, that such a thing can be. And the reasons refuted of all such as would call it but an imagination and melancholy humor.

Philomathes

Now, since you have satisfied me now so fully concerning magic or necromancy, I will pray you to do the like in sorcery or witchcraft.

Epistemon

That field is likewise very large; and although in the mouths and pens of many, yet few know the truth thereof so well as they believe themselves, as I shall so briefly as I can make you (God willing) as easily to perceive.

Philomathes

But I pray you before you go further, let me interrupt you here with a short digression, which is, that many can scarcely believe that there is such a thing as witchcraft. Whose reasons I will briefly allege unto you, that you may satisfy me as well in that as you have done in the rest.

For first, whereas the Scripture seems to prove witchcraft to be, by diverse examples, and specially by sundry of the same which you have alleged, it is thought by some that these places speak of magicians and necromancers only, and not of witches. As in special, these wise men of Pharaoh's that counterfeited Moses's miracles were magicians, say they, and not witches; as likewise that Pythoness that Saul consulted with; and so was Simon Magus in the New Testament, as that very styling imports.[1]

Secondly, where you would oppose the daily practice and confession of so many, that is thought likewise to be but very melancholy imaginations of simple raving creatures.

Thirdly, if witches have such power of witching of folks to death (as they say they have), there had been none left alive long since in the world but they; at least, no good or godly person of whatsoever estate could have escaped their devilry.

Epistemon

Your three reasons, as I take, are grounded the first of them upon Scripture; the second affirmative upon physic; and the third upon the certain proof of existence.

As to your first, it is most true, indeed, that all these wise men of Pharaoh were magicians of art; as likewise it appears well that the Pythoness with whom Saul consulted was of that same profession; and so was Simon Magus. But you omitted to speak of the law of God wherein are all magicians, diviners, enchanters, sorcerers, witches, and whatsoever of that kind that consult with the Devil, plainly prohibited, and alike threatened against.[2] And besides that, she who had the spirit of the Python in the Acts, whose spirit was put to silence by the apostle (Acts 16), could be no other thing but a very sorcerer or witch, if you admit the vulgar distinction to be in a manner true, whereof I spoke in the beginning of our conference. For that spirit whereby she acquired such gain to her master was not at her raising or commanding, as she pleased to appoint, but spoke by her tongue, as well publicly as privately; whereby she seemed to draw nearer to the sort of demoniacs or possessed, if that conjunction between them had not been of her own consent, as it appeared by her not being tormented therewith, and by her acquiring of such gain to her masters (as I have already said).[3]

As to your second reason, grounded upon physic, in attributing their confessions of apprehensions to a natural melancholic humor, any that please medically to consider upon the natural humor of melancholy, according to all the physicians that ever wrote thereupon, they shall find that that will be over-short a cloak to cover their knavery with. For as the humor of melancholy in the self is black, heavy, and earthy, so are the symptoms thereof, in any persons that are subject thereunto, leanness, paleness, desire of solitude, and if they come to the highest degree thereof, mere folly and mania. Whereas, by the contrary, a great number of them that ever have been convicted or confessors of witchcraft, as may be presently seen by many that have at this time confessed, they are by the contrary, I say, some of them rich and worldly wise, some of them fat or corpulent in their bodies, and most part of them altogether given over to the pleasures of the flesh, continual haunting of company, and all kinds of merriness, both lawful and unlawful, which are things directly contrary to the symptoms of melancholy whereof I spoke.[4] And further experience daily proves how loath they are to confess without torture, which witnesses their guiltiness; whereby the contrary, the melancholics, never spare to betray themselves by their continual discourses, feeding thereby their humor in that which they think no crime.

As to your third reason, it scarcely merits an answer. For if the Devil, their master, were not bridled, as the Scriptures teach us, suppose there were no men nor women to be his instruments, he could find ways enough without any help of others to wreck all mankind; whereunto he employs his whole study, and goes about like a roaring lion (as Peter says) to that effect (I Peter 5). But the limits of his power were set down before the foundations of the world were laid, which he hath not power in the least jot to transgress.

But beside all this, there is overgreat a certainty to prove that they are [witches], by the daily experience of the harms that they do, both to men and whatsoever thing men possess, whom God will permit them to be the instruments so to trouble or visit, as in my discourse of that art you shall hear clearly proved.

NOTES TO BOOK II, CHAPTER I

Note 1: Refer to Acts 8:9–24. The name "Simon Magus" might be translated "Simon the Magician," since *magus* is a Persian word that signifies "magician." Irenaeus described a pre-Gnostic sect called the Simonians that supposedly traced its beginning to the teachings of Simon Magus. Simon was denounced by the Church fathers as the founder of Gnosticism, the source of all Gnostic doctrines, and the father of all heresy (Barnstone, *The Other Bible*, page 603). Saint Clement of Alexandria related the fable that when Simon was acting as court magician to Nero at Rome, Saint Peter went to confront him. To demonstrate his power, Simon flew out a window, whereupon Peter muttered a fervent prayer, and Simon dropped to the ground, breaking both his legs, and shortly thereafter died of his injuries.

If the story has any truth, it might be speculated that Simon was a stage magician, that he flew out the window on wires, and that while suspended high above the ground, something malfunctioned with his apparatus. It is difficult to see how the prayer spoken by Paul at the time differs in any significant way in its intention from the malevolent forespeaking of a sorcerer resulting in death, so strongly condemned by James.

Note 2: The condemnation in Deuteronomy 18:10–11 against all forms of occult practice is quite sweeping, and reads a bit like the all-inclusive language of James's own witchcraft statute of 1604. Prohibited are those who use divination, those who observe times (astrologers), enchanters, witches, charmers, consulters with familiar spirits, wizards, and necromancers.

Note 3: This passage is a bit convoluted, but what James is saying is that the woman who was possessed by a spirit of divination

(Acts 16:16–18) cannot be called a magician by the vulgar definition of his day—that is, one who commands the Devil—because she did not control the spirit that was using her voice. It might be assumed that she was merely possessed, something that was believed to happen to many innocent individuals, were it not that her prophecies brought great profit to her masters, and were it not that she obviously had consented to act as host for the spirit. The implied conclusion of James is that the spirit was her familiar.

Note 4: Ancient medicine recognized four humors, or subtle fluids, flowing through the body. These humors took their prevailing nature from the elements with which they corresponded. Choler was hot and dry, like the element Fire. The humor of blood was moist and hot, like Air. Phlegm was cold and moist, like Water. Melancholy was dry and cold, like Earth.

When the humors of the body were in balance, the result was physical and mental health. An imbalance of the humors resulted in disease. The primary pursuit of physicians was to restore the balance of the humors—hence, the practice of bleeding, which was designed to allow a superabundant humor to flow out of the body and restore a natural equipoise between the four. Imbalance in the humors not only produced sickness but eccentric and socially unacceptable behavior, and served as a source of amusement for the English playwrights of the late sixteenth century, as the titles of the comic plays by Ben Jonson, *Every Man in his Humour* (1598) and *Every Man out of his Humour* (1599), suggest. Shakespeare made extensive use of the theory of humors in the exaggeration of his characters, as did other Elizabethan and Jacobean playwrights such as Marlowe and Webster.

An ordinary excess of the cold and dry humor of melancholy results in what we call depression. It makes us sour, withdrawn, sullen, brooding, sluggish, and sad. However, there is another type of melancholy, sometimes called heroic melancholy, that creates a kind of frantic intensity in the mind, giving rise to unrealistic ambitions, fantastic visions, irrational plans, cynical but brilliant witticisms, intense periods of creativity, inspirations, emotional outbursts, persistent delusions, and obsessions. Heroic melancholy is what we might call manic depression. James referred to this second type of melancholy as the "highest degree thereof."

James was correct in asserting that witchcraft, as it is described in the testimonies of accused witches, does not correspond with common melancholy. Witches frequently testified that they gathered together, sang, danced, drank, made love, and otherwise enjoyed themselves in a manner quite out of keeping with the low form of melancholy, which results in withdrawal from society and inertia of mind and body. Whether witchcraft corresponds with heroic melancholy is a more interesting matter to consider. Some accused witches exhibited delusions of grandeur, related wild and unrealistic plans, and reported fantastic visions that are in harmony with the higher form of melancholy. However, since not all witches were the same, there is no reason to suppose that they all suffered from the same affliction. A minority of them probably could be classed as melancholics of the highest degree, but the majority does not appear to have shown any signs of melancholy humor, either of the common or the extreme kind.

CHAPTER II

ARGUMENT:
The etymology and signification of that word, sorcery.
The first entrance and apprenticeship of them that give
themselves to that craft.

———

Philomathes
Come on then, I pray you, and return where you left.

Epistemon
This word of sorcery is a Latin word, which is taken from casting of the lot, and therefore he that uses it is called *sortiarius, à sorte.*[1] As to the word witchcraft, it is nothing but a proper name given in our language.[2] The cause wherefore they were called *sortiarii* proceeded of their practices seeming to come of lot or chance: such as the turning of the riddle, the knowing of the form of prayers or such like tokens, if a person diseased would live or die. And in general, that name was given them for using of such charms and freits as that craft teaches them. Many points of their craft and practices are common between the magicians and them; for they serve both one master, although in diverse fashions.

And as I divided the necromancers into two sorts, learned and unlearned, so must I divide them in another two: rich and of better account, poor and of baser degree. These two degrees now of persons that practice this craft answer to the passions in them, which (I told you before) the Devil used as means to entice them to his service. For such of them as are in great misery and poverty, he allures to follow him by promising unto them great riches and worldly commodity. Such as, though rich, yet burn in desperate desire of revenge, he allures them by promises to get their turn satisfied to their heart's contentment.

It is to be noted now, that that old and crafty Enemy of ours assails none, though touched with any of these two extremes, except he first find an entrance ready for him, either by the great ignorance of the person he deals with, joined with an evil life, or else by their carelessness and contempt of God. And finding them in utter despair from one of these two former causes that I have spoken of, he prepares the way by feeding them craftily in their humor, and filling them further and further with despair, until he finds the time proper to reveal himself unto them. At which time, either upon their walking solitary in the fields, or else lying brooding in their bed, but always without the company of any other, he either by a voice or in likeness of a man, inquires of them what troubles them; and promises them a sudden and certain way of remedy upon condition on the other part that they follow his advice, and do such things as he will require of them.

Their minds being prepared beforehand, as I have already spoken, they easily agree unto that demand of his, and soon set another tryst where they may meet again. At which time, before he proceeds any further with them, he first persuades them to addict themselves to his service; which being easily obtained, he then reveals what he is unto them, makes them renounce their God and baptism directly, and gives them his mark upon some secret place of their body, which remains sore unhealed until his next meeting with them, and thereafter ever insensible, howsoever it be nipped or pricked in any way, as is daily proved; to give them a proof thereby, that as in that doing he could hurt and heal them, so all their ill and well doings thereafter must depend upon him. And besides that, the intolerable distress that they feel in that place where he has marked them serves to waken them, and not to let them rest until their next meeting again; fearing lest otherwise they might either forget him, being as new apprentices and not well enough founded yet in that fiendly folly: or else, remembering of that horrible promise they made him at their last meeting, they might balk at the same, and press to call it back.

At their third meeting he makes a show to be careful to perform his promises, either by teaching them ways how to get themselves revenged, if they be of that sort, or else by teaching them lessons how, by most vile and unlawful means, they may obtain gain and worldly commodity, if they be of the other sort.

NOTES ON BOOK II, CHAPTER II

Note 1: The word "sorcerer" is from the Latin *sortiarius*, "one who casts a lot" (*sortis*).

Note 2: James was mistaken about the word "witchcraft," but his error is understandable, in view of the difficulty we still have today in determining the origins of the word "witch." In Anglo-Saxon, *wicca* is the term for a male witch, *wicce* for a female witch, and *wiccian* for the verb "to witch or bewitch." *Webster's Dictionary* traces these forms back to the Indo-European root *weiq*, meaning

Figure 6

"violent strength." Skeat states that *wicca* is a corruption of the An-glo-Saxon *witga*, "prophet, soothsayer, or wizard." The word *witga*, originally a seer, is from *witan*, "to see," and is allied to the Anglo-Saxon word *witan*, "to know" (Skeat, *An Etymological Dictionary of the English Language*, page 714). If Skeat is correct, the word "witch" signifies "someone who is knowing or wise," and witchcraft is the craft of the wise.

CHAPTER III

ARGUMENT:

The witches' actions divided into two parts: the actions proper to their own persons, their actions towards others. The form of their conventions, and adoring of their master.

———

Philomathes

You have said now enough of their initiating into that order. It remains then that you discourse upon their practices, before they be passed apprentices: for I would fain hear what is possible to them to perform in very deed.

Epistemon[1]

Although they serve a common master with the necromancers (as I have before said), yet serve they him in another form. For as the means are diverse which allure them to these unlawful arts of serving of the Devil, so by diverse ways use they their practices, answering to these means which first the Devil used as instruments in them; though all tending to one end, to wit, the enlarging of Satan's tyranny, and crossing of the propagation of the Kingdom of Christ, so far as lies in the possibility, either of the one or other sort, or of the Devil their master.

For where the magicians, as allured by curiosity, in the most part of their practices seek principally the satisfying of the same, and to win to themselves a popular honor and estimation, these witches on the other part, being enticed either for the desire of revenge, or of worldly riches, their whole practice is either to hurt men and their goods, or what they possess, for satisfying of their cruel minds in the former; or else by the wreck, in whatsoever sort, of any whom God will permit them to have power of, to satisfy their greedy desire in the last point.

In two parts their actions may be divided: the actions of their own persons, and the actions proceeding from them towards any other. And this division being well understood, will easily resolve [for] you what is possible to them to do. For although all that they confess is no lie upon their part, yet doubtlessly, in my opinion, a part of it is not indeed according as they take it to be: and in this I mean by the actions of their own persons. For as I said before, speaking of magic, that the Devil deludes the senses of these scholars of his in many things, so say I the like of these witches.

Philomathes

Then I pray you, first to speak of that part of their own persons, and then you may come next to their actions toward others.

Epistemon

To the effect that they may perform such services of their false master as he employs them in, the Devil as God's ape counterfeits in his servants this service and form of adoration, that God prescribed and made his servants to practice. For as the servants of God publicly convene for serving of him, so makes him them in great numbers to convene (though publicly they dare not) for his service. As none convenes to the adoration and worshipping of God except they be marked with his seal, the sacrament of baptism, so none serves Satan and convenes to the adoring of him that are not marked with that mark, whereof I already spoke. As the minister sent by God teaches plainly at the time of their public conventions how to serve him in spirit and truth, so that unclean spirit, in his own person teaches his disciples at the time of their convening how to work all kinds of mischief; and craves accounting of all their horrible and detestable proceeding past, for advancement of his service. Yea, that he may the more vilely counterfeit and scorn God, he often times makes his slaves to convene in these very places which are destined and ordained for the convening of the servants of God (I mean by churches).

But this far, which I have yet said, I not only take it to be true in their opinions, but even so to be in deed. For the form that he used in counterfeiting God among the pagans makes me so to think: as God spoke by his oracles, spoke he not so by his? As God had as well bloody sacrifices, as others without blood, had not he the like? As God had churches sanctified to his service, with altars, priests, sacrifices, ceremonies, and prayers, had he not the like polluted to his service? As God gave responses by Urim and Thummim,[2] gave he not his responses by the entrails of beasts,[3] by the singing of fowls, and by their actions in the air?[4] As God by visions, dreams, and ecstasies revealed what was to come, and what was his will unto his servants, used he not the like means to forewarn his slaves of things to come? Yea, even as God loved cleanness, hated vice and impurity, and appointed punishments therefore, used he not the like (though falsely I grant, and but in eschewing the less inconvenient to drew them upon a greater); yet dissembled he not, I say, so far as to appoint his priests to keep their bodies clean and undefiled[5] before their asking responses of him? And feigned he not God, to be a protector of every virtue, and a just revenger of the contrary?

This reason then moves me, that as he is that same Devil, and as crafty now as he was then, so will he not spare openly in these actions that I have spoken of concerning the witches' persons. But further, witches oftentimes confess not only his convening in the church with them, but his occupying of the pulpit; yea, their form of adoration, to be the kissing of his hinder parts.[6] Which, though it seem ridiculous, yet may it likewise be true, seeing we read that in Calicut,[7] he appearing in form of a goat-buck, had publicly that dishonest homage done unto him by every one of the people. So ambitious is he, and greedy of honor (which procured his Fall) that he will even imitate God in that part, where it is said that Moses could see but the hinder parts of God, for the brightness of his glory (Exodus 33); and yet that speech is spoken but *anthropopathically*.[8]

NOTES TO BOOK II, CHAPTER III

Note 1: The text of the two paragraphs that follow is in the original work attributed to Philomathes. This is an obvious error. I have returned this section of text to Epistemon.

Note 2: Urim and Thummim were two mysterious objects carried by the high priest of Israel within the sacred breastplate bearing the twelve stones of the tribes (see Leviticus 8:8). They were used as an instrument of divination on important matters. When Joshua was publicly chosen to succeed Moses as leader of Israel, he was confirmed by the oracle of Urim (Numbers 27:21). The Hebrew word AVRIM means "lights"; the word ThMIM means "truth." Both are plural forms. Philo Judaeus believed these objects were two small images, the first representing revelation and the second truth. However, the biblical commentator Rashi states unequivocally that they were "the writing of the Divine Name," that is, the four Hebrew letters of Tetragrammaton.

In my book *Tetragrammaton* I speculate that the oracle consisted of two disks, one of gold (Urim) and the other of silver (Thummim). I believe they represented the Sun and the Moon, and each was engraved with two of the letters of the Divine Name, a single letter on each side of the two disks (Tyson, *Tetragrammaton*, pages 82–86). The manner of using the oracle is not known, but one of the disks may have indicated a yes and the other a no, when blindly drawn from within the breastplate; or the letters may have been used to spell out one of the twelve possible permutations of the letters of the Name, corresponding to the twelve tribes of Israel.

Note 3: Divination by the inspection of the still-warm entrails of a sacrificed beast was the method favored by the Etruscans, and was later adopted by the Romans as their preferred method of official divination. The Romans employed Etruscan priests to interpret the oracle. The appearance of the liver was critical. A healthy liver was a good sign, but a liver that was discolored, misshaped, or diseased portended disaster.

Note 4: The Romans placed great reliance on prognostication by the flight of birds. Of chief importance was the direction of their passage, but they also took note of the manner of their flight and their number, and of the species of the birds involved. The eagle was thought to give important oracles, since it was one of the primary symbols of the Roman state.

Figure 7

Note 5: Many of the pagan priestly casts observed scrupulous physical cleanliness. The Egyptian priests were particularly noted for it, going so far as to shave their entire bodies. Some orders of priests and priestesses also maintained a sexual cleanliness by remaining virgin. The reason for physical cleanliness was to avoid dishonoring the deities they served, but the reason for celibacy was to accumulate sexual energy so that it could be devoted to esoteric purposes.

Note 6: When James mentions the Devil occupying the pulpit of the church, and causing the witches at the gathering to kiss his buttocks in homage, he is referring to testimony that he heard with his own ears during the interrogations of the North Berwick witches six years earlier. These practices are described in the tract *News From Scotland*.

Note 7: Calicut is a town in southern India, on the Malabar Coast.

Note 8: Anthropopathy (ανθρωποπαθεια) is the ascription of human emotions to God. The Greek word James was looking for here was "anthropomorphic" (ανθρωπομορφοσ), not "anthropopathic." Anthropomorphism is the ascription of the human form and characteristics to God—in this case, buttocks.

CHAPTER IV

ARGUMENT:
What are the ways possible whereby the witches may transport
themselves to places far distant. And what are impossible and mere
illusions of Satan. And the reasons thereof.

———

Philomathes

But by what way say they or think you it possible that they can come to these unlawful conventions?

Epistemon

There is the thing which I esteem their senses to be deluded in, and though they lie not in confessing of it, because they think it to be true, yet not to be so in substance or effect: for they say that by diverse means they may convene, either to the adoring of their Master, or to the putting into practice any service of his committed unto their charge. One way is natural, which is natural riding, going, or sailing, at what hour their Master comes and advises them; and this way may be easily believed. Another way is somewhat more strange, and yet is it possible to be true: which is, by being carried by the force of the spirit which is their conductor, either above the earth or above the sea, swiftly to the place where they are to meet; which I am persuaded to be likewise possible, in respect that Habbacuc was carried by the angel in that form to the den where Daniel lay (*Apocrypha of Bel and the Dragon*).

So, think I, the Devil will be ready to imitate God as well in that, as in other things: which is much more possible to him to do, being a spirit, than to a mighty wind, being but a natural event, to transport from one place to another a solid body, as is commonly and daily seen in practice. But in this violent form they cannot be carried but a short bounds, agreeing with the space that they may retain their breath: for if it were longer, their breath could not remain unextinguished, their bodies being carried in such a violent and forcible manner. As, by example: if one fall off a small height, his life is but in peril, according to the hard or soft landing; but if one fall from a high and steep rock, his breath will be forcibly banished from the body before he can win to the earth, as it oft seen by experience.[1]

And in this transporting, they say to themselves that they are invisible to any other, except among themselves; which may also be possible in my opinion. For if the Devil may form what kind of impressions he pleases in the air, as I have said before, speaking of magic, why may he not far easier thicken and obscure so the air that is next above them by contracting is close together, that the beams of any other man's eyes cannot pierce through the same to see them?[2]

But the third way of their coming to their conventions is that wherein I think them deluded: for some of them say that being transformed into the likeness of a little beast or fowl, they will come and pierce through whatsoever house or church, though all ordinary passages be closed, by whatsoever opening the air may enter in at.

And some say that their bodies lying still, as in ecstasy, their spirits will be ravished out of their bodies,[3] and carried to such places. And for verifying thereof, will give evident tokens, as well by witnesses that have seen their bodies lying senseless in the meantime, as by naming persons with whom they met, and giving tokens what purpose was amongst them, whom otherwise they could not have known: for this form of journeying, they affirm to use the most when they are transported from one country to another.

Philomathes

Surely, I long to hear your own opinion of this, for they are like old wives' tattles about the fire.

Epistemon[4]

The reasons that move me to think that these are mere illusions are these. First, for them that are transformed in likeness of beasts or fowls, can enter through so narrow passages, although I may easily believe that the Devil could by his workmanship upon the air make them appear to be in such forms, either to themselves or to others, yet how can he contract a solid body within so little room? I think it is directly contrary to itself, for to be made so little, and yet not diminished; to be so tightly drawn together, and yet feel no pain. I think it is so contrary to the quality of a natural body, and so like to the little transubstantial God in the Papists' Mass, that I can never believe it. So to have a quantity, is so proper to a solid body, that as all philosophers conclude, it cannot be any more without one, than a spirit can have one. For when Peter came out of the prison, and the doors all locked (Acts 12), it was not by any contracting of his body in so little room, but by the giving place of the door, though unspied by the jailers. And yet is there no comparison when this is done, between the power of God, and of the Devil.

As to their form of ecstasy and spiritual transporting, it is certain the soul's going out of the body is the only definition of natural death: and who are once dead, God forbid we should think that it should lie in the power of all the devils in hell to restore them to their life again (although he can put his own spirit in a dead body, which the necromancers commonly practice, as you have heard), for that is the office properly belonging to God. And besides that, the soul once parted from the body cannot wander any longer in the world, but to the one resting place must it go immediately, abiding the conjunction of the body again at the Latter Day. And what Christ or the prophets did miraculously in this case, it cannot, in any Christian man's opinion, be made common with the Devil. As for any tokens that they give for proving of this, it is very possible to the Devil's craft to persuade them to these means. For he being a spirit, may he not so ravish their thoughts, and dull their senses, that their body lying as dead, he may appear to their spirits as it were in a dream, and (as the poets write of Morpheus[5]) represent such forms of persons, of places, and other circumstances, as he pleases to delude them with?

Yea, that he may deceive them with the greater efficacy, may he not at that same instant, by fellow angels of his, delude such other persons so in that same fashion, whom with he makes them to believe that they met: that all their reports and tokens, though separately examined, may every one agree with another. And that whatsoever actions, either in hurting men or beasts, or whatsoever other thing that they falsely imagine at that time to have done, may by himself or his minions at that same time be done indeed. So as, if they would give for a token of their being ravished at, the death of such a person within so short space thereafter whom they believe to have poisoned or witched at that instant, might he not at that same hour have smitten that same person by the permission of God, to the further deceiving of them, and to move others to believe them? And this is surely the likeliest way, and most according to reason, which my judgement can find out in this, and whatsoever other unnatural points of their confession.

And by these means shall we sail surely between Charybdis and Scylla,[6] in eschewing the not believing of them altogether on the one part, lest that draw us to the error that there are no witches; and on the other part in believing of it, make us to eschew the falling into innumerable absurdities, both monstrously against all theology divine, and philosophy humane.

NOTES TO BOOK II, CHAPTER IV

Note 1: Since the impact with the ground after a fall from a high place would cause death, it is difficult to know how James could assert that someone falling from a high place dies through loss of breath before striking the earth. This is nothing but a fable, but one that was still believed in recent times. When trains began to travel faster than a horse could run, many were afraid to ride in them because they believed that the speed of their progress would tear the breath from their lungs and suffocate them.

Note 2: The belief was that the sense of sight operated by means of beams or rays projected from the eyes to touch the objects seen. Only when the beams from our eyes contacted something could

Figure 8

we see it. The eye was thought to be an active, rather than a passive, organ. It is in this false but plausible context that the evil eye was assumed to function, by projecting rays that carried an occult contagion from the witch to the person overlooked.

Note 3: Astral projection during a trance state.

Note 4: The name of Epistemon does not appear here in the original text, but it is obvious that the following long and learned explanation belongs to him and not to Philomathes.

Note 5: Morpheus is the Greek god of dreams, the son of Hypnos, god of sleep.

Note 6: The Scylla is a great rock on the Italian side of the Straits of Messina, directly opposite the whirlpool known as Charybdis. It was perilous to sail between them, since in an effort to avoid one there was danger of running headlong into the other.

CHAPTER V

ARGUMENT:

Witches' actions towards others. Why there are more women
of that craft than men. What things are possible to them
to effectuate by the power of their Master. The reasons thereof.
What is the surest remedy of the harms done by them.

―――――

Philomathes

For truth, your opinion in this seems to carry most reason with it,
and since you have ended, then, the actions belonging properly to
their own persons, say forward now to their actions used toward
others.

Epistemon

In their actions used toward others, three things ought to be considered. First, the manner of their consulting thereupon; next, their
part as instruments; and last, their Master's part, who puts the same
into execution.

As to their consultations thereupon, they use them oftenest in
the churches, where they convene for adoring; at what time their
Master, enquiring at them what they would be at, every one of them
proposes unto him what wicked turn they would have done, either
for obtaining of riches, or for revenging them upon any whom they
have malice at: who, granting their demand, as no doubt willingly he
will since it is to do evil, he teaches them the means whereby they
may do the same. As for little trifling turns that women have ado

with, he causes them to disjoint dead corpses, and to make powders thereof,[1] mixing such other things there amongst as he gives unto them.

Philomathes

But before you go further, permit me, I pray you, to interrupt you one word, which you have put me in memory of, by speaking of women. What can be the cause that there are twenty women given to that craft, where there is one man?

Epistemon

The reason is easy, for as that sex is frailer than man is, so is it easier to be entrapped in these gross snares of the Devil, as was overwell proved to be true by the Serpent's deceiving of Eve at the beginning, which makes him the friendlier with that sex since then.

Philomathes

Return now where you left.

Epistemon

To some others at these times he teaches how to make pictures of wax or clay,[2] that by the roasting thereof, the persons that they bear the name of may be continually melted or dried away by continual sickness. To some he gives such stones or powders as will help to cure or cast on diseases. And to some he teaches kinds of uncouth poisons, which mediciners understand not (for he is far more cunning than man in the knowledge of all the occult properties of nature).

Not that any of these means which he teaches them (except the poisons, which are composed of things natural) can of themselves help any thing to these turns, that they are employed in, but only being God's ape, as well in that, as in all other things. Even as God by his sacraments, which are earthly of themselves, works a heavenly effect, though nowise by any cooperation in them, and as Christ by clay and spittle wrought together, opened the eyes of the blind man

(John 9), suppose there was no virtue in that which he outwardly applied, so the Devil will have his outward means to be shows, as it were, of his doing, which have no part of cooperation in his turns with him, how far that ever the ignorant be abused in the contrary.

And as to the effects of these two former parts, to wit, the consultations and the outward means, they are so wonderful as I dare not allege any of them, without joining a sufficient reason of the possibility thereof. For leaving all the small trifles among wives, and to speak of the principal points of their craft (for the common trifles thereof, they can do without converting well enough by themselves), these principal points, I say, are these.

They can make men or women to love or hate [each] other, which may be very possible to the Devil to effect, seeing he being a subtle spirit, knows well enough how to persuade the corrupted affection of them whom God will permit him so to deal with.

They can lay the sickness of one upon another, which likewise is very possible unto him: for since by God's permission, he laid sickness upon Job,[3] why may he not far easier lay it upon any other? For as an old physician, he knows well enough what humor dominates most in any of us, and as a spirit he can subtly waken up the same, making it peccant or to abound, as he thinks meet for troubling us, when God will so permit him. And for the taking off of it, no doubt he will be glad to relieve such of present pain, as he may think by these means to persuade to be caught in his everlasting snares and fetters.

They can bewitch and take the life of men or women, by roasting of the pictures, as I spoke before, which likewise is very possible to their Master to perform; for although (as I said before) that instrument of wax has no virtue in that turn doing, yet may he not very well even by that same measure that his conjured slaves melt that wax at the fire, may he not I say at these same times, subtly as a spirit, so weaken and scatter the spirits of life of the patient, as may make him on the one part, for faintness to sweat out the humor of his body, and on the other part, for the not concurrence of these spirits, which cause his digestion, so debilitate his stomach, that his humor radical continually, sweating out on the one part, and no new good suck being put in the place thereof, for lack of digestion on the other, he at last shall vanish away, even as his picture will do at the fire. And that knavish and cunning workman, by troubling him only at some times, makes a proportion so near between the working of the one and the other, that both shall end as it were at one time.

They can raise storms and tempests in the air, either upon sea or land, though not universally, but in such a particular place and prescribed bounds, as God will permit them so to trouble: which likewise is very easy to be discerned from any other natural tempests that are meteors,[4] in respect of the sudden and violent raising thereof, together with the short enduring of the same. And this is likewise very possible to their Master to do, he having such affinity with the air as being a spirit, and having such power of the forming and moving thereof, as you have heard me already declare. For in the Scripture, that styling of the Prince of the Air is given unto him (Ephesians 2).

They can make folks to become frantic or maniac, which likewise is very possible to their Master to do, since they are but natural sicknesses. And so he lays on these kinds, as well as any others. They can make spirits either to follow and trouble persons, or haunt certain houses, and affright oftentimes the inhabitants; as hath been known to be done by our witches at this time.[5] And likewise they can make some to be possessed with spirits, and so to become very demoniacs: and this last sort is very possible likewise to the Devil their Master to do, since he may easily send his own angels to trouble in what form he pleases, any whom God will permit him to so use.

Philomathes

But will God permit these wicked instruments by the power of the Devil their Master, to trouble by any of these means, any that believes in him?

Epistemon

No doubt, for there are three kinds of folks whom God will permit so to be tempted or troubled: the wicked for their horrible sins, to punish them in the like measure; the godly that are sleeping in any great sins or infirmities and weaknesses in faith, to waken them up the faster by such an uncouth form; and even some of the best, that their patience may be tried before the world, as Job's was. For why may not God use any kind of extraordinary punishment when it pleases him, as well as the ordinary rods of sickness or other adversities?

Philomathes

Who then may he free from these devilish practices?

Epistemon

No man ought to presume so far as to promise any impunity to himself, for God hath before all beginnings preordained as well the particular sorts of plagues as of benefits for every man, which in their own time he ordains them to be visited with; and yet ought we not to be the more afraid for that, of anything that the Devil and his wicked instruments can do against us, for we daily fight against the Devil in a hundred other ways. And therefore as a valiant captain fears no more being at the combat, nor stays from his purpose for the rummishing shot of a cannon nor the small clack of a pistol, suppose he be not certain what may light upon him, even so ought we boldly to go forward in fighting against the Devil without any greater terror for these his rarest weapons, than for the ordinary whereof we have daily the proof.

Philomathes

Is it not lawful then by the help of some other witches to cure the disease that is cast on by that craft?

Epistemon

Nowise lawful, for I gave you the reason thereof in that axiom of theology, which was the last word I spoke of magic.[6]

Philomathes

How then may these diseases be lawfully cured?

Epistemon

Only by earnest prayer to God, by amendment of their lives, and by sharply pursuing every one, according to his calling, of these instruments of Satan, whose punishment to the death will be a salutary sacrifice for the patient.[7] And this is not only the lawful way, but likewise the most sure. For by the Devil's means, can never the Devil be cast out (Mark 3), as Christ says. And when such a cure is used, it may well serve for a short time, but at the last, it will doubtlessly tend to the utter perdition of the patient, both in body and soul.

NOTES ON BOOK II, CHAPTER V

Note 1: The accusation that the North Berwick witches dug up corpses and removed their joints for working malicious magic occurs in the charges laid against them. The joints were specifically the joints of the fingers and toes, as well as the kneecaps. These joints were either used whole, or were dried and reduced to a power, to be mixed with other materials having occult virtues.

It was charged against John Fian at his trial of December 20, 1590, that at the command of the Devil he had dismembered the bodies of the dead, and especially unbaptised children. At the January 27, 1591, trial against Agnes Sampson she was accused of having fastened to the four legs of a cat four joints from a dead man, and of then having thrown the cat into the sea for the purpose of sinking a ship (the cat swam back to shore, and presumably was uninjured, apart from the assault on its dignity). She was also charged with having each night put the powder or "mwildis"

of pulverized joints from corpses under the bed of Effie McCalyan, beginning ten days before she gave birth, for the purpose of
reducing her labor pains. She was charged with participating at
the North Berwick church in the digging-up and dismembering
of four corpses, so that the witches present could divide between
them the joints of the fingers, toes, and knees—Agnes got two
joints and a winding sheet, which she "kept negligently."

Note 2: Small figures molded out of wax or clay, and made through
magic to possess a sympathetic link with their subjects. This is
perhaps the most characteristic of all forms of magic associated
with witchcraft down through the centuries. Anything done to
the image affects the subject of the image in a similar way. For example, a pin thrust into the head would induce a headache. Wax
figures were "roasted" or melted over a fire to cause a wasting
disease in their subjects—as the figure of wax dripped away, so
did the vitality of the person it depicted. For the image, which
was sometimes called a poppet, to be effective, it was necessary
that the link with the person it represented be strong. Hence,
such figures were embedded with the hair, nail clippings, or other
waste products of the body secretly gathered from their subjects,
baptized in the name of that person and inscribed with the name,
and dressed in a scrap of clothing worn or used by the subject.
The image might be made of almost any material. Indeed, onions
were used for this purpose in England, wrapped with a strip of
paper upon which the name of the intended victim was written,
and affixed with pins, then inserted into a kitchen chimney to be
constantly subjected to the heat and smoke of the fire (Elworthy,
The Evil Eye, page 55).

Note 3: Job 2:7.

Note 4: A "meteor" was for James any natural atmospheric phenomenon. The term was used much more broadly in the Jacobean
period than today, when it solely denotes a streak of light across

the heavens. There were aerial meteors (winds), aqueous meteors (rain, snow, hail, dew), luminous meteors (rainbows, the aurora, halos), and igneous meteors (lightning, shooting stars).

Note 5: One of the accusations against the North Berwick witches was that they entered houses by magical means to frighten the inhabitants. They were also supposed to be able to magically transport themselves onto ships for the purpose of sinking them. While on the ships, they remained invisible to the crews.

Figure 9

Note 6: That evil should never be done for a good cause. See the end of Book I, Chapter VII.

Note 7: This is one of the more evil instructions given by James in his book. He is saying that the best way to cure illnesses and misfortunes caused by witchcraft is to locate, arrest, and execute the witch who caused them. As a result, anyone believing in witchcraft who had the misfortune to fall sick from some lingering disease or infirmity would begin to look with suspicion at his neighbors, in the expectation that the death of one of them would cure the sickness. This attitude would increase the hysteria surrounding anyone accused of witchcraft, and multiply the accusations. Notice the use by James of the word "sacrifice." He seems to be suggesting that the execution of a witch is a kind of offering to God that will be compensated for by the lifting of the curses placed on the witch's victims.

CHAPTER VI

ARGUMENT:
What sort of folks are least or most subject to receive harm
by witchcraft. What power they have to harm the magistrate,
and upon what respects they have any power in prison.
And to what end may or will the Devil appear to them therein.
Upon what respects the Devil appears in different shapes to various
of them at any time.

———

Philomathes
But who dare take upon him to punish them, if no man can be sure to be free from their unnatural invasions?

Epistemon
We ought not the more of that restrain from virtue, that the way whereby we climb thereunto be narrow and perilous. But besides that, as there is no kind of person so subject to receive harm of them, as these that are of infirm and weak faith (which is the best buckler against such invasions), so have they so small power over none as over such as zealously and earnestly pursue them, without sparing for any worldly respect.[1]

Philomathes
Then they are like the pestilence, which smites these with most sickness, that fly it farthest and apprehend deepest the peril thereof.

Epistemon

It is even so with them. For either is it able to them to use any false cure upon a patient, except the patient first believe in their power, and so hazard the tinsel of his own soul, nor yet can they have less power to hurt any, than such as condemns most their doings, so being it comes of faith and not of any vain arrogance in themselves.

Philomathes

But what is their power against the magistrate?

Epistemon

Less or greater, according as he deals with them. For if he be slothful towards them, God is very able to make them instruments to waken and punish his sloth. But if he be the contrary, he according to the just law of God, and allowable law of all nations, will be diligent in examining and punishing them, God will not permit their Master to trouble or hinder so good a work.

Philomathes

But after they be once in hands and confinement, have they any further power in their craft?

Epistemon

That is according to the form of their detention. If they be but apprehended and detained of any private person, upon other private respects, their power no doubt either in escaping or in doing hurt, is no less than ever it was before. But if on the other part, their apprehending and detention be by the lawful magistrate, upon the just respects of their guiltiness in that craft, their power is then no greater than before that ever they meddled with their Master. For when God begins justly to strike by his lawful lieutenants, it is not in the Devil's power to defraud or bereave him of the office, or affect of his power and revenging scepter.[2]

Philomathes

But will never their Master come to visit them, after they be once apprehended and put in confinement?

Epistemon

That is according to the estate that these miserable wretches are in. For if they be obstinate in still denying, he will not spare, when he finds time to speak with them, either if he find them in any comfort, to fill them more and more with the vain hope of some manner of relief; or else if he find them in a deep despair, by all means to augment the same, and to persuade them by some extraordinary means to put themselves down, which very commonly they do.[3] But if they be penitent and confess, God will not permit him to trouble them any more with his presence and allurements.

Philomathes

It is not good using his counsel, I see then. But I would earnestly know when he appears to them in prison, what forms does he then take?

Epistemon

Diverse forms, even as he used to do at other times upon them. For as I told you, speaking of magic, he appears to that kind of craftsman ordinarily in a form, according as they agree upon it among themselves. Or if they be but apprentices, according to the quality of their circles or conjurations. Yet to these capped[4] creatures, he appears as he pleases, and as he finds best for their humors. For even at their public conventions he appears to diverse of them in diverse forms, as we have found by the difference of their confessions in that point. For he deluding them with vain impressions in the air, makes himself to seem more terrible to the grosser sort, that they may thereby be moved to fear and reverence him the more, and less monstrous and uncouth again to the craftier sort, lest otherwise they might stare and shudder at his ugliness.

Philomathes

How can he then be felt, as they confess they have done him, if his body be but of air?

Epistemon

I hear little of that among their confessions, yet may he make himself palpable, either by assuming any dead body, and using the ministry thereof, or else by deluding as well their sense of feeling as seeing; which is not impossible to him to do, since all our senses, as we are so weak, and even by ordinary sickness will be oftentimes deluded.

Philomathes

But I would spare one word further yet, concerning his appearing to them in prison,[5] which is this: may any that chance to be present at that time in the prison see him as well as they?

Epistemon

Sometimes they will, and sometimes not, as it pleases God.

NOTES ON BOOK II, CHAPTER VI

Note 1: This is another calculated statement by James. His assertion is that the more aggressively anyone seeks to locate and persecute those believed to be witches, the more God will defend that person's health and security against their magic. As a consequence of this belief, it was inevitable that neurotic and hysterical members of society—those most likely to see witches around every corner—would be the most active in making accusations against their neighbors, as a way of ensuring their own security against witchcraft.

Note 2: James refers to himself when he writes of the "revenging scepter" that punishes witches. These are his own personal beliefs, and the essential motives of his actions against witchcraft. According to his opinion, by vigorously pursuing the persecution of witches he was not only performing the will of God but was ensuring his own security against any spells that might have been worked against him. His motive for so active an involvement in the North Berwick affair becomes plain. He was not so much driven by righteous indignation, as he was by fear. He believed that by taking the most aggressive of all possible roles in the affair, and becoming its leader, he would guarantee the most complete protection for himself and his wife from the evil magic of the Devil.

Note 3: There is no way to estimate how many of those accused of witchcraft, and confined for long periods while undergoing extreme tortures, took their own lives. James asserts this to be very common, and no doubt it occurred with regularity. This may have been the fate of Robert Grierson, one of the North Berwick witches, who on April 15, 1591, was said to have died in prison "by the extremyty of the tortours applyed to him." Anyone confined in a prison cell who wanted to commit suicide would be forced to use "extraordinary means," as James put it, since the more common means would be unavailable.

Note 4: The cap and gown symbolized someone who had earned a degree from a university.

Note 5: John Fian testified that the Devil came to his prison cell in the middle of the night, dressed all in black, the same day he had made his initial confession under torture, which he later retracted. There is no mention of anyone else seeing the Devil in Fian's cell.

CHAPTER VII

ARGUMENT:
Two forms of the Devil's visible conversing in the earth,
with the reasons wherefore the one of them was commonest
in the time of the Papistry, and the other since then.
Those that deny the power of the Devil, deny the power of God,
and are guilty of the error of the Sadducees.

———

Philomathes

Has the Devil then power to appear to any other, except to such as are his sworn disciples: especially since all oracles, and suchlike kinds of illusions, were taken away and abolished by the coming of Christ?

Epistemon

Although it be true indeed that the brightness of the Gospel at his coming, scaled the clouds of all these gross errors in paganism, yet that these abusing spirits cease not ever since at some times to appear, daily experience teaches us. Indeed, this difference is to be marked between the forms of Satan's conversing visibly in the world. For of two different forms thereof, the one of them by the spreading of the Evangel,[1] and conquest of the white horse[2] in the sixth chapter of the Revelation, is much hindered and become rarer thereby: this, his appearing to any Christians, troubling of them outwardly, or possessing of them constrainedly.[3] The other of them is become commoner and more used since then, I mean by their unlawful arts, whereupon our whole purpose has been. This we find by experience in this isle to be true. For as we know, more ghosts and spirits were seen than tongue can tell in the time of blind Papistry in these countries, where now by the contrary, a man shall scarcely all his time hear once of such things. And yet were these unlawful arts far rarer at that time, and never were so much heard of, nor so rife as they are now.

Philomathes

What should be the cause of that?

Epistemon

The diverse nature of our sins procures at the justice of God diverse sorts of punishments answering thereunto. And therefore as in the time of the Papistry, our fathers erring grossly and through ignorance, that mist of errors overshadowed the Devil to walk the more familiarly among them, and as it were by childish and frightening terrors, to mock and accuse their childish errors. By the contrary, we now being sound of religion, and in our life rebelling to our profession [of faith], God justly by that sin of rebellion, as Samuel calls it, accuses our life [for] so willfully fighting against our profession.[4]

Philomathes

Since you are entered now to speak of the appearing of spirits, I would be glad to hear your opinion in that matter. For many deny that any such spirits can appear in these days, as I have said.

Epistemon

Doubtlessly, who denies the power of the Devil would likewise deny the power of God, if they could for shame. For since the Devil is the very contrary opposite to God, there can be no better way to know God, than by the contrary: as by the one's power (though a creature), to admire the power of the great Creator; by the falsehood of the one, to consider the truth of the other; by the injustice of the one, to consider the justice of the other; and by the cruelty of the one, to consider the mercifulness of the other. And so forth in all the rest of the essence of God, and qualities of the Devil. But I fear indeed, there be overmany Sadducees in this world, that deny all kinds of spirits, for convincing of whose error, there is cause enough, if there were no more, that God should permit at some times spirits visible to make known.

NOTES ON BOOK II, CHAPTER VII

Note 1: The Evangel (from the Greek: *euangelion*: "good news") is the Gospel, or teachings of Jesus. Usually the word is applied to the first four books of the New Testament.

Note 2: As I mentioned in the Introduction, James saw himself as the brave knight mounted on the white horse of Revelation 6:2 and 19:11, or at least as an agent serving that knight.

Note 3: Obsession and possession by spirits.

Note 4: The rebellion of rationalism against faith during the Elizabethan Age, which we now know as the English Renaissance, caused the rise in the number of incidences of witchcraft, which according to James is a punishment of God for the sin of rebellion. By contrast, in former times while Scotland was Catholic, the punishment of God took the form of numerous sightings of ghosts and other spiritual creatures, which was the punishment of God against the sin of ignorance. We have two sins described here— the skepticism of modern times, and the ignorance of past times.

THE THIRD BOOK

ARGUMENT

The description of all these kinds of spirits
that trouble men or women.
The conclusion of the whole dialogue.

CHAPTER I

ARGUMENT:
The division of spirits into four principal kinds.
The description of the first kind of them,
called spectra *and* umbriae mortuorum.
What is the best way to be free of their trouble.

———

Philomathes

I pray you now then go forward in telling what you think fabulous, or may be trusted in that case.

Epistemon

That kind of the Devil's conversing in the earth, may be divided in four different kinds, whereby he frightens and troubles the bodies of men; for of the abusing of the soul, I have spoken already. The first is, where spirits trouble some houses or solitary places. The second, where spirits follow upon certain persons, and at diverse hours trouble them. The third, when they enter within them and possess them. The fourth is these kinds of spirits that are called vulgarly the fairies. Of the three former kinds, you heard already how they may artificially be made by witchcraft to trouble folk. Now it rests to speak of their natural coming, as it were, when not raised by witchcraft.

But generally I must forewarn you of one thing before I enter into this purpose: that is, that although in my discoursing of them, I divided them into diverse kinds, you must notwithstanding thereof note my phrase of speaking in that; for doubtlessly they are in effect, but all one kind of spirits, who for abusing the more of mankind take on these sundry shapes, and use diverse forms of outward action, as if some were of nature better than others. Now I return to my purpose.

As to the first kind of these spirits, they were called by the ancients by diverse names, according as their actions were. For if they were spirits that haunted some houses, by appearing in diverse and horrible forms, and making great din, they were called *lemures*[1] or *spectra*.[2] If they appeared in likeness of any deceased to some friends of his, they were called *umbrae mortuorum*.[3] And so innumerable stylings they got, according to their actions, as I have said already. As we see by experience, how many stylings they have given them in our language in the like manner. Of the appearing of these spirits, we are certified by the Scriptures, where the prophet Isaiah, chapters 13 and 34, threatening the destruction of Babylon and Edom (Isaiah 13; Jeremiah 50), declares that it shall not only be wrecked, but shall become so great a solitude, as it shall be the habitation of owlettes,[4] and of ZIIM and IIM,[5] which are the proper Hebrew names for these spirits.

The cause why they haunt solitary places, it is by reason that they may frighten and shake the more the faith of such as them alone frequenting such places. For our nature is such, as in company we are not so soon moved to any such kind of fear, as being solitary, which the Devil knowing well enough, he will not therefore assail us but when we are weak. And besides that, God will not permit him so to dishonor the societies and companies of Christians, as in public times and places to walk visibly among them. On the other part, when he troubles certain houses that are dwelt in, it is a sure token either of gross ignorance, or of some gross and slanderous sins among the inhabitants thereof, which God by that extraordinary rod punishes.

Philomathes

But by what way or passage can these spirits enter in these houses, seeing they allege that they will enter, door or window being shut?

Epistemon

They will choose the passage for their entrance, according to the form that they are in at that time. For if they have assumed a dead body, whereinto they lodge themselves, they can easily enough open without din any door or window, and enter thereat. And if they enter as a spirit only, any place where the air may come in at is large enough an entry for them: for as I said before, a spirit can occupy no quantity.

Philomathes

And will God then permit these wicked spirits to trouble the rest of a dead body, before the resurrection thereof? Or if he will so, I think it should be of the reprobate only.

Epistemon

What more is the rest troubled of a dead body, when the Devil carries it out of the grave to serve his turn for a space, than when the witches take it up and disjoint it, or when swine root up the graves? The rest, of them that the Scripture speaks of, is not meant by a local remaining continually in one place, but by their resting from their travails and miseries of this world, until their latter conjunction again with the soul, at that time to receive full glory in both.

And that the Devil may use as well the ministry of the bodies of the faithful in these cases, as of the unfaithful, there is no inconvenience; for his hauntings with their bodies after they are dead can nowise defile them, in respect of the soul's absence. And for any dishonor it can be unto them, by what reason can it be greater than the hanging, beheading, or many such shameful deaths that good men will suffer? For there is nothing in the bodies of the faithful more worthy of honor, or freer from corruption by nature, than in these of the unfaithful, until the time they be purged and glorified in the latter day, as is daily seen by the vile diseases and corruptions that the bodies of the faithful are subject unto, as you will see clearly proved, when I speak of the possessed and demoniacs.

Philomathes

Yet there are some that affirm to have haunted such places, where these spirits are alleged to be, and could never hear nor see anything.

Epistemon

I think well: for that is only reserved to the secret knowledge of God, whom he will permit to see such things and whom not.

Philomathes

But where these spirits haunt and trouble any houses, what is the best way to banish them?

Epistemon

By two means may only the remedy of such thing be procured. The one is ardent prayer to God, both of these persons that are troubled with them, and of that church whereof they are. The other is the purging of themselves by amendment of life from such sins, as have procured that extraordinary plague.

Philomathes

And what means then these kinds of spirits, when they appear as the shade of a person newly dead, or to die, to his friends?

Epistemon

When they appear upon that occasion, they are called wraiths in our language. Among the pagans the Devil used that much, to make them believe that it was some good spirit that appeared to them then, either to forewarn them of the death of their friend, or else to discover unto them the will of the deceased, or what was the way of his slaughter, as is written in the book of the *Histories Prodigious*. And this way he easily deceived the pagans, because they knew not God. And to that same effect is it, that he now appears in that manner to some ignorant Christians. For he dare not so delude any that know that neither can the spirit of the deceased return to his friend, or yet an angel use such forms.

Philomathes

And are not our werewolves one sort of these spirits also, that haunt and trouble some houses or dwelling places?

Epistemon

There has indeed been an old opinion of such like things; for by the Greeks they were called *lukanthropoi*, which signifies man-wolves.[6] But to tell you simply my opinion in this, if any such thing has been, I take it to have proceeded but of a natural superabundance of melancholy, which as we read, that it has made some think themselves pitchers, and some horses, and some one kind of beast or other. So suppose I that it has so vitiated the imagination and memory of some, as *per lucida interualla*,[7] it has so highly occupied them, that they have thought themselves very wolves indeed at times, and so have counterfeited their actions in going on their hands and feet, pressing to devour women and children, fighting and snatching with all the town dogs, and in using suchlike other brutish actions, and so to become beasts by a strong apprehension, as Nebuchadnezzar was seven years (Daniel 4).[8] But as to their having and hiding of their hard and shelly sloughs, I take that to be but learned by uncertain report, the author of all lies.

NOTES TO BOOK III, CHAPTER I

Note 1: *Lemures*, or ghosts of the dead, were sometimes divided into two classes by the Romans—*lares*, the ghosts of good men, and *larvae*, the ghosts of evil men.

Note 2: Our word "specter" comes from the Latin *spectrum*, "an appearance or apparition."

Note 3: "Shades of the dead."

Note 4: Certain night spirits known to the Romans as stirges were believed to come in the form of owls. "Large are their heads, fixed is their gaze, for plunder are their beaks adapted; on their wings is a grayish colour, crooked talons are on their claws. By night they fly, and they seek the children unprotected by the nurse, and pollute their bodies, dragged from their cradles. With their beaks they are said to tear the entrails of the sucklings, and they have their maws distended with the blood which they have swallowed" (Ovid, *Fasti*, page 216). This is evidently the same sort of winged night spirit that was fabled to visit Jewish children and stop their breath. It was identified by Kabbalists with Lilith, originally a Babylonian demoness who was elevated by Jewish Kabbalists to the rank of queen of hell. Both spirits may have their origin in the phenomenon known as crib death, or sudden infant death syndrome. A small percentage of very young children, for no apparent reason, simply stop breathing in the middle of the night and die.

Note 5: The spirits called in Hebrew ZIIM and IIM are mentioned in the notes of the King James Bible. Both are translated simply as "wild beasts," the ZIIM as the "wild beasts of the desert" (Isaiah 13:21) and IIM as the "wild beasts of the islands" (Isaiah 13:22). Gesenius identifies TzIIM (ציים) as "dwellers in the desert," in this case wild animals such as the jackal and ostrich, although the term was also applied to desert nomads (Gesenius, *Hebrew and Chaldee Lexicon*, page 708).

Note 6: The word "lycanthrope" is from the Greek λυκανθρωποσ —λυκοσ: a wolf; ανθρωποσ: a man. Summers quotes Richard Rowlands, who in 1605 wrote on the topic: "The were-wolves are certaine sorcerers, who hauing annoynted their bodyes, with an oyntment which they make by the instinct of the deuil; and putting on a certaine inchanted gridel, do not only vnto the view of others seeme as wolues, but to their own thinking haue both the shape and nature of wolues, so long as they weare the said girdel.

Figure 10

And they do dispose themselues as very wolues, in wurrying and killing, and moste of humaine creatures" (Summers, *The Werewolf*, page 3).

The account of the murders committed by Peter Stumpp in Germany, who was executed for his crimes in 1589, shows that the belief in werewolves was still very much alive at the time the North Berwick witches were supposed to be seeking the deaths of James and Anne, and that it was inextricably mingled with a belief in the power of sorcery and malice of the Devil. A year after Stumpp's execution, a tract was published in London detailing his activities. Contained in it is the following account of how Stumpp, called in the tract Stubbe Peeter, became a werewolf:

> The Devil, who saw him a fit instrument to perform mischief as a wicked fiend pleased with the desire of wrong and destruction, gave unto him a girdle which, being put around him, he was straight transformed into the likeness of a greedy, devouring wolf, strong and mighty, with eyes great and large, which in the night sparkled like unto brands of fire, a mouth great and wide, with most sharp and cruel teeth, a huge body

and mighty paws. And no sooner should he put off the same girdle, but presently he should appear in his former shape, according to the proportion of a man, as if he had never been changed. (Bores, *The Damnable Life and Death of Stubbe Peeter*, 1590).

Note 7: "during lucid intervals"

Note 8: Nebuchadnezzar, the king of Babylon, lost his reason for seven years and lived in the open like a beast on wild plants, so that his hair and beard became unkempt and his fingernails and toenails grew long. See Daniel 4:33.

CHAPTER II

ARGUMENT:

The description of the next two kinds of spirits, whereof the one follows outwardly, the other possesses inwardly, the persons that they trouble. That since all prophecies and visions are now ceased, all spirits that appear in these forms are evil.

———

Philomathes

Come forward now to the rest of these kinds of spirits.

Epistemon

As to the next two kinds, that is, either these that outwardly trouble and follow some persons, or else inwardly possess them: I will conjoin them in one, because as well the causes are alike in the persons they are permitted to trouble, as also the ways whereby they may be remedied and cured.

Philomathes

What kind of persons are they that are used to being so troubled?

Epistemon

Two kinds especially: either such as being guilty of grievous offences, God punishes by that horrible kind of scourge, or else being persons of the best nature peradventure, that you shall find in all the country about them, God permits them to be troubled in that sort, for the trial of their patience, and wakening up of their zeal, for admonishing of the beholders not to trust overmuch in themselves, since they are made of no better stuff, and peradventure blotted with no smaller sins (as Christ said, speaking of them upon whom the tower in Siloam fell (Luke 13)); and for giving likewise to the spectators, matter to praise God, that they meriting no better, are yet spared from being corrected in that fearful form.

Philomathes

These are good reasons for the part of God, which apparently moves him so to permit the Devil to trouble such persons. But since the Devil has ever a contrary respect in all the actions that God employs him in, which is, I pray you, the end and mark he shoots at in this turn?

Epistemon

It is to obtain one of two things thereby, if he may. The one is the tinsel of their life, by inducing them to such perilous places at such times as he either follows or possesses them, which may procure the same: and such like, so far as God will permit him, by tormenting them to weaken their bodies, and cast them into incurable diseases. The other thing that he wishes to obtain by troubling of them, is the tinsel of their soul, by enticing them to mistrust and blaspheme God, either for the intolerableness of their torments, as he assayed to have done with Job (Job 10), or else for his promising unto them to leave the troubling of them, in case they would so do, as is known by experience at this same time by the confession of a young one that was so troubled.

Philomathes

Since you have spoken now of both these kinds of spirits, comprehending them in one, I must now go back again in casting some questions of every one of these kinds in particular. And first for these that follow certain persons, you know that there are two sorts of them: one sort that troubles and torments the persons that they haunt with, and another sort that are serviceable unto them in all kinds of their necessities, and omit never to forewarn them of any sudden peril that they are to be in. And so in this case, I would understand whether both these sorts be but wicked and damned spirits, or if the last sort be rather angels (as should appear by their actions) sent by God to assist such as he specially favors. For it is written in the Scriptures, that God sends legions of angels to guard and watch over his elect (Genesis 32; I Kings 6; Psalms 34).

Epistemon

I know well enough wherefrom that error which you allege has proceeded: for it was the ignorant pagans that were the fountain thereof. Who for that they knew not God, they forged in their own imaginations, every man to be still accompanied with two spirits, whereof they called the one *genius bonus*, the other *genius malus*.[1] The Greeks called them *endaimona* and *kakodaimona*, whereof the former they said, persuaded him to all the good he did, the other enticed him to all the evil. But praised be God we that are Christians, and walk not among the Cimmerian[2] conjectures of man, know well enough that it is the good spirit of God only, who is the fountain of all goodness, that persuades us to the thinking or doing of any good; and that it is our corrupted flesh and Satan that entice us to the contrary. And yet the Devil for confirming in the heads of ignorant Christians, that error first maintained among the pagans, he bides among the first kind of spirits that I speak of, appeared in time of Papistry and blindness, and haunted diverse houses, without doing any evil, but doing as it were necessary tasks up and down the house: and this spirit they called brownie[3] in our language, who appeared like a rough man; yea, some were so blinded, as to believe that their house was all the more prosperous, as they called it, that such spirits resorted there.

Philomathes

But since the Devil's intention in all his actions is ever to do evil, what evil was there in that form of doing, since their actions outwardly were good?

Epistemon

Was it not evil enough to deceive simple ignorants, in making them to take him for an angel of light, and so to account of God's enemy, as of their particular friend: where by the contrary, all we that are Christians ought assuredly to know that since the coming of Christ in the flesh, and establishing of his church by the apostles, all miracles, visions, prophecies, and appearances of angels or good spirits are ceased.[4] Which served only for the first sowing of faith, and planting of the church. Where now the church being established, and the white horse[5] whereof I spoke before, having made his conquest, the law and prophets are thought sufficient to serve us, or make us inexcusable, as Christ says in his parable of Lazarus and the rich man (Luke 16).

NOTES TO BOOK III, CHAPTER II

Note 1: The good spirit and the evil spirit. It is from this ancient pagan belief that we get the Christian fable that everyone has a angel on their right shoulder and a devil on their left shoulder, forever whispering suggestions into their ears.

Note 2: The distant northern land of Cimmeria was said by the Greek poet Homer to be a land of perpetual mists and darkness.

Note 3: "The Nis, Kobold, or Goblin, appears in Scotland under the name of Brownie. Brownie is a personage of small stature, wrinkled visage, covered with short curly brown hair, and wearing a brown mantle and hood. His residence is the hollow of an old tree, a ruined castle, or the abode of man. He is attached to particular families, with whom he has been known to reside, even for centuries, threshing the corn, cleaning the house, and doing everything done by his northern and English brethren" (Keightley, *The Fairy Mythology*, pages 357–358).

Note 4: By denying the possibility of any form of miracle, prophecy, or vision since the time of Christ, James is able to class all supernatural events as devilish, no matter what their nature or utility. His sweeping statement excludes the miracles of God, the angels, and the saints that have been given formal recognition by the Catholic Church. From the perspective of James, the appearance of the stigmata, or wounds of Christ, on the hands of a pious Christian would be regarded as devilish, and a sign of some hidden sin; the miraculous restoration of sight to the blind at Lourdes would be dismissed as a ruse by Satan intended to beguile the ignorant. There is something of the fanatic in this comprehensive rejection of even the possibility of any divine supernatural event, coupled with a willingness to believe in the most fantastic supernatural evils.

Note 5: Another reference to the white horse of Revelation 19:11, which was a symbol of profound personal significance to James.

CHAPTER III

ARGUMENT:

The description of a particular sort of that kind of following spirit,
called incubi and succubi. And what is the reason wherefore
these kinds of spirits haunt most the northern
and barbarous parts of the world.

———

Philomathes

The next question that I would speak, is likewise concerning this first of these two kinds of spirits that you have conjoined, and it is this: you know how it is commonly written and reported, that among the rest of the sorts of spirits that follow certain persons, there is one more monstrous than all the rest, in respect as it is alleged they have intercourse naturally with them whom they trouble and haunt with? And therefore I would know in two things your opinion herein: first, if such a thing can be; and next, if it be, whether there be a difference of sexes among these spirits, or not.

Epistemon

That abominable kind of the Devil's abusing of men or women was called of old incubi and succubi, according to the difference of the sexes that they had congress with.[1] By two means this great kind of abuse might possibly be performed. The one, when the Devil only as a spirit, and stealing out the sperm of a dead body, abuses them that way, they not clearly seeing any shape or feeling any thing, but that which he so conveys in that part: as we read of a monastery of nuns which were burnt for their being that way abused. The other means it when he borrows a dead body and so visibly, and as it seems unto them naturally, as a man copulates with them.

But it is to be noted, that in whatsoever way he uses it, that sperm seems intolerably cold to the person abused. For if he steals out the nature of a living person, it cannot be so quickly carried, but it will both lose the strength and heat by the way, which it could never have had for lack of agitation, which in the time of procreation is the procurer and wakener up of these two natural qualities. And if he occupying the dead body as his lodging, expel the same out thereof in the due time, it must likewise be cold by the participation with the qualities of the dead body whereout of it comes.

And whereas you inquire if these spirits be divided in sexes or not, I think the rules of philosophy may easily resolve a man of the contrary: for it is a sure principle of that art, that nothing can be divided in sexes, except such living bodies as must have a natural seed to generate by. But we know spirits have no seed proper to themselves, nor yet can they engender one with another.

Philomathes

How is it then that they say various monsters have been gotten by that way?

Epistemon

These tales are nothing but *aniles fabulae*.[2] For that they have no semen of their own, I have shown you already. And that the cold semen of a dead body can work nothing in generation, it is more than plain, as being already dead of itself as well as the rest of the body is, wanting the natural heat, and such other natural operations, as are necessary for working that effect. And in case such a thing were possible (which were all utterly against all rules of nature), it would breed no monster, but only such a natural offspring as would have come between that man or woman and that other abused person, in case they both being alive had had ado with [each] other.

For the Devil's part therein is but the naked carrying or expelling of that substance, and so it could not participate with no quality of the same.

Indeed, it is possible to the craft of the Devil to make a woman's belly to swell after he hath that way abused her, which he may do either by stirring up her own humor, or by herbs, as we see beggars daily do;[3] and when the time of her delivery should come to make her labor with great anguish, like unto that natural course, and then subtly to slip into the midwife's hands sticks, stones, or some monstrous child brought from some other place. But this is more reported and guessed at by others, than believed by me.

Philomathes

But what is the cause that this kind of abuse is thought to be most common in such wild parts of the world, as Lapland and Finland,[4] or in our north isles of Orkney and Shetland?

Epistemon

Because where the Devil finds greatest ignorance and barbarity, there assails he most grossly, as I gave you the reason wherefore there were more witches of womenkind than men.

Philomathes

Can any be so unhappy as to give their willing consent to the Devil's vile abusing them in this form?

Epistemon

Yea, some of the witches have confessed that he has persuaded them to give their willing consent thereunto, that he may thereby have them tangled the deeper in his snares; but as the other compelled sort is to be pitied and prayed for, so is this most highly to be punished and detested.

Philomathes

It is not the thing which we call the mare, which takes folks sleeping in their beds, a kind of these spirits, whereof you are speaking?

Epistemon

No, that is but a natural sickness, which the mediciners have given that name of incubus unto, *ab incubando*, because it being a thick phlegm, falling into our breast upon the heart while we are sleeping, intercedes so our vital spirits, and takes all power from us, as to make us think that there were some unnatural burden or spirit lying upon us and holding us down.[5]

NOTES TO BOOK III, CHAPTER III

Note 1: The incubus is a sexual spirit in the form of a male, and the succubus a sexual spirit in the form of a female. It was believed by many demonologists that this appearance of gender was not an essential part of the nature of these spirits, but that they could change from male to female at will, depending on the sex of the person with whom they intended to have intercourse. How spirits copulated with humans, whether they stole human semen to inject into the womb during these unions, and whether it was possible that such lovemaking could result in pregnancy, were all topics of hot debate. However, there was general agreement that the incidence of willing sexual union with spirits had increased in recent times.

But the theory that modern witches are tainted with this sort of diabolical filthiness is not substantiated only in our opinion, since the expert testimony of the witches themselves has made all these things credible; and that they do not now, as in times past, subject themselves unwillingly, but willingly embrace this most foul and miserable servitude. For how many women have we left to be punished by secular law in various dioceses, especially in Constance and the town of Ratisbon, who have been for many years addicted to these abominations, some from their twentieth and some from their twelfth or thirteenth year, and always with a total or partial abnegation of the Faith?

All the inhabitants of these places are witnesses of it. For without reckoning those who secretly repented, and those who returned to the Faith, no less than forty-eight have been burned in five years. (Kramer and Sprenger, *Malleus Maleficarum*, page 111)

Note 2: "old wives' tales"

Note 3: James seems to mean that in his day one could often see female beggars who had eaten specific herbs in order to swell their bellies and make themselves appear pregnant, and so increase the amount of charity they might receive. However, it may have been the case that beggars would eat wild herbs merely to ease their hunger, and end up with distended stomachs as a result of the noxious properties of the plants they had consumed. Even in the absence of herbs, hunger itself will distend the belly.

Note 4: That sexual unions with spirits were more common in Lapland, Finland, and other northerly parts of the world is probable

Figure 11

since shamanism survived as an active religion in these places during the Jacobean period, and a feature of shamanism is marriage between the shaman and supernatural beings, who act as the shaman's tutelary and serving spirits.

Note 5: This is now referred to as "sleep paralysis." The theory is that the body is naturally held immobile in dreams to prevent us thrashing around and injuring ourselves, and sometimes we become conscious while this physical inhibitor is still in effect, making us feel as through we are being pressed or stifled. Having personally experienced the mare on numerous occasions, I can state that it is a very clear and distinct feeling of palpable weight pressing on a particular part of the body, but not on the rest of the body. Sometimes there is a sensation of the weight shifting, as though whatever causes it were moving around. This sensation of weight is accompanied by an inability to move the limbs that must be consciously and willfully thrown off. I suspect that the sensation of weight, and the inability to move, are not directly connected; that the first is caused by a spiritual creature, and the second by our natural sleep paralysis.

CHAPTER IV

ARGUMENT:
The description of the demoniacs and possessed.
By what reason the Papists may have power to cure them.

———

Philomathes

Well, I have told you now all my doubts, and you have satisfied me therein, concerning the first of these two kinds of spirits that you have conjoined. Now I am to inquire only two things at you concerning the last kind, I mean the demoniacs. The first is, whereby shall these possessed folks be discerned from them that are troubled with a natural frenzy or mania? The next is, how can it be that they can be remedied by the Papist's church, whom we count as heretics? It should appear that one devil should not cast out another, for then would his kingdom be divided in itself, as Christ said (Matthew 12; Mark 3).

Epistemon

As to your first question, there are diverse symptoms whereby that heavy trouble may be discerned from a natural sickness, and specially three, omitting the diverse vain signs that the Papists attribute unto it, such as the raging at holy water, their fleeing aback from the cross, their not abiding the hearing of God named, and innumerable such like vain things that were alike tiresome and worthless to recite.

But to come to these three symptoms then, whereof I spoke, I account the one of them to be the incredible strength of the possessed creature, which will far exceed the strength of six of the stoutest and strongest of any other men that are not so troubled.[1] The next is the rising up so far of the patient's breast and belly, with such an unnatural stirring and vehement agitation with them, and such an iron hardness of his sinews so stiffly bended out, that it were not possible to prick out, as it were, the skin of any other person so far: so mightily works the Devil in all the members and senses of his body, he being locally within the same; although of his soul and affections thereof, he has no more power than over any other man's. The last is the speaking of different languages, which the patient is known by them that were acquainted with him never to have learned, and that with an uncouth and hollow voice, and all the time of his speaking, a greater motion being in his breast than in his mouth.[2] But from this last symptom is excepted such as are altogether, in the time of their possessing, bereft of all their senses, being possessed with a dumb and blind spirit, whereof Christ relieved one, in the twelfth chapter of Matthew.

And as to your next demand, it is first to be doubted if the Papists or any not professing the only true religion, can relieve any of that trouble. And next, in case they can, upon what respects it is possible unto them. As to the former, upon two reasons it is grounded. First, that it is known so many of them to be counterfeit, which deception the clergy invents for confirming of their rotten religion. The next is, that by experience we find that few who are possessed indeed are fully cured by them: but rather the Devil is content to release the bodily hurting of them, for a short space, thereby to obtain the perpetual hurt of the souls of so many that by these false miracles may be induced or confirmed in the profession of that erroneous religion: even as I told you before that he does in the false cures, or casting off of diseases by witches.

As to the other part of the argument, in case they can, which rather (with reverence of the learned thinking otherwise) I am induced to believe, by reason of the faithful report that men sound of religion have made according to their sight thereof, I think if so be, I say these may be the respects whereupon the Papists may have that power. Christ gave a commission and power to his apostles to cast out devils, which they accordingly thereunto put into execution. The rules he had them observe in that action were fasting and prayer, and the action itself [was] to be done in his name. This power of theirs proceeded not, then, of any virtue in them, but only in him who directed them. As was clearly proved by Judas, his having as great power in that commission as any of the rest. It is easy, then, to be understood that the casting out of devils is by the virtue of fasting and prayer, and invoking of the name of God, even though many imperfections be in the person that is the instrument, as Christ himself teaches us of the power that false prophets shall have to cast out devils (Matthew 7). It is no wonder, then, these respects of this action being considered, that it may be possible to the Papists, though erring in various points of religion, to accomplish this, if they use the right form prescribed by Christ herein. For what the worse is that action, that they err in other things, more than their baptism is the worse that they err in the other sacrament, and have added many vain freits to the baptism itself.

Philomathes

Surely it is no little wonder that God should permit the bodies of any of the faithful to be so dishonored, as to be a dwelling place to that unclean spirit.

Epistemon

There is it which I told right now, would prove and strengthen my argument of the Devil's entering in the dead bodies of the faithful. For if he is permitted to enter in their living bodies, even when they are joined with the soul, how much more will God permit him to enter in their dead carcasses, which is no more man, but the filthy and corruptible case of man. For as Christ says, it is not anything

that enters within man that defiles him, but only that which proceeds and comes out of him (Mark 7).

NOTES ON BOOK III, CHAPTER IV

Note 1: James was himself the witness of a case of possession on
Christmas Eve, 1590, during the interrogation of John Fian. It
is described in *News From Scotland*. Fian confessed to having bewitched a man so that for one hour every day he fell into a raving
fit. It seems likely that Fian was aware of this man's bizarre mental illness, which was probably well-known in the area where he
lived, and in an attempt to avoid more torture, Fian confessed to
having caused the fits through witchcraft.

James had the man brought before him in the King's chamber,
and watched the possession happen. Suddenly the man gave a
screech and began to bend his body and caper about and spring
up so that his head touched the ceiling of the room. Those with
James who were watching this Christmas entertainment tried to
hold the man down, but he was too strong for them. More attendants had to be called in so that he could be tied up until his
fit passed. When he came to his senses, James asked him what
awareness he retained of his actions, and the man told him that
he had been asleep.

Note 2: In Greek and Roman times, those from whom issued the
voices of spirits were known as belly-speakers, or ventriloquists
(*venter:* "belly," *loquor:* "to speak"). They were characterized in this
way because the voices of the spirits did not seem to come from
the mouths of the possessed individuals, but from their abdom-
inal regions. The term is now applied to stage performers who
pretend to throw their voices outside themselves.

CHAPTER V

ARGUMENT:

The description of the fourth kind of spirits called the fairies.
What is possible therein, and what is but illusion. How far this
dialogue entreats of all these things, and to what end.

Philomathes

Now I pray you, come on to that fourth kind of spirits.

Epistemon

That fourth kind of spirits, which by the pagans was called Diana and her wandering court,[1] and among us was called the fairies (as I told you), or our Good Neighbours,[2] was one of the sorts of illusions that was rifest in the time of Papistry. For although it was held odious to prophesy by the Devil, yet whom this kind of spirits carried away and informed, they were thought to be luckiest and of best life. To speak of the many vain prattles founded upon that illusion, how there was a king and queen of fairy, of such a jolly court and train as they had, how they had a tithe and duty, as it were, of all goods, how they naturally rode and went, ate and drank, and did all other actions like natural men and women, I think it more like Virgil's *Campi Elysii*,[3] than anything that ought to be believed by Christians, except in general, that as I spoke various times before, the Devil deludes the senses of many simple creatures, in making them believe that they saw and heard such things as were nothing so indeed.

Philomathes

But how can it be then, that many witches have gone to death with that confession, that they have been transported with the fairies to such a hill,[4] which opening, they went in, and there saw a fairy queen, who being now lighter, gave them a stone[5] that had various virtues, which at different times has been produced in judgement?

Epistemon

I say that, even as I said before of that imaginary ravishing of the spirit forth of the body. For may not the Devil present to their fantasy, their senses being dulled, and as it were asleep, such hills and houses within them, such glistening courts and trains, and whatsoever such like wherewith he pleases to delude them? And in the meantime, their bodies being senseless, to convey into their hands any stone or such like thing, which he makes them to imagine to have received in such a place.

Philomathes

But what say you to their foretelling the death of various persons, whom they allege to have seen in these places? That is a sooth-dream (as they say) since they see it walking.

Epistemon

I think that either they have not been sharply enough examined, that gave so blunt a reason for their prophecy, or otherwise, I think it likewise as possible that the Devil may prophesy to them when he deceives their imaginations in that sort, as well as when he plainly speaks unto them at other times; for their prophesying is but a kind of vision, as it were, wherein he commonly counterfeits God among the pagans, as I told you before.

Philomathes

I would know now whether these kinds of spirits may only appear to witches, or if they may also appear to any other.

Epistemon

They may do to both. To the innocent sort, either to affright them, or to seem to be a better sort of folk than unclean spirits are; and to the witches, to be a color of safety[6] for them, that ignorant magistrates may not punish them for it, as I told even now. But as the one sort, for being perforce troubled with them ought to be pitied, so ought the other sort (who may be discerned by their taking upon them to prophesy by them), that sort I say, ought as severely to be punished as any other witches, and rather the more, in that they go dissemblingly to work.

Philomathes

And what makes the spirits have so different names from others?

Epistemon

Even the knavery of that same Devil, who as he deludes the necromancers with innumerable feigned names for him and his angels, as in particular making Satan, Beelzebub, and Lucifer to be three different spirits, where we find the two former but different names given to the prince of all the rebelling angels by the Scripture. As by Christ, the prince of all the devils is called Beelzebub in that place which I alleged against the power of any heretics to cast out devils. By John in the Revelation, the old tempter is called Satan, the prince of all the evil angels. And last, to wit, Lucifer is but by allegory taken from the Day Star[7] (so named in diverse places of the Scriptures) because of his excellence (I mean the prince of them) in his creation before his fall. Even so I say he deceives the witches by attributing to himself diverse names, as if every different shape that he transforms himself into were a different kind of spirit.

Philomathes

But I have heard many more strange tales of these fairies, than you have yet told me.

Epistemon

As well I do in that, as I did in all the rest of my discourse. For because the ground of this conference of ours proceeded of your inquiring at me at our meeting, if there were such a thing as witches or spirits, and if they had any power, I therefore have framed my whole discourse only to prove that such things are and may be, by such number of examples as I show to be possible by reason, and keep myself from dipping any further in playing the part of a dictionary, to tell whatever I have read or heard in that purpose, which both would exceed faith, and rather would seem to teach such unlawful arts, not to disallow and condemn them, as it is the duty of all Christians to do.

NOTES ON BOOK III, CHAPTER V

Note 1: Summers quotes from the work *De ecclesiasticis disciplinis* of the Abbot Regino of Prüm, written in 906:

> This too must by no means be passed over that certain utterly abandoned women, turning aside to follow Satan, being seduced by the illusions and phantasmical shows of demons firmly believe and openly profess that in the dead of night they ride upon certain beasts along with the pagan goddess Diana and a countless horde of women, and that in those silent hours they fly over vast tracts of country and obey her as their mistress, whilst on certain other nights they are summoned to do her homage and pay her service (Summers, *The History of Witchcraft and Demonology*, page 121).

Note 2: Fairies were sometimes referred to as "the good folk" as a form of avertive magic, to propitiate them and turn aside their wrath. It is exactly the same impulse of human nature that caused the Greeks to refer to the Furies, who originally were named the Erinyes (Angry Ones) as the Eumenides (Gracious Ones). The true character of fairies was strange and terrifying, and no man or woman wished to encounter them alone in the mists of twilight.

Figure 12

Note 3: The Elysian Fields, described by the Roman poet Virgil in his epic the *Aeneid*, Book VI, lines 637–659.

Note 4: "There is scarcely a district of the Highlands without its fairy knoll, generally the greenest hillock in the place" (Evans-Wentz, *The Fairy-Faith in Celtic Countries*, page 86). The fairies were thought to dwell in the depths of these hills in hidden caverns and passageways. Those who climbed the hill might chance to see the fairies dancing in a ring on the grass. If they inadvertently offended the good people, for example by refusing an offer of hospitality, they might find themselves suddenly swept under the hill and unable to escape. Entire palaces were said to be beneath these hills.

Note 5: This perhaps refers to the elf-shot or fairy arrow (*saighead sith*), a stone arrowhead, or a stone shaped like an arrowhead, which was believed to have been made by fairies, and to possess magical properties. It was thrown or shot by unseen fairies at those who ventured too near their habitations.

Note 6: In Scottish law, a "color" was a plea that seems probable but was actually without solid merit—what we might today refer to as a "technicality." It was usually raised in an attempt to get a decision moved from the hands of the jury into the hands of the judges.

Note 7: The planet Venus, when seen in the mornings in the east, is known as the Morning Star, and was sometimes poetically referred to as Lucifer, a name that literally means "light-bringing" or "light-bearer" (*lucis*: "light," *ferre*: "to bear"). It is fabled to be the original name of Satan before his expulsion from heaven.

CHAPTER VI

ARGUMENT:

Of the trial and punishment of witches. What sort of accusation ought to be admitted against them. What is the cause of the increasing so far of their number in this age.

———

Philomathes

Then to make an end of our conference, since I see it draws late, what form of punishment think you merit these magicians and witches? For I see that you account them to be all alike guilty.

Epistemon

They ought to be put to death according to the law of God, the civil and imperial law, and municipal law of all Christian nations.

Philomathes

But what kind of death, I pray you?

Epistemon

It is commonly used by fire, but that is an indifferent thing to be used in every country, according to the law or custom thereof.

Philomathes

But ought no sex, age, nor rank to be exempted?

Epistemon

None at all (being so used by the lawful magistrate),[1] for it is the highest point of idolatry, wherein no exception is admitted by the law of God.

Philomathes

Then children may not be spared?

Epistemon

Yea, not a hair the less of my conclusion. For they are not that capable of reason as to practice such things. And for any being in company and not revealing thereof, their less and ignorant age will no doubt excuse them.

Philomathes

I see you condemn them all that are of the counsel of such crafts.

Epistemon

No doubt, for as I said, speaking of magic, the consulters, trusters in, overlookers, entertainers, or stirrers up of these craftsfolk, are equally guilty with themselves that are the practitioners.

Philomathes

Whether may the prince, then, or supreme magistrate, spare or overlook any that are guilty of that craft, upon some great respects known to him?

Epistemon

The prince or magistrate for further trials' cause, may delay the punishing of them such a certain space as he thinks convenient: but in the end, to spare the life, and not to strike when God bids strike, and so severely punish in so odious a fault and treason against God, it is not only unlawful, but doubtless no less sin in that magistrate than it was in Saul's sparing of Agag (I Samuel 15). And so comparable to the sin of witchcraft itself, as Samuel alleged at that time.

Philomathes

Surely then, I think since this ought to be so severely punished, judges ought to beware to condemn any, but such as they are sure are guilty; neither should the clattering report of an accused old woman serve in so weighty a case.

Epistemon

Judges ought indeed to beware whom they condemn, for it is as great a crime (as Solomon says) to condemn the innocent, as to let the guilty escape free (Proverbs 17); neither ought the report of any one infamous person be admitted for a sufficient proof, which can stand of no law.

Philomathes

And what may a number then of guilty persons' confessions work against one that is accused?

Epistemon

The assize must serve for interpreter of our law in that respect. But in my opinion, since in a matter of treason against the prince, children or wives or never so defamed persons may of our law serve for sufficient witnesses and proofs, I think surely that by a far greater reason, such witnesses may be sufficient in matters of high treason against God. For who but witches can be proofs, and so witnesses, of the doings of witches?

Philomathes

Indeed, I trust they will be loath to prosecute any honest man upon their counsel. But what if they accuse folk to have been present at their imaginary conventions in the spirit, when their bodies lie senseless, as you have said?

Epistemon

I think they are not a hair the less guilty, for the Devil dared never have borrowed their shade or likeness to that turn, if their consent had not been at it, and the consent in these turns is death under the law.

Philomathes

Then Samuel was a witch: for the Devil resembled his shape, and played his person, in giving response to Saul.

Epistemon

Samuel was dead as well before that, and so none could slander him with meddling in that unlawful art. For the cause why, as I take it, that God will not permit Satan to use the shapes or similitudes of any innocent person at such unlawful times, is that God will not permit that any innocent person shall be slandered with that vile defection.[2] For then the Devil would find ways anew to calumniate the best. And this we have in proof by them that are carried with the fairies, who never see the shades of any in that court, but of them that thereafter are tried for having been brethren and sisters of that craft. And this was likewise proved by the confession of a young lass, troubled with spirits, laid on her by witchcraft. That although she saw the shapes of diverse men and women troubling her, and named the persons whom these shades represented, yet never one of them was found to be innocent, but all clearly tried to be most guilty, and the most part of them confessed the same.

And besides that, I think it has been seldom heard tell of, that any whom persons guilty of that crime accused, as having known them to be their companions by eyesight, and not by hearsay, but such as were so accused of witchcraft could not be clearly tried upon them, were at the least publicly known to be of a very evil life and reputation: so jealous is God I say, of the fame of them that are innocent in such causes. And besides that, there are two other good helps that may be used for their trial. The one is the finding of their mark, and the trying of the insensibleness thereof. The other is their floating on the water: for as in a secret murder, if the dead carcass be at any time thereafter handled by the murderer, it will gush out of blood, as if the blood were crying to the heaven for revenge of the murderer, God having appointed that secret supernatural sign, for trial of that secret unnatural crime; so it appears that God has appointed (for a supernatural sign of the monstrous impiety of the witches) that the water shall refuse to receive them in her bosom, that have shaken off them the sacred water of baptism, and willfully refused the benefit thereof. No, not so much as their eyes are able to shed tears (threaten and torture them as you please) before first they repent (God not permitting them to dissemble their obstinacy in so horrible a crime), albeit the womenkind especially, be able otherwise to shed tears at every light occasion when they will; yea, although it were dissemblingly, like the crocodiles.

Philomathes

Well, we have made this conference to last as long as leisure would permit. And to conclude then, since I am to take my leave of you, I pray God to purge this country of these devilish practices: for they were never so rife in these parts, as they are now.

Epistemon

I pray God that so be, too. But the causes are over manifest, that makes them to be so rife. For the great wickedness of the people on the one part, procures this horrible defection, whereby God justly punishes sin, by a greater iniquity; and on the other part, the consummation of the world, and our deliverance drawing near, makes Satan to rage the more in his instruments, knowing his kingdom to be so near an end (Revelation 2). And so, farewell for this time.

NOTES TO BOOK III, CHAPTER VI

Note 1: James asserts that no exceptions should be made to the punishment of witches based on age, other than those that are commonly recognized in the law for other crimes.

Figure 13

Note 2: The implications of this bit of reasoning are chilling. As far as James was concerned, anyone accused of witchcraft must be guilty, since God would never allow an innocent to be so slandered. Even those accused of having been present at imaginary sabbats of witches, which the magistrate and members of the jury know to have been imaginary, are to be condemned and executed since God would not permit them to be identified as present unless they had themselves consented to be present at the imaginary gatherings.

Newes from Scotland,

Declaring the Damna=

ble life and death of Doctor Fian, *a*
notable Sorcerer, who was burned at
Edenbrough in Ianuary laſt.
1591.

Which Doctor was regeſter to the Diuell
that ſundry times preached at North Barrick Kirke, to a number of ncto-
nous Witches.

With the true examinations of the ſaide Doctor
and Witches, as they vttered them in the pre-
ſence of the Scottiſh King.

Diſcouering how they pretended

to bewitch and drowne his Maieſtie in the Sea
comming from Denmarke, with ſuch
other wonderfull matters as the like
hath not been heard of at
any time.

Publiſhed according to the Scottiſh Coppie.

AT LONDON
Printed for William
Wright.

Figure 14

NEWS FROM SCOTLAND,

Declaring the damnable
life and death of Doctor Fian,
a notable Sorcerer, who was burned at
Edinburgh, in January last,
1591.

Which Doctor was Register to the Devil
that sundry times preached at North Berwick Kirk,
to a number of notorious witches.

With the true examinations of the said Doctor
and Witches as they uttered them
in the presence of the Scottish King.

Discovering how they pretended
to bewitch and drown his Majesty in the Sea
coming from Denmark, with such
other wonderful matters as the like
has not been heard of at
any time.

Published according to the Scottish copy.
AT LONDON
Printed for William Wright.

TO THE READER

The manifold untruths which are spread abroad concerning the detestable actions and apprehension of those witches whereof this history following truly treats, has caused me to publish the same in print: and the rather for that a number of written copies are lately dispersed thereof, containing, that the said witches were first discovered by means of a poor peddler traveling to the town of Tranent,[1] and that by a wonderful manner he was in a moment conveyed at midnight, from Scotland to Bordeaux in France (being places of no small distance between) into a merchant's cellar there, and after being sent from Bordeaux into Scotland by certain Scottish merchants to the King's Majesty, that he discovered those witches and was the cause of their apprehension: with a number of matters miraculous and incredible, all which in truth are most false.

Nevertheless, to satisfy a number of honest minds, who are desirous to be informed of the verity and truth of their confession, which for certain is more strange than the common report runs, and yet with more truth, I have undertaken to publish this short treatise, which declares the true discourse of all that has happened, and as well what was pretended by those wicked and detestable witches against the King's Majesty, as also by what means they wrought the same.

All which examinations (gentle reader) I have here truly published, as they were taken and uttered in the presence of the King's Majesty, praying thee to acccept it for verity, the same being so true as cannot be reproved.[2]

NOTES ON *TO THE READER*

Note 1: This mythical peddler is depicted twice in a woodcut that accompanies the early editions of *News From Scotland*. He is shown reclining on his side, his head propped up on his elbow and resting on his hand. In the upper panel of the woodcut he lies beside a group of witches, and in the lower panel he is shown similarly posed inside a wine cellar in Bordeaux.

Note 2: The authorship of *News From Scotland* is unknown. It is based on the actual court records, or a detailed account of them, probably the latter. The "Scottish copy" referred to on the title page may have been penned by James Carmichael, Minister of Haddington, who composed a record of the entire North Berwick witchcraft affair. Sir James Melville wrote in 1592 in his *Memoirs* that Carmichael had written "the history whereof, with their whole depositions." It seems unlikely that *News From Scotland* is the actual text of Carmichael's account of the affair, due to the incomplete state of the charges and testimony in the tract, and the interpolation of a fanciful tale of a lovesick cow that was obviously inspired by a similar account in the *Golden Ass* of Lucius Apuleius, but it may well have been based on Carmichael's document.

Internal evidence suggests that the tract itself was written by an Englishman in the latter part of 1591, and underwent extensive editorial revision after the two original woodcuts that accompany it had already been made, since there is matter in the woodcuts that is not referred to in the text. For an excellent analysis of these woodcuts, see the paper by Edward H. Thompson "More *Newes from Scotland*: the woodblock illustrations of a witchcraft pamphlet," presented at the conference for Authorship, Reading and Publishing held at the University of Edinburgh in 1995.

A TRUE DISCOURSE

Of the apprehension of sundry
witches lately taken in Scotland: whereof
some are executed, and some are
yet imprisoned.

With a particular recital of their examinations,
taken in the presence of the King's Majesty.

God by his omnipotent power, has at all times and daily does take
such care, and is so vigilant, for the well-being and preservation of
his own, that thereby he disappoints the wicked practices and evil
intentions of all such as by any means whatsoever seek indirectly
to conspire anything contrary to his holy will. Yea, and by the same
power, he has lately overthrown and hindered the intentions and
wicked dealings of a great number[1] of ungoldy creatures (no better
than devils, who suffered themselves to be allured and enticed by the
Devil whom they served, and to whom they were privately sworn)
entered into the detestable art of witchcraft, which they studied and
practiced so long a time, that in the end they had seduced by their
sorcery a number of others to be as bad as themselves, dwelling in
the bounds of Lothian, which is the principal shire or part of Scotland, where the King's Majesty used to make his chief residence or
abode.

And to the end that their detestable wickedness which they privately had pretended against the King's Majesty, the commonweal
of that country, with the nobility and subjects of the same, should

come to light, God of his unspeakable goodness did reveal and lay it open in very strange sort, thereby to make known unto the world, that their actions were contrary to the law of God, and the natural affection which we ought generally to bear one to another. The manner of the revealing whereof was as followeth.

Within the town of Tranent[2] in the kingdom of Scotland, there dwells one David Seaton,[3] who being deputy-bailiff in the said town, had a maid servant called Gilly Duncan, who used secretly to be absent and to lie forth of her master's house every other night. This Gilly Duncan took in hand to help all such as were troubled or grieved with any kind of sickness or infirmity, and in a short space did perform many matters most miraculous, which things forasmuch as she began to do them upon a sudden, having never done the like before, made her master and others to be in great admiration, and wonder thereat, by means whereof the said David Seaton had his maid in some great suspicion, that she did not those things by natural and lawful ways, but rather supposed it to be done by some extraordinary and unlawful means.

Whereupon, her master began to grow very inquisitive, and examined her which way and by what means she was able to perform matters of so great importance. Whereat, she gave no answer. Nevertheless, her master, to the intent that he might the better try and find out the truth of the same, did with the help of others, torment her with the torture of the pilliwinks[4] upon her fingers, which is a grievous torture, and binding or wrenching her head with a cord or rope,[5] which is a most cruel torment also. Yet would she not confess anything.

Whereupon they, suspecting that she had been marked by the Devil (as commonly witches are), made dilligent search about her, and found the Enemy's mark to be in her forecrag, or forepart of her throat. Which being found, she confessed that all her doings were done by the wicked allurements and inticements of the Devil, and that she did them by witchcraft.

Figure 15

After this her confession, she was committed to prison, where she continued for a season, where immediately she accused these persons following to be notorious witches, and caused them forthwith to be apprehended one after another, viz. Agnes Sampson, the eldest witch of them all, dwelling in Haddington; Agnes Tompson[6] of Edinburgh; Doctor Fian, alias John Cunningham, master of the school at Saltpans[7] in Lothian, of whose life and strange acts, you shall hear more largely in the end of this discourse. These were by the said Gilly Duncan accused, as also George Mott's wife, dwelling in Saltpans; Robert Grierson, skipper; and Janet Bandilandis; with the porter's wife of Seaton, the smith at the brig Hallis, with innumerable others in that parts, and dwelling in those bounds aforesaid. Of whom, some are already executed, the rest remain in prison to receive the doom of judgement at the King Majesty's will and pleasure.

The said Gilly Duncan also caused Euphemia McCalyan[8] to be apprehended, who conspired and performed the death of her godfather, and who used her art upon a gentleman, being one of the Lords and Justices of the Session, for bearing goodwill to her daughter. She also caused to be apprehended one Barbara Napier,[9] for bewitching to death Archibald, last Earl of Angus, who languished to death by witchcraft, and yet the same was not suspected, but that he died of so strange a disease, as the physician knew not how to cure or remedy the same. But of all other the said witches, these two last before recited, were reputed for as civil honest women as any that dwelled within the city of Edinburgh, before they were apprehended. Many other besides were taken dwelling in Leith, who are detained in prison, until his Majesty's further will and pleasure be known, of whose wicked doings you shall particularly hear, which were as followeth.

This aforesaid Agnes Sampson[10] who was the elder witch, was taken and brought to Holyrood House before the King's Majesty and various others of the nobility of Scotland, where she was narrowly examined, but all the persuasions which the King's Majesty used to her with the rest of his Council, might not provoke or induce her to confess anything, but [she] stood stiffly in the denial of all that was laid to her charge. Whereupon they caused her to be conveyed away to prison, there to receive such torture as has been lately provided for witches in that country.

And foreasmuch as by due examination of witchcraft and witches in Scotland, it has lately been found that the Devil does generally mark them with a private mark, by reason the witches have confessed themselves, that the Devil does lick them with his tongue in some private part of their body, before he does receive them to be his servants, which mark commonly is given them under the hair in some part of their body, whereby it may not easily be found out or seen, although they be searched. And generally, so long as the mark is not seen to those which search them, so long the parties that have the mark will never confess anything. Therefore by special commandment this Agnes Sampson had all her hair shaved off, in each part of her body, and her head thrawn with a rope according to the custom of that country, being a pain most grievous, which she continued almost an hour, during which time she would not confess anything until the Devil's mark was found upon her privates. Then she immediately confessed whatsoever was demanded of her, and testified those persons aforesaid to be notorious witches.

Item, the said Agnes Sampson was afterwards brought again before the King's Majesty and his Council, and being examined of the meetings and detestable dealings of these witches, she confessed that upon the night of All Hallows' Eve last, she was accompanied as well with the persons aforesaid, as also with a great many other witches, to the number of two hundred,[11] and that all they together went by sea each one in a riddle or sieve,[12] and went in the same very substantially with flaggons of wine, making merry and drinking by the way in the same riddles or sieves, to the kirk[13] of North Berwick in Lothian, and that after they had landed, took hands on the land and danced this reel, or short dance, singing all with one voice.

Comer go ye before, comer go ye,
If ye will not go before, comer let me.

At which time she confessed, that this Gilly Duncan did go before them playing this reel or dance upon a small trump, called a Jew's trump,[14] until they entered into the kirk of North Berwick.[15]

These confessions made the King in a wonderful admiration, and [he] sent for the said Gilly Duncan, who upon the like trump did play the said dance before the King's Majesty, who in respect of the strangeness of these matters took great delight to be present at their examinations.

Item, the said Agnes Sampson confessed that the Devil being then at North Berwick Kirk, attending their coming in the habit or likeness of a man,[16] and seeing that they tarried overlong, he at their coming enjoined them all to a pennance, which was, that they should kiss his buttocks, in sign of duty to him: which being put over the pulpit bar, everyone did as he had enjoined them. And having made his ungodly exhortations, wherein he did greatly inveigh against the King of Scotland, he received their oaths for their good and true service towards him, and departed. Which done, they returned to sea, and so home again.

At which time the witches demanded of the Devil why he did bear such hatred to the King, who answered, by reason the King is the greatest enemy he hath in the world: all which their confessions and depositions are still extant upon record.

Item, the said Agnes Sampson confessed before the King's Majesty various things which were so miraculous and strange, as that his Majesty said they were all extreme liars, whereat she answered, she would not wish his Majesty to suppose her words to be false, but rather to believe them, in that she would discover such matter unto him as his Majesty should not any way doubt of.

And thereupon taking his Majesty a little aside, she declared unto him the very words which passed between the King's Majesty and his Queen at Oslo in Norway the first night of their marriage,[17] with their answer each to other. Whereat the King's Majesty wondered greatly, and swore by the living God, that he believed that all the devils in hell could not have discovered the same, acknowledging her words to be most true, and therefore gave the more credit to the rest which is before declared.

Touching this Agnes Sampson, she is the same woman who by the Devil's persuasion should have intended and put in execution the King Majesty's death, in this manner.

She confessed that she took a black toad, and did hang the same up by the heels three days, and collected and gathered the venom as it dropped and fell from it into an oyster shell, and kept the same venom close covered, until she should obtain any part or piece of fouled linen cloth, that had appertained to the King's Majesty, as shirt, handkerchief, napkin, or any other thing, which she practiced to obtain by means of one John Kers, who being attendant in his Majesty's chamber, desired him for old acquaintance between them, to help her to one or a piece of such a cloth as is aforesaid. Which thing the said John Kers denied to help her to, saying he could not help her to it.

And the said Agnes Sampson, by her dispositions since her apprehension, said that if she had obtained any one piece of linen cloth which the King had worn and fouled, she had bewitched him to death, and put him to such extraordinary pains, as if he had been lying upon sharp thorns and ends of needles.

Moreover, she confessed that at the time when his Majesty was in Denmark, she being accompanied with the parties before specially named, took a cat and christened it,[18] and afterward bound to each part of that cat, the chiefest parts[19] of a dead man, and several joints of his body,[20] and that in the night following, the said cat was conveyed into the midst of the sea by all these witches sailing in their riddles or sieves as is aforesaid, and so left the said cat right before the town of Leith in Scotland. This done, there did arise such a tempest in the sea, as a greater hath not been seen, which tempest was the cause of the perishing of a boat or vessel coming over from the town of Burntis-land to the town of Leith, wherein were many jewels and rich gifts, which should have been presented to the new Queen of Scotland, at her Majesty's coming to Leith.

Again it is confessed, that the said christened cat was the cause that the King's Majesty's ship at his coming forth from Denmark had a contrary wind to the rest of his ships, then being in his company, which thing was most strange and true, as the King's Majesty acknowledged, for when the rest of the ships had a fair and good wind, then was the wind contrary and altogether against his Majesty.

And further the said witch declared, that his Majesty had never come safely from the sea, if his faith had not prevailed above their intentions.

Moreover, the said witches being demanded how the Devil would use them when he was in their company, they confessed that when the Devil did receive them for his servants, and that they had vowed themselves unto him, then he would carnally use them, albeit to their little pleasure, in respect of his cold nature:[21] and would do the like at various other times.

As touching the aforesaid Doctor Fian, alias John Cunningham, the examination of his acts since his apprehension declares the great subtlety of the Devil, and therefore makes things to appear the more miraculous: for being apprehended by the accusation of the said Gilly Duncan aforesaid, who confessed he was their Register,[22] and that there was not one man suffered to come to the Devil's readings but only he,[23] the said doctor was taken and imprisoned, and used with the accustomed pain provided for those offenses, inflicted upon the rest as is aforesaid.

First, by wringing of his head with a rope, whereat he would confess nothing.

Secondly, he was persuaded by fair means to confess his follies, but that would prevail as little.

Lastly, he was put to the most severe and cruel pain in the world, called the boots,[24] which after he had received three strokes, being enquired if he would confess his damnable acts and wicked life, his tongue would not serve him to speak, in respect whereof the rest of the witches willed to search his tongue, under which was found two pins thrust up into the head, whereupon the witches did chant, now is the charm stinted, and showed that those charmed pins were the cause he could not confess anything. Then he was immediately released of the boots, brought before the King, his confession was taken, and his own hand willingly set thereunto, which contained as follows.

Figure 16

First, that at the general meetings of those witches, he was always present; that he was clerk to all those that were in subjection to the Devil's service, bearing the name of witches; that always he did take their oaths for their true service to the Devil; and that he wrote for them such matters as the Devil still pleased to command him.

Item, he confessed that by his witchcraft he did bewitch a gentleman dwelling near to the Saltpans, where the said doctor kept school, only for being enamoured of a gentlewoman whom he loved himself, by means of which his sorcery, witchcraft, and devilish practices, he caused the said gentleman that once in twenty-four hours he fell into a lunacy and madness, and so continued one whole hour together. And for the proving of the same, he caused the gentleman to be brought before the King's Majesty, which was upon the twenty-fourth day of December last.[25]

And being in his Majesty's chamber, suddenly he gave a great screech and fell into a madness, sometimes bending himself, and sometimes capering so directly up, that his head did touch the ceiling of the chamber, to the great admiration of his Majesty and others then present, so that all the gentlemen in the chamber were not able to hold him, until they called in more help, who together bound him hand and foot. And suffering the said gentleman to lie still until his fury was past, he within an hour came again to himself; when being demanded of the King's Majesty what he saw or did all that while, answered that he had been in a sound sleep.

Item, the said doctor did also confess that he had used means at various times to obtain his purpose and wicked intent of the same gentlewoman, and seeing himself disappointed of his intention, he determined by all ways he might to obtain the same, trusting by conjuring, witchcraft, and sorcery to obtain it in this manner.

It happened this gentlewoman being unmarried, had a brother who went to school with the said doctor, who calling his scholar to him, demanded if he did lie with his sister, who answered he did. By means whereof he thought to obtain his purpose, and therefore secretly promised to teach him without stripes, so he would obtain for him three hairs of his sister's privates, at such time as he should spy best occasion for it. Which the youth promised faithfully to perform, and vowed speedily to put it in practice, taking a piece of conjured paper of his master to wrap them in when he had gotten them. And thereupon the boy practiced nightly to obtain his master's purpose, especially when his sister was asleep.

But God, who knoweth the secrets of all hearts, and revealeth all wicked and ungodly practices, would not suffer the intents of this devilish doctor to come to that purpose which he supposed it would, and therefore to declare that he was heavily offended with his wicked intent, did so work by the gentlewoman's own means, that in the end the same was discovered and brought to light. For she being one night asleep, and her brother in bed with her, suddenly cried out to her mother, declaring that her brother would not suffer her to sleep, whereupon her mother having a quick capacity, did vehemently suspect Doctor Fian's intention, by reason she was a witch of herself, and therefore presently arose, and was very inquisitive of the boy to understand his intent, and the better to know the same, did beat him with many stripes, whereby he discovered the truth unto her.

The mother therefore being well practiced in witchcraft, did think it most convenient to meet with the doctor in his own art, and thereupon took the paper from the boy, wherein he should have put the same hairs, and went to a young heifer which never had born calf nor gone to the bull, and with a pair of shears, clipped off three hairs from the udder of the cow, and wrapped them in the same paper, which she again delivered to the boy, then willing him to give the same to his said master, which he immediately did.

The schoolmaster so soon as he had received them, thinking them indeed to be the maid's hairs, went straight and wrought his art upon them. But the doctor had no sooner done his intent to them, but presently the heifer or cow whose hairs they were indeed, came unto the door of the church wherein the school master was, into which the heifer went, and made towards the schoolmaster, leaping and dancing upon him, and following him forth of the church and to what place soever he went, to the great admiration of all the townsmen of Saltpans, and many others who did behold the same.[26]

The report whereof made all men imagine that he did work it by the Devil, without whom it could never have been so sufficiently effected. And thereupon, the name of the said Doctor Fian (who was but a very young man) began to grow so common among the people of Scotland, that he was secretly nominated for a notable conjurer.

All which although in the beginning he denied, and would not confess, yet having felt the pain of the boots (and the charm stinted, as aforesaid), he confessed all the aforesaid to be most true, without producing any witnesses to justify the same, and thereupon before the King's Majesty he subscribed the said confessions with his own hand, which for truth remain upon record in Scotland.

After that the depositions and examinations of the said Doctor Fian, alias Cunningham, were taken, as already is declared, with his

Figure 17

own hand willingly set thereunto, he was by the master of the prison committed to ward, and appointed to a chamber by himself, where foresaking his wicked ways, acknowledging his most ungodly life, showing that he had too much followed the allurements and enticements of Satan, and fondly practiced his conclusions by conjuring, witchcraft, enchantment, sorcery, and such like, he renounced the Devil and all his wicked works, vowed to lead the life of a Christian, and seemed newly connected towards God.

The morrow after upon conference had with him, he granted that the Devil had appeared unto him in the night before, appareled all in black, with a white wand in his hand, and that the Devil demanded of him if he would continue his faithful service, according to his first oath and promise made to that effect. Whom (as he then said) he utterly renounced to his face, and said unto him in this manner, avoid Satan, avoid, for I have listened too much unto you, and by the same you have undone me, in respect whereof I utterly foresake you. To whom the Devil answered, that once before you die you shall be mine. And with that (as he said) the Devil broke the white wand, and immediately vanished forth of his sight.

Thus all the day this Doctor Fian continued very solitary, and seemed to have care of his own soul, and would call upon God, showing himself penitent for his wicked life. Nevertheless the same night he found such means, that he stole the key of the prison door and chamber in the which he was, which in the night he opened and fled away to the salt pans, where he was always resident, and first apprehended. Of whose sudden departure, when the King's Majesty had intelligence, he presently commanded diligent inquiry to be made for his apprehension, and for the better effecting thereof, he sent public proclaimations into all parts of his land to the same effect. By means of whose hot and hard pursuit, he was again taken and brought to prison, and then being called before the King's Highness, he was reexamined as well touching his departure, as also touching all that had before happened.

But this doctor, notwithstanding that his own confession appeared remaining in the record under his own handwriting, and the same thereunto fixed in the presence of the King's Majesty and several of his Council, yet did he utterly deny the same.

Whereupon the King's Majesty perceiving his stubborn willfulness, conceived and imagined that in the time of his absence he had entered into new conference and league with the Devil his Master, and that he had been again newly marked, for the which he was narrowly searched, but it could not in any way be found. Yet for more trial of him to make him confess, he was commanded to have a most strange torment, which was done in the manner following.

His nails upon all his fingers were riven and pulled off with an instrument called in Scottish a turkas, which in England we call a pair of pincers, and under every nail there was thrust in two needles over even up to the heads. At all which torments notwithstanding the doctor never shrank any wit, neither would he then confess it the sooner for all the tortures inflicted upon him.

Then was he with all convenient speed, by commandment, conveyed again to the torment of the boots, wherein he continued a long time, and did abide so many blows in them, that his legs were crushed and beaten together as small as might be, and the bones and flesh so bruised, that the blood and marrow spurted forth in great abundance, whereby they were made unserviceable forever. And notwithstanding all these grievous pains and cruel torments, he would not confess anything, so deeply had the Devil entered into his heart, that he utterly denied all that which he had before avouched, and would say nothing thereupon but this, that what he had done and said before, was only done and said for fear of pains which he had endured.

Upon great consideration therefore taken by the King's Majesty and his Council, as well for the due execution of justice upon such detestable malefactors, as also for example's sake, to remain a terror to all others hereafter, that shall attempt to deal in the like wicked and ungodly actions, as witchcraft, sorcery, conjuration, and such like, the said Doctor Fian was soon after araigned, condemned, and adjudged by the law to die, and then to be burned according to the law of that land, provided in that behalf. Whereupon he was put into a cart, and being first strangled, he was immediately put into a great fire, being ready provided for that purpose, and there burned in the Castle Hill of Edinburgh on a Saturday in the end of January last past, 1591.

The rest of the witches which are not yet executed, remain in prison till further trial, and knowledge of his Majesty's pleasure.

This strange discourse before recited, may perhaps give some occasion of doubt to such as shall happen to read the same, and thereby conjecture that the King's Majesty would not hazard himself in the presence of such notorious witches, lest thereby might have ensured great danger to his person and the general state of the land, which thing in truth might well have been feared. But to answer generally to such, let this suffice: that first it is well-known that the King is the child and servant of God, and they but servants to the Devil; he is the Lord's annointed, and they but vessels of God's wrath; he is a true Christian, and trusts in God, they worse than infidels, for they only trust in the Devil, who daily serves them, till he has brought them to utter destruction.

But hereby it seems that his Highness carried a magnanimous and undaunted mind, not frightened with their enchantments, but resolute in this, that so long as God is with him, he fears not who is against him. And truly the whole scope of this treatise does so plainly lay open the wonderful providence of the Almighty, that if he had not been defended by his omnipotence and power, his Highness had never returned alive in his voyage from Denmark, so that there is no doubt but God would as well defend him on the land as on the sea, where they pretended their damnable practice.

FINIS

Figure 18

NOTES ON *NEWS FROM SCOTLAND*

Note 1: The principal accused witches in the affair were four: Agnes Sampson, John Fian, Effie McCalyan, and Barbara Napier. All were tortured, tried, and sentenced to death in 1591. By the extraordianry efforts of her family and friends, Barbara Napier avoided the fire. Agnes Sampson was strangled at the stake and her body burned on Castle Hill in Edinburgh, the usual manner and place of execution for convicted witches. Effie McCalyan was sentenced to be burned alive, perhaps because she refused to implicate the Earl of Bothwell, but at the end she was afforded the mercy of strangulation before being consumed by the fire. John Fian faced unimaginably severe tortures, which he withstood as bravely as any man could have done, and maintaining his innocence to the end was executed by strangulation and burning. Not one of the witches was burned alive.

Other key figures were Gilly Duncan, Richard Graham, Robert Grierson, and Francis, Earl of Bothwell. Gilly Duncan was tried but does not appear to have been executed. Her life may have been spared in return for her accusations of witchcraft against her friends and neighbors, and her public repentence. Robert Grierson died in prison on April 15, 1591, probably as a result of the severity of his torture, although it is possible he took his own life. Richard Graham was executed in the usual fashion on February 29, 1592, on Castle Hill. Bothwell was tried on August 10, 1593, but was acquitted by a jury of his peers. However, he found it prudent to change his residence from Scotland to Italy.

Lesser figures executed included Marion Ersche, Margaret Downey, Christian Todd, Begie Todd, Gilbert McGillis, John McGillis (Gilbert's son), John Gordon (known as Graymeal), Katherine Gray, Isabel Grierson, and Meg Dun.

Among those that went through the legal process were Donald Robinson, Meg Begton, Margaret Aicheson, Charles Watt,

Masie Aicheson, Anne Richardson, Thomas Fian, Janet Straton, Margaret Thomson, Catherine Duncan, Janet Gall, Annie Nairn, Janet Logan, Thomas Cockburn, Marion Ranking, Catherine McGillis, Bessie Cowan, Marion Congilton, Helen Lauder, Isabel Lauder, Duncan Buchanan, Marion Nicholson, Annie Simson, Janet Nicholson, Isobel Gylor, Bessie Wright, Marion Shaw, Janet Campbell, Bessie Brown, Marion Longniddry, Malie Geddie, Helen White, Katherine Muirhead, Christian Carrington, Janet Drummond, Archie Farquhar, Janet Fairley, Bessie Thomson, Marion Peterson, Alexander Whitelaw, Marion Bailzy, Catherine Wallace, Ninian Chirnside, porter's wife of Seaton (unnamed), Thomas Brounhill and his wife, John Ramsey's wife (unnamed), George Mott's wife (unnamed), and Nichol Murray's wife (un-named). A number of the accused managed to escape and flee to England, causing James to send the deputy-baliff of Tranent, David Seaton, who knew them all by sight, in pursuit. At least one of these witches was returned to Scotland by the English au-thorities for additional torture, and named additional names.

Some of the names of those accused of witchcraft in the con-fessions of the witches, extracted from them by torture, are Mar-ion Linkup, Michael Clark, John Sibbet, Janet Duncan, George Mott, Meg Stillcart, Agnes Stratton, John Cooper, Bessie Gwlene, Archie Henill's wife (unnamed), Sir Robert Bowes (the English ambassador), David Nesbitt, and Arran Lord Farneyer.

The spellings of the names of those involved in the affair are hopelessly corrupt in the documents of the period, and undoubt-edly there are instances when the same individual is mentioned under two different names as a result of this confusion. The most prominent instance in *News From Scotland* is where Agnes Sampson is referred to in several places as Agnes Tompson. I have corrected this duplication where it is unambiguous, and have at-tempted to modernize the names when a modern equivalent is obvious. Margaret Thomson and Bessie Thomson may be the same person.

The total numbers of persons executed, imprisoned, or tortured in the North Berwick affair are not known with certainty. According to the testimony of some of the accused, the number of witches supposed to be present at their conventions, or sabbats, ranged from around seventy to two hundred, but those actually named were fewer in number. Margaret Murray, acting under the questonable assumption that there was organized witchcraft going on, put the number of witches at thirty-nine, or three covens of thirteen. This number seems arbitrary and is inaccurate, and in any case groups of witches did not always contain thirteen members. An examination of the names shows that family members were often accused together, husband and wife, sister and sister, mother and daughter, father and son. The scale of the human tragedy is considerably larger than what is confirmed in the printed records.

Note 2: David Seaton was not only instrumental in initiating the North Berwick witch affair, which he did when he questioned his maid, but must have been involved throughout the entire process of identifying and arresting the accused. We can make this surmise because, after a number of the accused fled to England at the beginning of Feburary, 1591, James was willing to pay Seaton to hunt them down and bring them back. The King prepared letters of introduction for Seaton to the English nobles Sir John Foster, Sir Henry Woddrington, and Sir John Selby, instructing them to give Seaton every possible help in apprehending and confining the fugitives until they could be safely conveyed back to Scotland for trial. Seaton was also mentioned in the testimony of Agnes Sampson, who confessed that she had tried and failed to end Seaton's life with witchcraft. John Fian was accused of opening locks by magic in Seaton's house at Tranent, and also at the house of Seaton's mother.

Note 3: Tranent is a small town about ten miles east of Edinburgh.

Note 4: The pilliwinks was an instrument of torture similar to the thumbscrews, with which pressure was applied to the ends of the fingers by means of a screw to cause pain. Those who endured this type of torture reported that the blood would spurt from under the fingernails. By subjecting his maid to torture, Seaton was acting completely outside the authority of the law. However, at the end of the sixteenth century, it was common for the master of a household to physically discipline not only the members of his own family, but his servants as well. Seaton may have justified his actions on these grounds, although he greatly overstepped the bounds of custom.

Note 5: This torture, called "thrawing" in the Scottish dialect, involved tightening a binding around the head by twisting a stick through it, in a manner similar to that of a tourniquet. In this way strong pressure could be applied to the skull.

Note 6: "Agnes Tompson" may merely be a misreading of the name "Agnes Sampson."

Note 7: Saltpans, sometimes referred to as the salt pans or Saltpreston, seems to be the place presently known as Prestonpans, located in East Lothian on the south shore of the Firth of Forth, about two miles northwest of Tranent.

Note 8: Euphemia, or Effie, McCalyan, the daughter of Lord Cliftonhall, was arraigned on June 9, 1591. She was the wife of Patrick Moscrop, a wealthy man, and was defended at her trial by six lawyers, but James was determined to see her dead, and dismissed the foreman of the jury in order to procure a verdict of guilty. Her trial lasted from June 9 to June 13, a much longer period than the usual trial of the time, thanks to the exhaustive efforts of her lawyers, who "pleaded so subtillie for her, that the assise could not be resolved before the 13th of June." She was condemned to be burned alive, an extreme sentence usually only given to witches who refused to confess, or who confessed and then recanted their confession. Effie maintained her innocence throughout her ordeal.

James himself took an active part in directing her torture. He wrote to John Maitland, who was overseeing the interrogation: "Let Effie McCalyan see the stoop two or three days, and upon the sudden stay her in hope of a confession." The stoop was the wooden post to which the condemned was bound. It had to be set in the ground at each execution by a woodwright, who was paid ten shillings for the job. It seems that James hoped that by showing her the stake that would be used at her burning, she would break down and confess. The Earl of Bothwell and his supporters were quite nervous that she would accuse Bothwell, who was her friend, and hoped that her execution would proceed swiftly, as a way of closing her mouth. This does not necessarily imply any guilt on Bothwell's part, merely a concern that a woman would not be able to withstand torture as well as a man, and might say anything to relieve the pain. As it happened, they need not have worried, since she endured her ordeal with great courage and loyalty to Bothwell.

Accounts of her execution indicate that she was strangled before being burned on Castle Hill on June 25, 1591, though no reason is given as to why the severity of her sentence was mitigated. In her statement to the crowd at her execution, she "tooke it upon her conscience that she was innocent of all the crymes laid to her charge." The long delay between her sentencing and death was the result of an assertion by Effie, after the verdict was read against her, that she was pregnant. Since the unborn child of a convicted criminal was considered to be innocent, execution of a pregnant woman was delayed until after the birth of the baby.

Note 9: Barbara Napier, the sister-in-law of the Laird of Carschoggill, was convicted by a jury on May 8, 1591, for consulting with witches, specifically Richard Graham and Agnes Sampson. The other more serious charges against her, chief among them that she had attempted to kill the King with a "picture of wax," that she had caused a ferryboat to sink between Leith and Kinghorn, resulting in the loss of sixty lives, and that she was responsible for the death of the Earl of Angus, were dismissed by the jury. The partial acquittal was accomplished by packing the jury box with her friends. The English ambassador Sir Robert Bowes wrote in a letter to Lord Burghley: "By the counsel assigned to her, and by her challenges and shifts, she both put off the gentlemen returned to have been of her assize, in whose places others of this town— where she has many kinsfolk and friends of good credit—were received, and also continued the matter in debate until two of the clock in this morning, before the jury or assize—as they term it— could be chosen and charged."

Although they found her guilty of consultation with witches, no judgement was pronounced against her. As Bowes put it, she was at "the King's pleasure." Obviously the king was not pleased. She was sentenced to be strangled and burned on Castle Hill on May 11, but on that day, when the stake had been erected and piled all around with flammable materials ready for the torch, and the townsfolk had gathered to watch the show, her friends announced that she could not be put to death because she was pregnant.

James was beside himself with rage. He instructed John Maitland: "Try by the mediciners whether Barbara Napier be with child or not. Take no delaying answer. If you find she be not, to the fire with her presently, and cause bowel her publically." To bowel someone (Bowes spelled it "bouell") is to disembowel that person. James wanted her strangled at the stake, and her belly cut open to prove to the crowd that she had not been with child. He was determined not to allow this clever and able woman whom, as he believed, had made an attempt on not only his own life, but the life of his young queen, to escape the fire through legal trickery.

While Barbara's pregnancy was being examined, her friends were working hard in the background on her behalf. Because the act of Parliament against simple consultation with a witch had not actually been put into execution, it was decided that a death sentence was too harsh a punishment for her crime. James became convinced that her acquittal of the more serious charges, including the charge of high treason for attempting to end his life, was a plot against him intended to frustrate his will in the matter. He was particularly upset that the men he had hand-picked to be a part of the trial had been excluded through legal maneuvering. Clerics in Edinburgh began to criticize his lack of action publically from the pulpit.

On May 26, James had the jury members charged with an assize of error. Bowes wrote to Burghley, "The assize of error to reverse the verdict given in favor of Barbara Napier is proclaimed. The assizers are commanded to be here two days before their appearance in court, that the King may speak with them. Thus to reverse the verdict is lawful, but a great novelty, not hitherto practised." The speech James delivered to the jury on June 7, 1591, is his famous Tolbooth speech, the relevent portions of which are reproduced in Appendix C. James caused the court to be reassembled and ordered that Barbara Napier be strangled, burned, and her property forfeited to him. The original jury was then itself tried on the charge of acquitting a witch.

Although it would have seemed that Barbara Napier's fate was sealed by the extraordinary machinations of the King against her, there is no record of her execution. After a passage of time, her prosecution was quietly dropped without ever being resolved. This is difficult to explain. Perhaps she actually was pregnant, having had the foresight to put herself in this condition just prior to her trial. That would have bought her some time, almost a year. James may have allowed himself to be persuaded by his advisors that he was walking on thin ice, legally, and that it would be prudent to allow the matter to fade away. However it happened, her "many kinsfolk and friends of good credit" prevailed in her behalf, and she was the only one of the four principals in the North Berwick affair who was not burned.

Note 10: Agnes Sampson, known locally as the Wise Wife of Keith, was described by a contemporary as being "a woman not of the base and ignorant sort of witches, but matron-like, grave and settled in her answers, which were all to some purpose" (Spottiswoode, *History of the Church of Scotland*, Vol. II, pages 411–412). Her skills as both a midwife and a healer were held in high regard in Edinburgh and the surrounding towns. There can be little question that she relied upon magic practices and the occult virtues of herbs and stones for her cures. Many of the charges against her involved accurate diagnoses of diseases, and cures by occult means. One technique she used was to take the disease of the sick person onto herself, then, after suffering with it until the morning, cast it off onto a dog or cat.

She was also an accomplished seer. She kept a large black dog named Elva that may have served as the host for her familiar spirit, and used the dog for purposes of divination. A certain amount of theatrics must have been employed to impress onlookers. She would ask the dog questions, and the dog would answer her. The dog was summoned with the magic word "hola," which appears in several places in the North Berwick testimonies.

It was her practice to diagnose whether or not an individual would recover from sickness by reciting a prayer. If she stopped speaking once before the prayer was done, it was a sign that the sick person was bewitched, but if she stopped twice, it was a sure sign that the person would die. Sometimes when asked to come and heal, she would refuse after saying the prayer, on the grounds that there was nothing she could do, the person was going to die in any case.

When first accused of witchcraft, she denied all charges. Her torture was extreme. All the hair was shaved off from every part of her body, and she was pricked for the witch mark, a not only painful but humiliating experience. The mark was found on her vulva. A witch's bridle was placed on her head, an instrument of iron that pressed four sharp spikes into her mouth to prevent her from muttering or chanting magic charms. She was "thrawed" like Gilly Duncan and John Fian, and deprived of sleep for a prolonged period. Finally, her proud spirit broke and she began to implicate others, and to offer fantastic details of evil works and plots against the king. The list of charges made against her at her trial of January 27, 1591, is longer than that of any other accused. Robert Bowes wrote to Lord Burghley that of the one hundred and two charges that were brought against her, she confessed to fifty-eight. The sentence read against her was that she "be taken to the Castle of Edinburgh, and there bound to a stake and strangled until she was dead, and thereafter her body to be burned to ashes." The records do not show a date of execution, but it was probably no more than a few days following her conviction. At the stake she apologized for causing the death of the Earl of Douglas with a small figure of yellow wax.

Note 11: There was a belief that witches travelled across the sea using sieves for boats. A riddle is a coarse-screened sieve for separating chaff from grain. The witches related that while they were crossing the sea, and making merry with wine, they could see the Devil going before them over the waves, looking in the distance somewhat like a large rolling haystack (Scot, *Demonology and Witchcraft*, page 302). Agnes Sampson confessed that they went across the water in a boat shaped like a chimney, and that the Devil resembed a hayrick. It is tempting to think that when asked about these matters by her interrogators, she responded with the most absurd things that popped into her head, with the expectation that they were so silly they would not be believed. Instead they were solemnly pronounced against her at her trial.

Note 12: The transcript of the questioning of Agnes Sampson puts the number in the church on All Hallow's Eve at around ninety women and six men, not two hundred women. According to Barbara Napier, there were "seven score" present, or around 140 persons.

Note 13: "Kirk" is a Scottish term for a church.

Note 14: "Jew's trump" was the earlier name for the instrument known as the "Jew's harp." It consists of a metal frame with a flexible steel tongue. The frame is held between the teeth while the steel tongue is struck with the finger, and the twanging tone is varied by enlarging or diminishing the cavity of the mouth.

Note 15: The great sabbat meeting at North Berwick Kirk is one of the most notorious in all the records of the witch trials. It is supposed to have happened on Halloween in the year 1590, and if it was indeed a real event, probably took place around midnight—in her testimony concerning a previous solitary meeting with the Devil at the North Berwick Kirk, Agnes Sampson stated that it occured at eleven o'clock. North Berwick is located on a headland on the southern shore of the Firth of Forth, and the towns of Tranent, Edinburgh, and Leith are ranged to the west along the same side of this body of water, although Tranent is somewhat inland. Saltpans, presently known as Prestonpans, is located about two miles from Tranent on the coast. On that memorable night the witches stood or sat in their sieves and were borne, some of them as much as fifteen miles, over the sea along the southern shore of the Firth of Forth in an easterly direction, laughing, calling out to each other, and drinking wine, while the Devil in the form of a tumbling vortex went before them on top of the waves to lead the way.

When they landed next to the church, they all held hands and danced a reel on the green, singing "Comer, go you before, comer go you, if you will not go before, comer let me," as Gilly Duncan played on her Jew's harp to provide the music. Barbara Napier led the dance up and down the longest dimension of the kirkyard. The six male witches whirled themselves around nine times widdershins, or counterclockwise, with, according to the testimony of Agnes Sampson, John Fian leading the ring, his face covered or muffled with cloth. The far more numerous female witches twirled about six times in the same direction, widdershins. In magic, turning widdershins is usually done for works of evil. Doctor Fian blew his breath into the keyhole of the lock on the front doors of the church, causing the lock to spring open.

The church was illuminated inside with black candles that burned with a strange blue light. In the pulpit the Devil awaited them, dressed in the clothing of an ordinary man. He was described as a "black man" by Doctor Fian, although this may have meant only that he was clothed all in black garments. If this extraordinary meeting ever took place, it is likely that the man playing the part of the Devil had his face obscured in some manner, as did John Fian, to conceal his identity. The Devil was exceedingly annoyed at their late arrival, and ordered as a penance and a sign of their continuing loyalty that they kiss his buttocks, which he exposed by dropping his hose and extending his ass over the rail of the pulpit. One by one the witches filed up and kissed his backside before seating themselves for the meeting.

The purpose of the gathering was to work black magic against King James and cause his death. This was to be done using a wax image of the king that had previously been given to the Devil by Agnes Sampson for the Devil to bewitch. However, the Devil had neglected to bring the prepared image with him, which caused a good deal of irritation among his congregation. I will quote from the partial transcript of the accusations against Barbara Napier presented by Margaret A. Murray. I have modernized the text, since the original is quite difficult to read because of the archaic spelling.

And the Devil stood up in the pulpit like a great black man, having a black book in his hand, and called on every one of them, desiring them all to be good servants to him, and he should be a good master to them. Robert Grierson and John Fian stood on his left hand; and the said Robert found great fault with the Devil and cried out, that all witches were worried greatly here, because his Highness' picture was not given them, as was promised: the said Effie McCalyan remembered and bid the said Robert Grierson to inquire for the picture, meaning his Majesty's picture, which should have been roasted. Robert Grierson said these words: "Where is the thing you promised?" Meaning the picture of wax, devised for roasting and undoing his Highness' person, which Agnes Sampson gave to him; and Robert cried to "have the turn done"; yet his Highness' name was not named, until they that were women named him; craving in plain terms his Highness' picture. But he answered, "It should be gotten the next meeting; and he would hold the next assembly for that cause the sooner: it was not ready at that time." Robert Grierson answered, "You promised to us, and false it was." And four forthright women were very earnest and insistent to have it. And the said Barbara and Effie McCalyan got then a promise of the Devil, that his Highness' picture should be gotten to them two, and that right soon: and this matter of his Highness' picture was the cause of that assembly. (Murray, *Witch-cult in Western Europe*, page 55)

Much of the account of the meeting at North Berwick Kirk, and probably the whole of it, is fantasy. However, there is a plausibility about the homely details of the event that makes it difficult not to suspect that it may have had some basis in reality. It is scarcely to be believed that the witches would have stood up in the church and berated the Devil for being late with the king's portrait, but that they might treat a man representing the

Devil in this way, who was dressed in a black costume with his face masked or darkened with burnt cork, especially if they were drunk on wine, is more likely.

Note 16: The Devil of the witches' sabbat is so often described as a man, who is sometimes masked, rather than as some sort of fantastic monster, that Margaret Murray offered the opinion that he was always a human being: "The evidence of the witches makes it abundantly clear that the so-called Devil was a human being, generally a man, occasionally a woman" (Murray, *Witch-cult in Western Europe*, page 31).

Montague Summers identified the devil personage in the kirk as Francis Stewart, Earl of Bothwell, who wished to kill James in order to open his own claim to the throne. Bothwell was mentioned by name in the testimony of Agnes Sampson, who declared that she had constructed a wax figure of the king to be melted and consumed in the fire "at the instance of a noble man Francis Erle Bodowell" (Summers, *Geography of Witchcraft*, page 223). Summers pointed out that when Bothwell was living in Naples in 1610, he had the reputation of an accomplished necromancer. It was also the conviction of Margaret Murray that the devil of North Berwick Kirk was the Earl of Bothwell. She made this identification on the assumption that where there is a plot to murder, there must be motive, and Bothwell had the best reason of anyone to wish to see James dead.

This sort of speculation is entertaining but should not be given too much weight since it is unsupported by any hard evidence. We have no way of knowing if there ever was a collective meeting of witches presided over by a man wearing a devil's costume, much less that the man was Bothwell. It cannot be emphasized too often that the testimony extracted under torture is worthless, and no other evidence exists for Bothwell as the leader of the North Berwick witches.

Note 17: James and Anne romantically came together in Oslo after Anne's ship sprang a leak on the voyage to Scotland and was driven into the Norwegian port by bad weather, and James sailed north to meet her.

Note 18: The purpose for christening the cat was to transfer the identity of the intended victim into the cat, so that whatever was done to the cat would also, by magical sympathy, be done to the victim. Presumably it was christened in the name of King James.

Note 19: The "chiefest parts" of a man are probably his genitals. They symbolize the life force or vitality.

Note 20: The knucklebones from the fingers or toes of a corpse. Knucklebones have a long history in magic as an instrument of divination. They are cast in a way similar to dice.

Note 21: The explanation James might give for the coldness of the Devil's member is that the Devil caused a corpse to be animated for the purpose of intercourse with the witches. If the witches' conventions actually occurred, and the lover in the kirk was a man rather than a demon, the coldness might be explained in a more natural way as the result of the employment of a dildo to penetrate the witches, something that would likely be required due to the sheer number of witches that must be coupled with.

Note 22: John Fian was said to have acted as the clerk or recorder at the witch gatherings. Being a schoolteacher, he was the natural choice for this office. One of the woodcuts accompanying *News From Scotland* shows Fian seated at a desk with a pen in his left hand (the sinister side of the body), writing upon a sheet of paper, or perhaps into a records book.

Note 23: This statement is in disagreement with the testimony of Agnes Sampson, who confessed that six men were present at the North Berwick church during the Halloween gathering.

Note 24: The boot was a popular device of torture because it proved so effective in extracting confessions. A heavy wooden frame was

Figure 19

bound around the lower leg and foot of a seated victim, and large
wooden wedges were driven into the frame with a mallet in such
a way that its inner sides were forced together, crushing the foot,
ankle, and shin. We know this was the type of boot employed
against the witches since the records speak of specific numbers
of blows administered—that is, blows of the hammer upon the
wedges. Those who survived this form of interrogation were often
crippled for life. It is reported that no form of torture generated
greater agony than the boot.

Note 25: Christmas Eve, 1590. James and his courtiers seem to have regarded the entire affair of the witches as something of a recreational activity. This mentally ill man was brought to the King's bedchamber to provide the same sort of Christmas entertainment that might have been afforded by an acrobat or a juggler.

Note 26: This story is very old, and is related in a slightly different form in the *Golden Ass* of Lucius Apuleius. Any educated man of the late sixteenth century would know that it had been derived from this classic second-century Roman work. The novelist Sir Walter Scott, in his examination of the North Berwick witch trials, assumed that it had been injected into *News From Scotland* by its editor William Wright to enliven the content: "It is remarkable that the Scottish witchcrafts were not thought sufficiently horrible by the editor of this tract, without adding to them the story of a philtre being applied to a cow's hair instead of that of the young woman for whom it was designed, and telling how the animal came lowing after the sorcerer to his schoolroom-door, like a second Pasiphaë, the original of which charm occurs in the story of Apuleius" (Scott, *Demonology and Witchcraft*, page 301).

APPENDIX A
Original text of Daemonologie

DAEMONOLOGIE, IN FORME
of a Dialogue,
Diuided into three Bookes.

EDINBVRGH
Printed by Robert Walde-graue
Printer to the Kings Majestie. An. 1597.
Cum Privilegio Regio.

THE PREFACE
to the Reader.

THE fearefull abounding at this time in this countrie, of these detestable
slaues of the Deuill, the Witches or enchaunters, hath moved me (beloued
reader) to dispatch in post, this following treatise of mine, not in any wise
(as I protest) to serue for a shew of my learning & ingine, but onely (mo-
oued of conscience) to preasse / thereby, so farre as I can, to resolue the
doubting harts of many; both that such assaultes of Sathan are most certainly
practized, & that the instrumentes thereof, merits most severly to be pun-
ished: against the damnable opinions of two principally in our age, wherof
the one called SCOT an Englishman, is not ashamed in publike print to deny,

that ther can be such a thing as Witch-craft: and so mainteines the old error of the Sadducees, in denying of spirits. The other called VVIERVS, a German Phisition, sets out a publick apologie for al these craftesfolkes, whereby, procuring for their impunitie, he plainely bewrayes himselfe to haue bene one of that profession. And for to make this treatise the more pleasaunt and facill, I haue put it in forme of a Dialogue, which I haue diuided into three bookes: The first spea-/ king of Magie in general, and Necromancie in special. The second of Sorcerie and Witch-craft: and the thirde, conteines a discourse of all these kindes of spirits, & Spectres that appeares & trobles persones: together with a conclusion of the whol work. My intention in this labour, is only to proue two things, as I haue alreadie said: the one, that such diuelish artes haue bene and are. The other, what exact trial and seuere punishment they merite: & therefore reason I, what kinde of things are possible to be performed in these arts, & by what naturall causes they may be, not that I touch every particular thing of the Deuils power, for that were infinite: but onelie, to speak scholasticklie, (since this can not bee spoken in our language) I reason vpon genus *leauing* species, *and* differentia *to be comprehended therein. /As for example, speaking of the power of Magiciens, in the first book & sixt Chapter: I say, that they can suddenly cause be brought vnto them, all kindes of daintie disshes, by their familiar spirit: Since as a thiefe he delightes to steale, and as a spirite, he can subtillie & suddenlie inough transport the same. Now vnder this* genus, *may be comprehended al particulars, depending thereupon; Such as the bringing Wine out of a Wall, (as we haue heard oft to haue bene practised) and such others; which particulars, are sufficientlie proved by the reasons of the generall. And such like in the second booke of Witch-craft in speciall, and fift Chap. I say and proue by diuerse arguments, that Witches can, by the power of their Master, cure or cast on disseases: Now by these same reasones, that proues their power by the/Deuil of disseases in generall, is aswell proued their power in speciall: as of weakening the nature of some men, to make them vnable for women: and making it to abound in others, more then the ordinary course of nature would permit. And such like in all other particular sicknesses; But one thing I will pray thee to obserue in all these places, where I reason vpon the deuils power, which is the diferent ends & scopes,* that God as the first cause, and the Devill as his instrument and second cause shootes at in all these actiones of the Deuil, (as Gods hang-man:) For where the deuilles intention in them is euer to perish, either the soule or the body, or both of them, that he is so permitted to deale with: God by the contrarie, drawes euer out of that euill glorie to himselfe, either by the wracke of the wicked in his justice, or/by the tryall of the patient, and amendment of the faithfull, being wakened vp with that rod of correction. Hauing thus declared vnto thee then, my full intention in this Treatise, thou wilt easelie excuse, I doubt not, aswel my pretermitting, to declare the whole particular rites and secretes of these vnlawfull artes: as also their infinite and wounderfull practises, as being neither of them pertinent to my purpose: the reason whereof, is giuen in the hinder ende of the first Chapter of the thirde booke: and who likes to be curious in these thinges, he may reade, if he will here of their practises, BODINVS Dæmonomanie, collected with greater diligence, then written with judgement, together with their confessions, that haue bene at this time apprehened. If he would know what hath bene the opinion of the Aunci-/entes, concerning their power: he shall see it wel descrybed by HYPERIVS, & HEMMINGIVS, two, late Germaine writers: Besides innumerable other neoterick Theologues, that writes largelie vpon that subject: And if he woulde knowe what are the particuler rites, & curiosities of these black arts (which is both vnnecessarie and perilous,) he will finde it in the fourth book of CORNELIVS Agrippa, and in VVIERVS, whomof I spak. And so wishing my pains in this Treatise (beloued Reader) to be effectual, in arming al them that reades the same, against these aboue mentioned erroures, and recommending my good will to thy friendly acceptation, I bid thee hartely fare-well.

JAMES Rx.

DAEMONOLOGIE, IN FORME of ane Dialogue

FIRST BOOKE.

ARGVMENT,

The exord of the whole. The description of Magie in speciall.

CHAP. I. ARGVMENT.

Proven by the Scripture, that these vnlawfull artes in genere, have bene and may be put in practise.

PHILOMATHES and EPISTEMON reason the matter.

PHILOMATHES.

I AM surely verie glad to haue mette with you this daye, for I am of opinion, that ye can better resolue me of some thing, wherof I stand in great doubt, nor anie other whom-with I could haue mette.

EPI. In what I can, that ye like to speir at me, I will willinglie and freelie tell my opinion, and if I proue it not sufficiently, I am heartely content that a better reason carie it away then.

PHI. What thinke yee of these strange newes, which now one-lie furnishes purpose to al men at their meeting: I meane of these Witches?

EPI. Surelie they are wonderfull: And I think so cleare and plaine confessions in that purpose, haue neuer fallen out in anie age or cuntrey.

PHI. No question if they be true, but thereof the Doctours doubtes.

EPI. What part of it doubt ye of?

PHI. Even of all, for ought I can yet perceaue: and namelie, that there is such a thing as Witchcraft or Witches, and I would pray you to resolue me thereof if ye may: for I haue reasoned with sundrie in that matter, and yet could never be satisfied therein.

EPI. I shall with good will doe the best I can: But I thinke it the difficiller, since ye denie the thing it selfe in generall: for as it is said in the logick schools, *Contra negantem principia non est disputandum.* Alwaies for that part, that witchcraft, and Witches haue bene, and are, the former part is clearelie proved by the Scriptures, and the last by dailie experience and confessions.

PHI. I know Yee will alleadge me *Saules Pythonisse:* but that as appeares will not make much for you.

EPI. Not onlie that place, but divers others: But I marvel why that should not make much for me?

PHI. The reasones are these, first yee may consider, that *Saul* being troubled in spirit, [marginal gloss: *I Sam.28*] and having fasted long before, as the text testifieth, and being come to a woman that was bruted to have such knowledge, and that to inquire so important news, he having so guiltie a conscience for his hainous offences, and specially, for that same vnlawful curiositie, and horrible defection: and then the woman crying out vpon the suddaine in great admiration, for the vncouth sicht that she alledged to haue sene, discovering him to be the King, thogh disguysed, & denied by him before: it was no wounder I say, that his senses being thus distracted, he could not perceaue hir faining of hir voice, hee being himselfe in an other chalmer, and seeing nothing. Next what could be, or was raised? The spirit of *Samuel?* Prophane and against all Theologie: the Diuell in his likenes? as vnappeirant, that either God would permit him to come in the shape of his Saintes (for then could neuer the Prophets in those daies haue bene sure, what Spirit spake to them in their visiones) or then that he could fore-tell what was to come there after; for Prophecie proceedeth onelie of GOD: and the Devill hath no knowledge of things to come.

EPI. Yet if yee will marke the wordes of the text, ye will finde clearely, that *Saul* saw that apparition: for giving you that *Saul* was in an other Chalmer, at the making of the circles & conjurationes, needeful for that purpose (as none of that craft will permit any vthers to behold at that time) yet it is evident by the text, that how sone that once that vnclean spirit was fully risen, shee called in vpon *Saul*. For it is saide in the text, that *Saule knew him to be Samuel*, which coulde not haue bene, by the hearing tell onely of an olde man with an mantil, since there was many mo old men dead in *Israel* nor *Samuel*: And the common weid of that whole Cuntrey was mantils. As to the next, that it was not the spirit of *Samuel*, I grant: In the proving whereof ye neede not to insist, since all Christians of whatso-ever Religion agrees vpon that: and none but either mere ignorants, or Necromanciers or Witches doubtes thereof. And that the Diuel is permitted at som-times to put himself in the liknes of the Saintes, it is plaine in the Scriptures, [marginal gloss: *2.Cor.11.14.*] where it is said, that *Sathan can trans-forme himselfe into an Angell of light*. Neither could that bring any inconvenient with the visiones of the Prophets, since it is most certaine, that God will not permit him so to deceiue his own: but only such, as first wilfully deceiues them-selves, by running vnto him, whome God then suffers to fall in their owne snares, and justlie permittes them to be illuded with great efficacy of deceit, because they would not beleeue the trueth (as *Paul* sayth). And as to the diuelles foretelling of things to come, it is true that he knowes not all things future, but yet that he knowes parte, the Tragicall event of this historie declares it, (which the wit of woman could never haue fore-spoken) not that he hath any prescience, which is only proper to God: or yet knows anie thing by loking vpon God, as in a mirrour (as the good Angels doe) he being for euer debarred from the fauorable presence & countenance of his creator, but only by one of these two meanes, either as being worldlie wise, and taught by an continuall experience, ever since the creation, judges by likelie-hood of thinges to come, according to the like that hath passed before, and the naturall causes, in respect of the vicissitude of all thinges; worldly: Or else by Gods employing of him in a turne, and so foreseene thereof: as appeares to haue bin in this, whereof we finde the verie like in *Micheas* propheticque discourse to King *Achab*. [marginal gloss: *I.King.22.*] But to prooue this my first proposition, that there can be such a thing as witch-craft, &

witches, there are manie mo places in the Scriptures then this (as I said before). As first in the law of God, it is plainely prohibited: [marginal gloss: *Exod.22.*] But certaine it is, that the Law of God speakes nothing in vaine, nether doth it lay curses, or injoyne punishmentes vpon shaddowes, condemning that to be il, which is not in essence or being as we call it. Secondlie it is plaine, where wicked Pharaohs wise-men imitated ane number of *Moses* miracles, to harden the tyrants heart there by. [marginal gloss: *Exod. 7 & 8.*] Thirdly, said not *Samuell* to *Saull*, that *disobedience is as the sinne of Witch-craft?* [marginal gloss: *I.Sam.15.*] To compare to a thing that were not, it were too too absurd. Fourthlie, was not *Simon Magus*, a man of that craft? [marginal gloss: *Acts.8.*] And fiftlie, what was she that had the spirit of *Python?* [marginal gloss: *Acts 16*] beside innumerable other places that were irkesom to recite.

CHAP. II. ARGV.

What kyndie of sin the practizers of these vnlawfull artes committes.
The division of these artes. And quhat are the meanes
that allures any to practize them.

PHILOMATHES.

BVT I thinke it very strange, that God should permit anie mankynde (since they beare his owne Image) to fall in so grosse and filthie a defection.

EPI. Although man in his Creation was made to the Image of the Creator, [marginal gloss: *Gen.1.*] yet through his fall having once lost it, it is but restored againe in a part by grace onelie to the elect: So all the rest falling away from God, are given over in the handes of the Devill that enemie, to beare his Image: and being once so given over, the greatest and the grossest impietie, is the pleasantest, and most delytefull vnto them.

PHI. But may it not suffice him to haue indirectly the rule, and procure the perdition of so manie soules by alluring them to vices, and to the following of their own appetites, suppose he abuse not so many simple soules, in making them directlie acknowledge him for their maister.

EPI. No surelie, for hee vses everie man, whom of he hath the rule, according to their complexion and knowledge: And so whome he findes most simple, he plaineliest discovers himselfe vnto them. For hee beeing the enemie of mans Salvation, vses al the meanes he can to entrappe them so farre in his snares, as it may be vnable to them thereafter (suppose they would) to rid themselues out of the same.

PHI. Then this sinne is a sinne against the holie Ghost.

EPI. It is in some, but not in all.

PHI. How that? Are not all these that runnes directlie to the Devill in one Categorie.

EPI. God forbid, for the sin against the holie Ghost hath two branches: The one a falling backe from the whole service of GOD, and a refusall of all his preceptes. The other is the doing of the first with knowledge, knowing that they doe wrong against their own conscience, and the testimonie of the holie Spirit, having once had a tast of the sweetnes of Gods mercies. [marginal gloss: *Heb.6.10.*] Now in the first of these two, all sortes of Necromancers, Enchanters or Witches, ar comprehended: but in the last, none but such as erres with this knowledge that I haue spoken of.

PHI. Then it appeares that there are more sortes nor one, that are directlie professors of his service: and if so be, I pray you tell me how manie, and what are they?

EPI. There are principallie two sortes, wherevnto all the partes of that vnhappie arte are redacted; whereof the one is called *Magie* or *Necromancie*, the other *Sorcerie* or *Witch-craft.*

PHI. What I pray you? and how manie are the meanes, whereby the Devill allures persones in anie of these snares?

EPI. Even by these three passiones that are within our selues: Curiositie in great ingines: thrist of revenge, for some tortes deeply apprehended: or greedie appetite of geare, caused through great pouerty. As to the first of these, Curiosity, it is onelie the inticement of *Magiciens*, or *Necromanciers*: and the other two are the allureres of the *Sorcerers*, or *Witches*, for that olde and craftie Serpent, being a spirite, hee easilie spyes our affections, and so conformes himselfe thereto, to deceaue vs to our wracke.

CHAP. III ARGV.

The significations and Etymologies of the words of Magie *and* Necromancie. *The difference betuixt* Necromancie *and* Witch-craft: *What are the entressis, and beginninges, that brings anie to the knowledge thereof.*

PHILOMATHES.

I Would gladlie first heare, what thing is it that ye call *Magie* or *Necromancie*.

EPI. This worde *Magie* in the *Persian* toung, importes as muche as to be ane contemplator or Interpretour of Divine and heavenlie sciences: which being first vsed amongs the *Chaldees*, through their ignorance of the true divinitie, was esteemed and reputed amongst them, as a principall vertue: And therefore, was named vnjustlie with an honorable stile, which name the *Greekes* imitated, generally importing all these kindes of vnlawfull artes. And this word *Necromancie* is a Greek word, compounded of Νεκρων & μαντεια, which is to say, the Prophecie by the dead. This last name is given, to this black & vnlawfull science by the figure *Synedoche*, because it is a principal part of that art, to serue them selues with dead carcages in their diuinations.

PHI. What difference is there betwixt this arte, and Witch-craft.

EPI. Surelie, the difference vulgare put betwixt them, is verrie merrie, and in a maner true; for they say, that the Witches ar servantes onelie, and slaues to the Devil; but the Necromanciers are his maisters and commanders.

PHI. How can that be true, yt any men being specially adicted to his service, can be his comanders?

EPI. Yea, they may be: but it is onelie *secundum quid*: For it is not by anie power that they can haue over him, but *ex pacto* allanerlie: whereby he oblices himself in some trifles to them, that he may on the other part obteine the fruition of their body & soule, which is the onlie thing he huntes for.

PHI. An verie in-æquitable contract forsooth: But I pray you discourse vnto mee, what is the effect and secreets of that arte?

EPI. That is over large an fielde ye giue mee: yet I shall doe goodwill, the most summarlie that I can, to runne through the principal points thereof. As there are two sorts of folkes, that may be entysed to this arte, to wit, learned or vnlearned: so is there two meanes, which are the first steerers vp & feeders of their curiositie, thereby to make them to giue themselves over to the same: Which two meanes, I call the Divels schoole, and his rudimentes. The learned haue their curiositie wakened vppe; and fedde by that which I call his schoole: this is the *Astrologie* judiciar. For divers men having attained to a great perfection in learning, & yet remaining overbare (alas) of the spirit of regeneration and frutes thereof: finding all naturall thinges common, aswell to the stupide pedants as vnto them, they assaie to vendicate vnto them a greater name, by not onlie knowing the course of things heavenlie, but likewise to clim to the knowledge of things to come thereby. Which, at the first face appearing lawfull vnto them, in respect the ground therof seemeth to proceed of naturall causes onelie: they are so allured thereby, that finding their practize to prooue true in sundry things, they studie to know the cause thereof: and so mounting from degree to degree, vpon the slipperie and vncertaine scale of curiositie; they are at last entised, that where lawfull artes or sciences failes, to satisfie their restles mindes, even to seeke to that black and vnlawfull science of *Magie*. Where, finding at the first, that such diuers formes of circles & conjurations right-lie joyned thereunto, will raise such divers formes of spirites, to res-olue them of their doubts: and attributing the doing thereof, to the power inseparablie tyed, or inherent in the circles: and manie words of God, confusedlie wrapped in; they blindlie glorie of themselves, as if they had by their quicknes of ingine, made a conquest of *Plutoes* dominion, and were become Emperours over the *Stygian* habitacles. Where, in the meane time (miserable wretches) they are become in verie deede, bond-slaues to their mortall enemie: and their knowl-edge, for all that they presume thereof, is nothing increased, except in knowing evill, and the horrors of Hell for punishment thereof, as *Adams* was [marginal gloss: *Gen. 3.*] by the eating of the forbidden tree.

CHAP. IIII. ARGV.

The Description of the Rudiments and Schoole, which are the entresses to the arte of Magie: *And in speciall the differences betwixt* Astronomie *and* Astrologie: *Diuision of* Astrologie *in diuers partes.*

PHILOMATHES.

BVt I pray you likewise forget not to tell what are the Deuilles rudi-mentes.

EPI. His rudimentes, I call first in generall, all that which is called vulgarly the vertue of worde, herbe, & stone: which is vsed by vn-lawful charmes, without naturall causes. As likewise all kinde of practicques, freites, or other like extraordinarie actiones, which can-not abide the true toutche of naturall reason.

PHI. I would haue you to make that playner, by some particular examples; for your proposition is verie generall.

EPI. I meane either by such kinde of Charmes as commonlie dafte wiues vses, for healing of forspoken goodes, for preseruing them from euill eyes, by knitting roun-trees, or sundriest kinde of herbes, to the haire or tailes of the goodes: By curing the Worme, by stemming of blood, by healing of Horse-crookes, by turning of the riddle, or doing of such like innumerable things by wordes, without applying anie thing, meete to the part offended, as Mediciners doe; Or else by staying maried folkes, to haue naturallie adoe with other, (by knitting so manie knottes vpon a poynt at the time of their mariage) And such-like things, which men vses to practise in their merrinesse: For fra vnlearned men (being naturallie curious, and lacking the true knowledge of God) findes these practises to prooue true, as sundrie of them will doe, by the power of the Devill for deceauing men, and not by anie inherent vertue in these vaine wordes and freites; & being desirous to winne a reputation to themselues in suchlike turnes, they either (if they be of the shamefaster sorte) seeke to bee learned by some that are experimented in that Arte, (not knowing it to be euill at the first) or else being of the grosser sorte, runnes directlie to the Deuill for ambition or desire of gaine, and plainelie contractes with him thereupon.

PHI. But me thinkes these meanes which yee call the Schoole and rudimentes of the Deuill, are thinges lawfull, and haue bene approoued for such in all times and ages: As in special, this science of *Astrologie*, which is one of the speciall members of the *Mathematicques*.

EPI. There are two thinges which the learned haue obserued from the beginning, in the science of the Heauenlie Creatures, the Planets, Starres, and such like: The one is their course and ordinary motiones, which for that cause is called *Astronomia*: Which word is a compound of νομοζ & αστερων that is to say, the law of the Starres: And this arte indeed is one of the members of the *Mathematicques*, & not onelie lawful, but most necessarie and commendable. The other is called *Astrologia*, being compounded of αστερων &

λογοζ which is to say, the word, and preaching of the starres: Which is deuided in two partes: The first by knowing thereby the powers of simples, and sickenesses, the course of the seasons and the weather, being ruled by their influence; which part depending vpon the former, although it be not of it selfe a parte of *Mathematicques*: yet it is not vnlawful, being moderatlie vsed, suppose not so necessarie and commendable as the former. The second part is to truste so much to their influences, as thereby to fore-tell what common-weales shall florish or decay: what, persones shall be fortunate or vnfortunate: what side shall winne in anie battell: What man shall obteine victorie at singular combate: What way, and of what age shall men die: What horse shall winne at matche-running; and diuerse such like incredible things, wherein *Cardanus*, *Cornelius Agrippa*, and diuerse others haue more curiouslie then profitably written at large. Of this roote last spoken of, springs innumerable branches; such as the knowledge by the natiuities; the *Cheiromancie*, *Geomantie*, *Hydromantie*, *Arithmantie*, *Physiognomie*: & a thousand others: which were much practised, & holden in great reuerence by the *Gentles* of olde. And this last part of *Astrologie* whereof I haue spoken, which is the root of their branches, was called by them *pars fortunæ*. This parte now is vtterlie vnlawful to be trusted in, or practized amongst christians, as leaning to no ground of natural reason: & it is this part which I called before the deuils schole.

PHI. But yet manie of the learned are of the contrarie opinion.

EPI. I grant, yet I could giue my reasons to fortifie & maintaine my opinion, if to enter into this disputation it wold not draw me quite off the ground of our discours; besides the mis-spending of the whole daie thereupon: One word onely I will answer to them, & that in the Scriptures (which must be an infallible ground to all true Christians) That in the Prophet *Ieremie* [marginal gloss: *Ierem. 10.*] it is plainelie forbidden, to beleeue or hearken vnto them that Prophecies & fore-speakes by the course of the Planets & Starres.

CHAP. V. ARGV.

How farre the vsing of Charmes is lawfull or vnlawfull:
The description of the formes of Circkles and Coniurationes.
And what causeth the Magicianes *themselues to wearie thereof.*

PHILOMATHES.

WEL, Ye haue said far inough in that argument. But how prooue ye now that these charmes or vnnaturall practicques are vnlawfull: For so, many honest & merrie men & women haue publicklie practized some of them, that I thinke if ye would accuse them al of Witch-craft, ye would affirme more nor ye will be beleeued in.

EPI. I see if you had taken good tent (to the nature of that word, whereby I named it,) ye would not haue bene in this doubt, nor mis-taken me, so farre as ye haue done: For although, as none can be schollers in a schole, & not be subject to the master thereof: so none can studie and put in practize (for studie the alone, and knowledge, is more perilous nor offensiue; and it is the practise only that makes the greatnes of the offence.) The cirkles and art of *Magie*, without committing an horrible defection from God: And yet as they that reades and learnes their rudiments, are not the more subject to anie schoole-master, if it please not their parentes to put them to the schoole thereafter; So they who ignorantly proues these practicques, which I cal the deuilles rudiments, vnknowing them to be baites, casten out by him, for trapping such as God will permit to fall in his hands: This kinde of folkes I saie, no doubt, ar to be judged the best of, in respect they vse no invocation nor help of him (by their knowledge at least) in these turnes, and so haue neuer entred them-selues in Sathans seruice; Yet to speake truely for my owne part (I speake but for my selfe) I desire not to make so neere riding: For in my opinion our enemie is ouer craftie, and we ouer weake (except the greater grace of God) to assay such hazards, wherein he preases to trap vs.

PHI. Ye haue reason forsooth; for as the common Prouerbe saith: They that suppe keile with the Deuill, haue neede of long spoones. But now I praie you goe forwarde in the describing of this arte of *Magie*.

EPI. Fra they bee come once vnto this perfection in euill, in hauing any knowledge (whether learned or vnlearned) of this black art: they then beginne to be wearie of the raising of their Maister, by conjured circkles; being both so difficile and perilous, and so commeth plainelie to a contract with him, wherein is speciallie conteined formes and effectes.

PHI. But I praye you or euer you goe further, discourse me some-what of their circkles and conjurationes; And what should be the cause of their wearying thereof: For it should seeme that that forme should be lesse fearefull yet, than the direct haunting and societie, with that foule and vncleane Spirite.

EPI. I thinke ye take me to be a Witch my selfe, or at the least would faine sweare your selfe prentise to that craft: Alwaies as I may, I shall shortlie satisfie you, in that kinde of conjurations, which are conteined in such bookes, which I call the Deuilles Schoole: There are foure principall partes; the persons of the conjurers; the action of the conjuration; the wordes and rites vsed to that effect; and the Spirites that are conjured. Ye must first remember to laye the ground, that I tould you before: which is, that it is no power inherent in the circles, or in the holines of the names of God blasphemouslie vsed: nor in whatsoeuer rites or ceremonies at that time vsed, that either can raise any infernall spirit, or yet limitat him perforce within or without these circles. For it is he onelie, the father of all lyes, who hauing first of all prescribed that forme of doing, feining himselfe to he cornmanded & restreined thereby, wil be loath to passe the boundes of these injunctiones; aswell thereby to make them glory in the impiring ouer him (as I saide before:) As likewise to make himselfe so to be trusted in these little thinges, that he may haue the better commoditie thereafter, to deceiue them in the end with a tricke once for all; I meane the euerlasting perdition of their soul & body. Then laying this ground, as I haue said, these conjurationes must haue few or mo in number of the persones conjurers (alwaies passing the singuler number) according to the qualitie of the circle, and forme of apparition. Two principall thinges cannot well in that errand be wanted: holie-water (whereby the Deuill mockes the *Papistes*) and some present of a liuing thing vnto him. There ar likewise certaine seasons, dayes and houres, that they obserue in this purpose: These things being all readie, and prepared, circles are made triangular, quadrangular, round, double or single, according to the forme of apparition that they craue. But to speake of the diuerse formes of the circles, of the innumerable characters and crosses that are within and without, and out-through the same, of the diuers formes of apparitiones, that that craftie spirit illudes them with, and of all such particulars in that action, I remit it to ouer-manie that haue busied their heades in describing of the same; as being but curious, and altogether vnprofitable. And this farre onelie I touch, that when the conjured Spirit appeares, which will not be while after manie circumstances, long praiers, and much muttring and murmuring of the conjurers; like a *Papist* priest, dispatching a hunting *Masse*: how sone I say, he appeares, if they haue missed one iote of all their rites; or if any of their feete once slyd ouer the circle through terror of his feareful apparition, he payes himselfe at that time in his owne hande, of that due debt which they ought him; and other-wise would haue delayed longer to haue payed him: I meane hee carries them with him bodie and soule. If this be not now a just cause to make them wearie of these formes of conjuration, I leaue it to you to judge vpon; considering the long-somenesse of the labour, the precise keeping of dayes and houres (as I haue said) The terriblenesse of apparition, and the present perrell that they stande in, in missing the least circumstance or freite, that they ought to obserue: And on the other parte, the Deuil is glad to mooue them to a plaine and square dealing with him as I said before.

CHAP. VI ARGV.

The Deuilles contract with the Magicians: *The diuision thereof in two partes: What is the difference betwixt Gods miracles and the Deuils.*

PHILOMATHES.

INdeede there is cause inough, but rather to leaue him at all, then to runne more plainlie to him, if they were wise he delt with. But goe forwarde now I pray you to these turnes, fra they become once deacons in this craft.

EPI. From time that they once plainelie begin to contract with him: The effect of their contract consistes in two thinges; in formes and effectes, as I be gan to tell alreadie, were it not yee interrupted me (for although the contract be mutuall; I speake first of that part, wherein the Deuill oblishes himselfe to them) by formes, I meane in what shape or fashion he shall come vnto them, when they call vpon him. And by effectes, I vnderstand, in what special sorts of seruices he bindes himselfe to be subject vnto them. The qualitie of these formes and effectes, is lesse or greater, according to the skil and art of the *Magician.* For as to the formes, to some of the baser sorte of them he oblishes him selfe to appeare at their calling vpon him, by such a proper name which he shewes vnto them, either in likenes of a dog, a Catte, an Ape, or such-like other beast; or else to answere by a voyce onlie. The effects are to answere to such demands, as concernes curing of disseases, their own particular menagery: or such other base things as they require of him. But to the most curious sorte, in the formes he will oblish himselfe, to enter in a dead bodie, and there out of to giue such answers, of the euent of battels, of maters concerning the estate of commonwelths, and such like other great questions: yea, to some he will be a continuall attender, in forme of a Page: He will permit himselfe to be conjured, for the space of so many yeres, ether in a tablet or a ring, or such like thing, which they may easely carrie about with them: He giues them power to sel such wares to others, whereof some will bee dearer, and some better cheape; according to the lying or true speaking of the Spirit that is conjured therein. Not but that in verie deede, all Devils must be lyars; but so they abuse the simplicitie of these wretches, that becomes their schollers, that they make them beleeue, that at the fall of *Lucifer*, some Spirites fell in the aire, some in the fire, some in the water, some in the lande: In which Elementes they still remaine. Whereupon they build, that such as fell in the fire, or in the aire, are truer then they, who fell in the water or in the land, which is al but meare trattles, & forged be the author of al deceit. For they fel not be weight, as a solide substance, to stick in any one parte: But the principall part of their fal, consisting in qualitie, by the falling from the grace of God wherein they were created, they continued still thereafter, and shal do while the latter daie, in wandring through the worlde, as Gods hang-men, to execute such turnes as he employes them in. And when anie of them are not occupyed in that, re-turne they must to their prison in hel (as it is plaine in the miracle that CHRIST wrought at *Gennezareth*) [marginal gloss: *Mat. 8.*] therein at the latter daie to be all enclosed for euer: and as they deceiue their schollers in this, so do they, in imprinting in them the opinion that there are so manie Princes, Dukes, and Kinges amongst them, euerie one commanding fewer or mo Legions, and impyring in diuers artes, and quarters of the earth. For though that I will not denie that there be a forme of ordour amongst the Angels in Heauen, and consequentlie, was amongst them before their fall; yet, either that they bruike the same sensine; or that God will permit vs to know by damned Deuils, such heauenlie mysteries of his, which he would not reueale to vs neither by Scripture nor Prophets, I thinke no Christiane will once thinke it. But by the contrarie of all such mysteries, as he hath closed vp with his seale of secrecie; it becommeth vs to be contented with an humble ignorance, they being thinges not necessarie for our saluation. But to returne to the purpose, as these formes, wherein Sathan oblishes himselfe to the greatest of the *Magicians*, are wounderfull curious; so are the effectes correspondent vnto the same: For he will oblish himselfe to teach them artes and sciences, which he may easelie doe, being so learned a knaue as he is: To carrie them newes from anie parte of the worlde, which the agilitie of a Spirite may easelie performe: to reueale to them the secretes of anie persons, so being they bee once spoken, for the thought none knowes but GOD; except so far as yee may ghesse by their countenance, as one who is doubtleslie learned inough in the *Physiognomie*: Yea, he will make his schollers to creepe in credite with Princes, by fore-telling them manie greate thinges; parte true, parte false: For if all were false, he would tyne credite at all handes; but alwaies doubtsome, as his Oracles were. And he will also make them to please Princes, by faire banquets and daintie dishes, carryed in short space fra the farthest part of the worlde. For no man doubts but he is a thiefe, and his agilitie (as I spake before) makes him to come suche speede. Such-like, he will guard his schollers with faire armies of horse-men and foote-men in appearance, castles and fortes: Which all are but impressiones in the aire, easelie gathered by a spirite, drawing so neare to that substance himselfe: As in like maner he will learne them manie juglarie trickes at Cardes, dice, & such like, to deceiue mennes senses thereby: and such innumerable false practicques; which are prouen by ouer-manie in this age: As they who ar acquainted with that Italian called SCOTO yet liuing, can reporte. And yet are all these thinges but deluding of the senses, and no waies true in substance, as were the false miracles wrought by King *Pharaoes* Magicians, for counterfeiting *Moyses*: For that is the difference betuixt Gods myracles and the Deuils, God is a creator, what he makes appeare in miracle, it is so in effect. As *Moyses* rod being casten downe, was no doubt turned in a natural Serpent: where as the Deuill (as Gods Ape) counterfetting that by his *Magicians*, maid their wandes to appeare so, onelie to mennes outward senses: as kythed in effect by their being deuoured by the other. For it is no wonder, that the Deuill may delude our senses, since we see by common proofe, that simple juglars will make an hundreth thinges seeme both to our eies and eares otherwaies then they are. Now as to the *Magicians* parte of the contract, it is in a word that thing, which I said before, the Deuill hunts for in all men.

PHI. Surelie ye haue said much to me in this arte, if all that ye haue said be as true as wounderfull.

EPI. For the trueth in these actiones, it will be easelie confirmed, to anie that pleases to take paine vpon the reading of diuerse authenticque histories, and the inquiring of daily experiences. And as for the trueth of their possibilitie, that they may be, and in what maner, I trust I haue alleaged nothing whereunto I haue not joyned such probable reasons, as I leaue to your discretion, to waie and consider: One word onlie I omitted; concerning the forme of making of this contract, which is either written with the *Magicians* owne bloud: or else being agreed vpon (in termes his schole-master) touches him in some parte, though peraduenture no marke remaine: as it doth with all Witches.

CHAP. VII. ARGV.

The reason why the art of Magie *is vnlawfull. What punishment they merite: And who may he accounted guiltie of that crime.*

PHILOMATHES.

SVRELIE Ye haue made this arte to appeare verie monstruous & detestable. But what I pray you shall be said to such as mainteines this art to be lawfull, for as euill as you haue made it?

EPI. I say, they sauour of the panne them selues, or at least little better, And yet I would be glad to heare their reasons.

PHI. There are two principallie, that euer I heard vsed; beside that which is founded vpon the comon Prouerb (that the *Necromancers* commands the Deuill, which ye haue already refuted) The one is grounded vpon a receiued custome: The other vpon an authoritie, which some thinkes infallible. Vpon custome, we see that diuerse Christian Princes and Magistrates seuere punishers of Witches, will not onelie ouer-see *Magicians* to liue within their dominions; but euen some-times delight to see them prooue some of their practicques. The other reason is, that *Moyses* being brought vp (as it is expreslie said in the Scriptures) *in all the sciences of the AEgyptians*; whereof no doubt, this was one of the principalles. And he notwithstanding of this arte, pleasing God, as he did, consequentlie that art professed by so godlie a man, coulde not be vnlawfull.

EPI. As to the first of your reasones, grounded vpon custome: I saie, an euill custome can neuer be accepted for a good law, for the ouer great ignorance of the worde in some Princes and Magistrates, and the contempt thereof in others, moues them to sinne heavelie against their office in that poynt. As to the other reasone, which seemes to be of greater weight, if it were formed in a Syllogisme; it behooued to be in manie termes, and full of fallacies (to speake in termes of *Logicque*) for first, that that generall proposition; affirming *Moyses* to be taught *in all the sciences of the AEgyptians*, should conclude that he was taught in *Magie*, I see no necessity. For we must vnderstand that the spirit of God there, speaking of sciences, vnderstandes them that are lawfull; for except they be lawfull, they are but *abusiuè* called sciences, & are but ignorances indeede: *Nam homo pictus, non est homo.* Secondlie, giuing that he had bene taught in it, there is great difference, betwixt knowledge and practising of a thing (as I said before) For God knoweth all thinges, being alwaies good, and of our sinne & our infirmitie proceedeth our ignorance. Thirdlie, giuing that he had both studied and practised the same (which is more nor monstruous to be beleeued by any Christian) yet we know well inough, that before that euer the spirite of God began to call *Moyses*, he was fled out of *AEgypt*, being fourtie yeares of age, for the slaughter of an *AEgyptian*, and in his good-father *Iethroes* lande, first called at the firie bushe, hauing remained there other fourtie yeares in exile: so that suppose he had beene the wickeddest man in the worlde before, he then became a changed and regenerat man, and very litle of olde *Moyses* remained in him. *Abraham* was an Idolater in *Vr* of *Chaldæa*, before he was called: And *Paule* being called *Saule*, was a most sharp persecutor of the Saintes of God, while that name was changed.

PHI. What punishment then thinke ye merites these *Magicians* and *Necromancers*?

EPI. The like no doubt, that *Sorcerers* and *Witches* merites; and rather so much greater, as their error proceedes of the greater knowledge, and so drawes nerer to the sin against the holy Ghost. And as I saye of them, so saye I the like of all such as consults, enquires, entertaines, & ouersees them, which is seene by the miserable endes of many that askes councell of them: For the Deuill hath neuer better tydings to tell to any, then he tolde to Saule: neither is it lawfull to vse so vnlawfull instrumentes, were it neuer for so good a purpose: for that axiome in Theologie is most certaine and infallible: [marginal gloss: *Ast 3.*] *Nunquam faciendum est malum vt bonum inde eueniat.*

THE SECONDE BOOKE OF DÆMONOLOGIE

ARGVMENT.

The description of Sorcerie an Witch-craft in speciall.

CHAP. I. ARGV.

Proued by the Scripture, that such a thing can be:
And the reasones refuted of all such as would call it but an
imagination and Melancholicque humor.

PHILOMATHES.

NOW Since yee haue satisfied me nowe so fullie, concerning *Magie* or *Necromancie* I will pray you to do the like in *Sorcerie* or *Witchcraft*.

EPI. That fielde is likewise verie large: and althought in the mouthes; and pennes of manie, yet fewe knowes the trueth thereof, so wel as they beleeue themselues, as I shall so shortely as I can, make you (God willing) as easelie to perceiue.

PHI. But I pray you before ye goe further, let mee interrupt you here with a shorte digression: which is, that manie can scarcely beleeue that there is such a thing as Witch-craft. Whose reasons I wil shortely alleage vnto you, that ye may satisfie me as well in that, as ye haue done in the rest. For first, whereas the Scripture seemes to prooue Witchcraft to be, by diuerse examples, and speciallie by sundrie of the same, which ye haue alleaged, it is thought by some, that these places speakes of *Magicians* and *Necromancers* onlie, & not of Witches. As in special, these wise men of *Pharaohs*, that counterfeited *Moyses* miracles, were *Magicians* say they, & not Witches: As likewise that *Pythonisse* that *Saul* consulted with: And so was *Simon Magus* in the new Testament, as that very stile importes. Secondlie, where ye would oppone the dailie practicque, & confession of so manie, that is thought likewise to be but verie melancholicque imaginations of simple rauing creatures. Thirdly, if Witches had such power of Witching of folkes to death, (as they say they haue) there had bene none left aliue long sence in the world, but they: at the least, no good or godlie person of whatsoeuer estate, coulde haue escaped their deuilrie.

EPI. Your three reasons as I take, ar grounded the first of them *negativè* vpon the Scripture: The second *affirmativè* vpon Physicke: And the thirde vpon the certaine proofe of experience. As to your first, it is most true indeede, that all these wise men of *Pharaoh* were *Magicians* of art: As likewise it appeares wel that the *Pythonisse*, with whom *Saul* consulted, was of that same profession: & so was *Simon Magus.* But yee omitted to speake of the Lawe of God, wherein are all *Magicians,* Diuines, Enchanters, Sorcerers, Witches, & whatsouer of that kinde that consultes with the Deuill, plainelie prohibited, and alike threatned against. And besides that, she who had the Spirite of *Python,* in the Actes [marginal gloss: *Act. 16.*], whose Spirite was put to silence by the Apostle, coulde be no other thing but a verie Sorcerer or Witch, if ye admit the vulgare distinction, to be in a maner true, whereof I spake in the beginning of our conference. For that spirit whereby she conquested such gaine to her Master, was not at her raising or commanding, as she pleased to appoynt, but spake by her toung, aswel publicklie, as priuatelie: Whereby she seemed to draw nearer to the sort of *Demoniakes* or possessed, if that conjunction betwixt them, had not bene of her owne consent: as it appeared by her, not being tormented therewith: And by her conquesting of such gaine to her masters (as I haue alreadie said.) As to your second reason grounded vpon Physick, in attributing their confessiones or apprehensiones, to a naturall melancholicque humour: Anie that pleases Physicallie to consider vpon the naturall humour of melancholie, according to all the Physicians, that euer writ thereupon, they sall finde that that will be ouer short a cloak to couer their knauery with: For as the humor of Melancholie in the selfe is blacke, heauie and terrene, so are the symptomes thereof, in any persons that are subject therevnto, leannes, palenes, desire of solitude: and if they come to the highest degree therof, mere folie and *Manie*: where as by the contrarie, a great nomber of them that euer haue bene convict or confessors of Witchcraft, as may be presently scene by manie that haue at this time confessed: they are by the contrarie, I say, some of them rich and worldly-wise, some of them fatte or corpulent in their bodies, and most part of them altogether giuen ouer to the pleasures of the flesh, continual haunting of companie, and all kind of merrines, both lawfull and vnlawfull, which are thinges directly contrary to the symptomes of Melancholie, wherof I spake, and further experience daylie proues how loath they are to confesse without torture, which witnesseth their guiltines, where by the contrary, the Melancholicques neuer spares to bewray themselues, by their continuall discourses, feeding therby their humor in that which they thinke no crime. As to your third reason, it scarselie merites an answere. For if the deuill their master were not bridled, as the scriptures teacheth vs, suppose there were no men nor women to be his instrumentes, he could finde waies inough without anie helpe of others to wrack al mankinde: wherevnto he employes his whole study, and *goeth about like a roaring Lyon* (as PETER saith) to that effect, [marginal gloss: *I.Pet.5.*] but the limites of his power were set down before the foundations of the world were laid, which he hath not power in the least jote to transgresse. But beside all this, there is ouer greate a certainty to proue that they are, by the daily experience of the harmes that they do, both to men, and whatsoeuer thing men possesses, whome God will permit them to be the instrumentes, so to trouble or visite, as in my discourse of that arte, yee shall heare clearelie proued.

CHAP. II ARGV.

The Etymologie and signification of that word of Sorcerie. *The first entresse and prentishippe of them that giues themselues to that craft.*

PHILOMATHES.

Come on then I pray you, and returne where ye left.

EPI. This word of *Sorcerie* is a *Latine* worde, which is taken from casting of the lot, & therefore he that vseth it, is called *Sortiarius à sorte*. As to the word of *Witchcraft*, it is nothing but a proper name giuen in our language. The cause wherefore they were called *sortiarij*, proceeded of their practicques seeming to come of lot or chance: Such as the turning of the riddle: the knowing of the forme of prayers, or such like tokens: If a person diseased woulde liue or dye. And in generall, that name was giuen them for vsing of such charmes, and freites, as that Crafte teacheth them. Manie poynts of their craft and practicques are common betuixt the *Magicians* and them: for they serue both one Master, althought in diuerse fashions. And as I deuided the *Necromancers*, into two sorts, learned and vnlearned; so must I denie them in other two, riche and of better accompt, poore and of basser degree. These two degrees now of persones, that practises this craft, answers to the passions in them, which (I told you before) the Deuil vsed as meanes to intyse them to his seruice, for such of them as are in great miserie and pouertie, he allures to follow him, by promising vnto them greate riches, and worldlie commoditie. Such as though riche, yet burnes in a desperat desire of reuenge, hee allures them by promises, to get their turne satisfied to their hartes contentment. It is to be noted nowe, that that olde and craftie enemie of ours, assailes none, though touched with any of these two extremities, except he first finde an entresse reddy for him, either by the great ignorance of the person he deales with, ioyned with an euill life, or else by their carelesnes and contempt of God: And finding them in an vtter despair, for one of these two former causes that I haue spoken of; he prepares the way by feeding them craftely in their humour, and filling them further and further with despaire, while he finde the time proper to discouer himself vnto them. At which time, either vpon their walking solitarie in the fieldes, or else lying pansing in their bed; but alwaies with-

out the company of any other, he either by a voyce, or in likenesse
of a man inquires of them, what troubles them: and promiseth
them, a suddaine and certaine waie of remedie, vpon condition on
the other parte, that they follow his advise; and do such thinges as he
wil require of them: Their mindes being prepared before hand, as I
haue alreadie spoken, they easelie agreed vnto that demande of his:
And syne settes an other tryist, where they may meete againe. At
which time, before he proceede any further with them, he first per-
swades them to addict themselues to his seruice: which being easely
obteined, he then discouers what he is vnto them: makes them to
renunce their God and *Baptisme* directlie, and giues them his marke
vpon some secreit place of their bodie, which remaines soare vn-
healed, while his next meeting with them, and thereafter euer insensible, how soeuer it be nipped or pricked by any, as is dailie proued,
to giue them a proofe thereby, that as in that doing, hee could hurte
and heale them; so all their ill and well doing thereafter, must de-
pende vpon him. And besides that, the intollerable dolour that they
feele in that place, where he hath marked them, serues to waken
them, and not to let them rest, while their next meeting againe: fearing least otherwaies they might either forget him, being as new Prentises, and not well inough founded yet, in that fiendlie follie: or else
remembring of that horrible promise they made him, at their last
meeting, they might skunner at the same, and preasse to call it back.
At their thirde meeting, he makes a shew to be carefull, to performe
his promises, either by teaching them waies howe to get themselues
reuenged, if they be of that sort: Or els by teaching them lessons,
how by moste vilde and vnlawfull meanes, they may obtaine gaine,
and worldlie commoditie, if they be of the other sorte.

CHAP. III. ARGV.

The Witches actiones diuided in two partes. The actiones proper to
their owne persones. Their actiones toward others. The forme of
their conuentiones, and adoring of their Master.

PHILOMATHES.

YE haue said now inough of their initiating in that ordour. It restes then that ye discourse vpon their practises, fra they be passed Prentises: for I would faine heare what is possible to them to performe in verie deede. Although they serue a common Master with the *Necromancers*, (as I haue before saide) yet serue they him in an other forme. For as the meanes are diuerse, which allures them to these vnlawfull artes of seruing of the Deuill; so by diuerse waies vse they their practises, answering to these meanes, which first the Deuill, vsed as instrumentes in them; though al tending to one end: To wit, the enlargeing of Sathans tyrannie, and crossing of the propagation of the Kingdome of CHRIST, so farre as lyeth in the possibilitie, either of the one or other sorte, or of the Deuill their Master. For where the *Magicians*, as allured by curiositie, in the most parte of their practises, seekes principallie the satisfying of the same, and to winne to themselues a popular honoure and estimation: These Witches on the other parte, being intised ether for the desire of reuenge, or of worldly riches, their whole practises are either to hurte men and their gudes, or what they possesse, for satisfying of their cruell mindes in the former, or else by the wracke in quhatsoeuer sorte, of anie whome God will permitte them to haue power off, to satisfie their greedie desire in the last poynt.

EPI. In two partes their actiones may be diuided; the actiones of their owne persones, and the actiones proceeding from them towardes anie other. And this diuision being wel vnderstood, will easilie resolue you, what is possible to them to doe. For although all that they confesse is no lie vpon their parte, yet doubtlesly in my opinion, a part of it is not indeede, according as they take it to be: And in this I meane by the actiones of their owne persones. For as I said before, speaking of *Magie* that the Deuill illudes the senses of these schollers of his, in manie thinges, so saye I the like of these Witches.

PHI. Then I pray you, first to speake of that part of their owne persons, and syne ye may come next to their actiones towardes others.

EPI. To the effect that they may performe such seruices of their false Master, as he employes them in, the deuill as Gods Ape, counterfeites in his seruantes this seruice & forme of adoration, that God prescribed and made his seruantes to practise. For as the seruants of GOD, publicklie vses to conveene for seruing of him, so makes he them in great numbers to conveene (though publickly they dare not) for his seruice. As none conueenes to the adoration and worshipping of God, except they be marked with his seale, the Sacrament of *Baptisme*: So none serues Sathan, and conueenes to the adoring of him, that are not marked with that marke, wherof I alredy spake. As the Minister sent by God, teacheth plainely at the time of their publick conuentions, how to serue him in spirit & truth: so that vncleane spirite, in his owne person teacheth his Disciples, at the time of their conueening, how to worke all kinde of mischiefe: And craues compt of all their horrible and detestable proceedinges passed, for aduancement of his seruice. Yea, that he may the more viuelie counterfeit and scorne God, he oft times makes his slaues to conveene in these verrie places, which are destinat and ordeined for the conveening of the servantes of God (I meane by Churches) But this farre, which I haue yet said, I not onelie take it to be true in their opiniones, but euen so to be indeede. For the forme that he vsed in counterfeiting God amongst the *Gentiles*, makes me so to thinke: As God spake by his Oracles, spake he not so by his? As GOD had aswell bloudie Sacrifices, as others without bloud, had not he the like? As God had Churches sanctified to his seruice, with Altars, Priests, Sacrifices, Ceremonies and Prayers; had he not the like polluted to his seruice? As God gaue responses by *Vrim* and *Thummim*, gaue he not his responses by the intralls of beastes, by the singing of Fowles, and by their actiones in the aire? As God by visiones, dreames, and extases reueiled what was to come, and what was his will vnto his scruantes; vsed he not the like meanes to forwarne his slaues of things to come? Yea, euen as God loued cleannes, hated vice, and impuritie, & appoynted punishmentes therefore: vsed he not the like (though falselie I grant, and but in eschewing the lesse inconuenient, to draw them vpon a greater) yet dissimuled he not I say, so farre as to appoynt his Priestes to keepe their bodies cleane and vndefiled, before their asking responses of him? And feyned he not God to be a protectour of euerie vertue, and a iust reuenger of the contrarie? This reason then moues me, that as he is that same Deuill; and as craftie nowe as he was then; so wil hee not spare a pertelie in these actiones that I haue spoken of, concerning the witches persones: But further, Witches oft times confesses not only his conueening in the Church with them, but his occupying of the Pulpit: Yea, their forme of adoration, to be the kissing of his hinder partes. Which though it seeme ridiculous, yet may it likewise be true, seeing we reade that in *Calicute*, he appearing in forme of a *Goate*-bucke, hath publicklie that vn-honest homage done vnto him, by euerie one of the people: So ambitious is he, and greedie of honour (which procured his fall) that he will euen imitate God in that parte, where it is said, that *Moyses* could see but the *hinder partes of God, for the brightnesse of his glorie*: [marginal gloss: *Exo. 33*] And yet that speache is spoken but ανθρωπωπαθειαν

CHAP. IIII. ARGV.

What are the waies possible, wherby the witches may transport themselues to places far distant. And what ar impossible &mere illusiones of Sathan. And the reasons therof.

PHILOMATHES.

BVt by what way say they or think ye it possible that they can com to these vnlawful cõuentiõs?

EPI. There is the thing which I esteeme their senses to be deluded in, and though they lye not in confessing of it, because they

thinke it to be true, yet not to be so in substance or effect: for they
saie, that by diuerse meanes they may conueene, either to the adoring of their Master, or to the putting in practise any seruice of his,
committed vnto their charge: one way is natural, which is natural
riding, going or sayling, at what houre their Master comes and adu-
ertises them. And this way may be easelie beleued: an other way is
some-what more strange: and yet is it possible to be true: which is
by being carried by the force of the Spirite which is their conducter,
either aboue the earth or aboue the Sea swiftlie, to the place where
they are to meet: which I am perswaded to be likewaies possible, in
respect that as *Habakkuk* was carryed by the Angell in that forme, to
the denne where *Daniell* laie; [marginal gloss: *Apocrypha of Bel and
the Dragon.*] so thinke I, the Deuill will be reddie to imitate God, as
well in that as in other thinges: which is much more possible to him
to doe, being a Spirite, then to a mighty winde, being but a naturall
meteore, to transporte from one place to an other a solide bodie, as
is commonlie and dailie seene in practise: But in this violent forme
they cannot be carryed, but a shorte boundes, agreeing with the
space that they may reteine their breath: for if it were longer, their
breath could not remaine vnextinguished, their bodie being carryed
in such a violent & forceable maner, as be example: If one fall off an
small height, his life is but in perrell, according to the harde or soft
lighting: But if one fall from an high and stay rocke, his breath wilbe
forceablie banished from the bodie, before he can win to the earth,
as is oft seen by experience. And in this transporting they say themselues, that they are inuisible to anie other, except amongst themselues; which may also be possible in my opinion. For if the deuil may
forme what kinde of impressiones he pleases in the aire, as I haue
said before, speaking of *Magie*, why may he not far easilier thicken
& obscure so the air, that is next about them by contracting it strait
together, that the beames of any other mans eyes, cannot pearce
thorow the same, to see them? But the third way of their comming
to their conuentions, is, that where in I think them deluded: for

some of them sayeth, that being transformed in the likenesse of a little beast or foule, they will come and pearce through whatsoeuer house or Church, though all ordinarie passages be closed, by whatsoeuer open, the aire may enter in at. And some sayeth, that their bodies lying stil as in an extasy, their spirits wil be rauished out of their bodies, & caried to such places. And for verefying therof, wil giue euident tokens, aswel by witnesses that haue seene their body lying senseles in the meane time, as by naming persones, whomwith they mette, and giuing tokens quhat purpose was amongst them, whome otherwaies they could not haue knowen: for this forme of journeing, they affirme to vse most, when they are transported from one Countrie to another.

PHI. Surelie I long to heare your owne opinion of this: For they are like old wiues trattles about the fire.

EPI. The reasons that moues me to thinke that these are meere illusiones, ar these. First for them that are transformed in likenes of beastes or foules, can enter through so narrow passages, although I may easelie beleeue that the Deuill coulde by his woorkemanshippe vpon the aire, make them appeare to be in such formes, either to themselues or to others: Yet how he can contract a solide bodie within so little roome, I thinke it is directlie contrarie to it selfe, for to be made so little, and yet not diminished: To be so straitlie drawen together, and yet feele no paine; I thinke it is so contrarie to the qualitie of a naturall bodie, and so like to the little transubstantiat god in the *Papistes Masse*, that I can neuer beleeue it. So to haue a quantitie, is so proper to a solide bodie, that as all Philosophers concludes, it cannot be any more without one, then a spirite can haue one. For when PETER *came out of the prison, and the doores all locked*: [marginal gloss: *Act. 12.*] It was not by any contracting of his bodie in so little roome: but by the giuing place of the dore, though vn-espyed by the Gaylors. And yet is there no comparison, when this is done, betuixt the power of God, and of the Deuill. As to their forme of extasie and spirituall transporting, it is certaine the soules going out of the bodie, is the onely difinition of naturall death: and who are once dead, God forbid wee should thinke that it should lie in the power of all the Deuils in Hell, to restore them to their life againe: Although he can put his owne spirite in a dead bodie, which the *Necromancers* commonlie practise, as yee haue harde. For that is the office properly belonging to God; and besides that, the soule once parting from the bodie, cannot wander anie longer in the worlde, but to the owne resting place must it goe immediatlie, abiding the conjunction of the bodie againe, at the latter daie. And what CHRIST or the Prophets did miraculouslie in this case, it cannot in no Christian mans opinion be maid common with the Deuill. As for anie tokens that they giue for proouing of this, it is verie possible to the Deuils craft, to perswade them to these meanes. For he being a spirite, may hee: not so rauishe their thoughtes, and dull their sences, that their bodie lying as dead, hee may object to their spirites as it were in a dreame, & (as the Poets write of *Morpheus*) represente such formes of persones, of places, and other circumstances, as he pleases to illude them with? Yea, that he maie deceiue them with the greater efficacie, may hee not at that same instant, by fellow angelles of his, illude such other persones so in that same fashion, whome with he makes them to beleeue that they mette; that all their reportes and tokens, though seuerallie examined, may euerie one agree with an other. And that whatsoeuer actiones, either in hurting men or beasts: or whatsoeuer other thing that they falselie imagine, at that time to haue done, may by himselfe or his marrowes, at that same time be done indeede; so as if they would giue for a token of their being rauished at the death of such a person within so shorte space thereafter, whom they beleeue to haue poysoned, or witched at that instante, might hee not at that same houre, haue smitten that same person by the permission of GOD, to the farther deceiuing of them, and to mooue others to beleeue them? And this is surelie the likeliest way, and most according to reason, which my judgement can finde out in this, and whatsoeuer vther vnnaturall poyntes of their confession. And by these meanes shall we saill surelie, betuixt *Charybdis* and

Scylla, in eschewing the not beleeuing of them altogether on the one part, least that drawe vs to the errour that there is no Witches: and on the other parte in beleeuing of it, make vs to eschew the falling into innumerable absurdities, both monstruouslie against all Theologie diuine, and Philosophie humaine.

CHAP. V ARGV.

Witches actiones towardes others. Why there are more women of that craft nor men? What thinges are possible to them to effectuate by the power of their master. The reasons thereof. What is the surest remedie of the harmes done by them.

PHILOMATHES.

FOrsooth your opinion in this, seemes to carrie most reason with it, and sence yee haue ended, then the actions belonging properly to their owne persones: say forwarde now to their actiones vsed towardes others.

EPI. In their actiones vsed towardes others, three thinges ought to be considered: First the maner of their consulting thereupon: Next their part as instrumentes: And last their masters parte, who puts the same in execution. As to their consultationes thereupon, they vse them oftest in the Churches, where they conveene for ador-ing: at what time their master enquiring at them what they would be at: euerie one of them propones vnto him, what wicked turne they would haue done, either for obteining of riches, or for reueng-ing them vpon anie whome they haue malice at: who granting their demande, as no doubt willinglie he wil, since it is to doe euill, he teacheth them the means, wherby they may do the same. As for lit-tle trifling turnes that women haue ado with, he causeth them to ioynt dead corpses, & to make powders thereof, mixing such other thinges there amongst, as he giues vnto them.

PHI. But before yee goe further, permit mee I pray you to interrupt you one worde, which yee haue put mee in memorie of, by speaking of Women. What can be the cause that there are twentie women giuen to that craft, where ther is one man?

EPI. The reason is easie, for as that sexe is frailer then man is, so is it easier to be intrapped in these grosse snares of the Deuill, as was ouer well proued to be true, by the Serpents deceiuing of *Eua* at the beginning, which makes him the homelier with that sexe sensine.

PHI. Returne now where ye left.

EPI. To some others at these times hee teacheth, how to make Pictures of waxe or clay: That by the rosting thereof, the persones; that they beare the name of, may be continuallie melted or dryed awaie by continuall sicknesse. To some hee giues such stones or poulders, as will helpe to cure or cast on diseases: And to some he teacheth kindes of vncouthe poysons, which Mediciners vnderstandes not (for he is farre cunningner then man in the knowledge of all the occult proprieties of nature) not that anie of these meanes which hee teacheth them (except the poysons which are composed of thinges naturall) can of them selues helpe any thing to these turnes, that they are employed in, but onelie being Gods Ape, as well in that, as in all other thinges. Even as God by his Sacramentes which are earthlie of themselues workes a heavenlie effect, though no waies by any cooperation in them: And as CHRIST by clay & spettle wrought together, *opened the eies of the blynd man*, [marginal gloss: *Iohn. 9.*] suppose there was no vertue in that which he outwardlie applyed, so the Deuill will haue his out-warde meanes to be shewes as it were of his doing, which hath no part of cooperation in his turnes with him, how farre that euer the ignorantes be abused in the contrarie. And as to the effectes of these two former partes, to wit, the consultationes and the outward meanes, they are so wounderfull as I dare not allege anie of them, without ioyning a sufficient reason of the possibilitie thereof. For leauing all the small trifles among wiues, and to speake of the principall poyntes of their craft. For the common

trifles thereof, they can do without conuerting well inough by themselues: These principall poyntes I say are these: They can make men
or women to loue or hate other, which may be verie possible to the
Deuil to effectuat, seing he being a subtile spirite, knowes well inough how to perswade the corrupted affection of them whom God
will permit him so to deale with: They can lay the siknesse of one
vpon an other, which likewise is verie possible vnto him: For since
by Gods permission, he layed siknesse vpon IOB, why may he not
farre easilier lay it vpon any other: For as an old practisian, he knowes
well inough what humor domines most in anie of vs, and as a spirite hee can subtillie walken vp the same, making it peccant, or to
abounde, as he thinkes meete for troubling of vs, when God will so
permit him. And for the taking off of it, no doubt he will be glad to
reliue such of present paine, as he may thinke by these meanes to
perswade to bee catched in his euerlasting snares and fetters. They
can be-witch and take the life of men or women, by rosting of the
Pictures, as I spake of before, which likewise is verie possible to their
Master to performe, for although, (as I saide before) that instrumente
of waxe haue no vertue in that turne doing, yet may hee not verie
well euen by that same measure that his conjured slaues meltes that
waxe at the fire, may he not I say at these same times, subtilie as a
spirite so weaken and scatter the spirites of life of the patient, as may
make him on th'one part, for faintnesse to sweate out the humour of
his bodie: And on the other parte, for the not concurrence of these
spirites, which causes his digestion, so debilitat his stomak, that his
humour radicall continually, sweating out on the one parte, and no
new good suck being put in the place thereof, for lack of digestion on
the other, hee at last shall vanish awaie, euen as his picture will doe
at the fire. And that knauish and cunning woorkeman, by troubling
him onely at some times, makes a proportion so neare betuixt the
woorking of the one and the other, that both shall ende as it were
at one time. They can rayse stormes and tempestes in the aire, either vpon Sea or land, though not vniuersally, but in such a particu-

lar place and prescribed boundes, as God will permitte them so to trouble: Which likewise is verie easie to be discerned from anie other naturall tempestes that are meteores, in respect of the suddaine and violent raising thereof, together with the short induring of the same. And this is likewise verie possible to their master to do, he hauing such affinitie with the aire as being a spirite, and hauing such power of the forming and moouing thereof, as ye haue heard me alreadie declare: For in the Scripture, that stile of *the Prince of the aire* is giuen vnto him [marginal gloss: *Ephes. 2*]. They can make folkes to becom phrenticque or Maniacque, which likewise is very possible to their master to do, sence they are but naturall sicknesses: and so he may lay on these kindes, aswell as anie others. They can make spirites either to follow and trouble persones, or haunt certaine houses, and affraie oftentimes the inhabitantes: as hath bene knowen to be done by our Witches at this time. And likewise they can make some to be possessed with spirites, & so to becom verie Dæmoniacques: and this last sorte is verie possible likewise to the Deuill their Master to do, since he may easilie send his owne angells to trouble in what forme he pleases, any whom God wil permit him so to vse.

PHI. But will God permit these wicked instrumentes by the power of the Deuill their master, to trouble by anie of these meanes, anie that beleeues in him?

EPI. No doubt, for there are three kinde of folkes whom God will permit so to be tempted or troubled; the wicked for their horrible sinnes, to punish them in the like measure; The godlie that are sleeping in anie great sinnes or infirmities and weakenesse in faith, to waken them vp the faster by such an vncouth forme: and euen some of the best, that their patience may bee tryed before the world, as IOBS was. For why may not God vse anie kinde of extraordinarie punishment, when it pleases him; as well as the ordinarie roddes of sicknesse or other aduersities.

PHI. Who then may he free from these Deuilish practises?

EPI. No man ought to presume so far as to promise anie impu-nitie to himselfe: for God hath before all beginninges preordinated aswell the particular sortes of Plagues as of benefites for euerie man, which in the owne time he ordaines them to be visited with, & yet ought we not to be the more affrayde for that, of any thing that the Deuill and his wicked instrumentes can do against vs: For we dailie fight against the Deuill in a hundreth other waies: And therefore as a valiant Captaine, affraies no more being at the combat, nor stayes from his purpose for the rummishing shot of a Cannon, nor the small clack of a Pistolet: suppose he be not certaine what may light vpon him; Euen so ought we boldlie to goe forwarde in fighting against the Deuill without anie greater terrour, for these his rarest weapons, nor for the ordinarie whereof wee haue daily the proofe.

PHI. Is it not lawfull then by the helpe of some other Witche to cure the disease that is casten on by that craft?

EPI. No waies lawfull: For I gaue you the reason thereof in that axiome of Theologie, which was the last wordes I spake of *Magie*.

PHI. How then may these diseases he lawfullie cured?

EPI. Onelie by earnest prayer to GOD, by amendement of their liues, and by sharp persewing euerie one, according to his calling of these instrumentes of Sathan, whose punishment to the death will be a salutarie sacrifice for the patient. And this is not onely the lawfull way, but likewise the most sure: For by the Deuils meanes, *can neuer the Deuill be casten out*, as Christ sayeth. [marginal gloss: *Mark. 3*] And when such a cure is vsed, it may wel serue for a shorte time, but at the last, it will doubtleslie tend to the vtter perdition of the patient, both in bodie and soule.

CHAP. VI. ARGV.

What sorte of folkes are least or most subiect to receiue harme by
Witchcraft. What power they haue to harme the Magistrate, and vpon
what respectes they haue any power in prison: And to what end may or
will the Deuill appeare to them therein. Vpon what respectes the Deuill
appeires in sundry shapes to sundry of them at any time.

PHILOMATHES.

BVt who dare take vpon him to punish them, if no man can be sure to be free from their vnnaturall inuasiones?

EPI. We ought not the more of that restraine from vertue, that the way wherby we climbe thereunto be straight and perrilous. But besides that, as there is no kinde of persones so subject to receiue harme of them, as these that are of infirme and weake faith (which is the best buckler against such inuasiones:) so haue they so smal power ouer none) as ouer such as zealouslie and earnestlie persewes them, without sparing for anie worldlie respect.

PHI. Then they are like the Pest, which smites these sickarest, that flies it farthest, and apprehends deepliest the perrell thereof.

EPI. It is euen so with them: For neither is it able to them to vse anie false cure vpon a patient, except the patient first beleeue in their power, and so hazard the tinsell of his owne soule, nor yet can they haue lesse power to hurte anie, nor such as contemnes most their doinges, so being it comes of faith, and not of anie vaine arrogancie in themselues.

PHI. But what is their power against the Magistrate?

EPI. Lesse or greater, according as he deales with them. For if he be slouthfull towardes them, God is verie able to make them instrumentes to waken & punish his slouth. But if he be the contrarie, he according to the iust law of God, and allowable law of all Nationes, will be diligent in examining and punishing of them: GOD will not permit their master to trouble or hinder so good a woorke.

PHI. But fra they be once in handes and firmance, haue they anie further power in their craft?

EPI. That is according to the forme of their detention. If they be but apprehended and deteined by anie priuate person, vpon other priuate respectes, their power no doubt either in escaping, or in doing hurte, is no lesse nor euer it was before. But if on the other parte, their apprehending and detention be by the lawfull Magistrate, vpon the iust respectes of their guiltinesse in that craft, their power is then no greater then before that euer they medled with their master. For where God beginnes iustlie to strike by his lawfull Lieutennentes, it is not in the Deuilles power to defraude or bereaue him of the office, or effect of his powerfull and reuenging Scepter.

PHI. But will neuer their master come to visite them, fra they be once apprehended and put in firmance?

EPI. That is according to the estaite that these miserable wretches are in: For if they be obstinate in still denying, he will not spare, when he findes time to speake with them, either if he finde them in anie comfort, to fill them more and more with the vaine hope of some maner of reliefe: or else if hee finde them in a deepe dispaire, by all meanes to augment the same, and to perswade them by some extraordinarie meanes to put themselues downe, which verie commonlie they doe. But if they be penitent and confesse, God will not permit him to trouble them anie more with his presence and aluremente.

PHI. It is not good vsing his counsell I see then. But I woulde earnestlie know when he appeares to them in Prison, what formes vses he then to take?

EPI. Diuers formes, euen as he vses to do at other times vnto them. For as I told you, speking of *Magie*, he appeares to that kinde of craftes-men ordinarily in an forme, according as they agree vpon it amongst themselues: Or if they be but prentises, according to the qualitie of their circles or conjurationes: Yet to these capped creatures, he appeares as he pleases, and as he findes meetest for their humors. For euen at their publick conuentiones, he appeares to diuers of them in diuers formes, as we haue found by the difference of their confessiones in that point: For he deluding them with vaine impressiones in the aire, makes himselfe to seeme more terrible to the grosser sorte, that they maie thereby be moued to feare and reuerence him the more: And les monstrous and vncouthlike againe to the craftier sorte, least otherwaies they might sturre and skunner at his vglinesse.

PHI. How can he then be felt, as they confesse they haue done him, if his bodie be but of aire?

EPI. I heare little of that amongst their confessiones, yet may he make himselfe palpable, either by assuming any dead bodie, and vsing the ministrie thereof, or else by deluding as wel their sence of feeling as seeing; which is not impossible to him to doe, since all our senses, as we are so weake, and euen by ordinarie sicknesses will be often times deluded.

PHI. But I would speere one worde further yet, concerning his appearing to them in prison, which is this. May any other that chances to be present at that time in the prison, see him as well as they.

EPI. Some-times they will, and some-times not, as it pleases God.

CHAP. VII. ARGV.

Two formes of the deuils visible conuersing in the earth, with the reasones wherefore the one of them was communest in the time of Papistrie: *And the other sensine. Those that denies the power of the Deuill, denies the power of God, and are guiltie of the errour of the* Sadduces.

PHILOMATHES.

HAth the Deuill then power to appeare to any other, except to such as are his sworne disciples: especially since al Oracles, & such like kinds of illusiones were taken awaie and abolished by the cumming of CHRIST?

EPI. Although it be true indeede, that the brightnesse of the Gospell at his cumming, scaled the cloudes of all these grosse errors in the Gentilisme: yet that these abusing spirites, ceases not sensine at sometimes to appeare, dailie experience teaches vs. Indeede this difference is to be marked betwixt the formes of Sathans conuersing visiblie in the world. For of two different formes thereof, the one of

them by the spreading of the Euangell, and conquest of the white
horse, in the sixt Chapter of the Reuelation, is much hindred and
become rarer there through. This his appearing to any Christians,
troubling of them outwardly, or possessing of them constraynedly.
The other of them is become communer and more vsed sensine, I
meane by their vnlawfull artes, whereupon our whole purpose hath
bene. This we finde by experience in this Ile to be true. For as we
know, moe Ghostes and spirites were seene, nor tongue can tell, in
the time of blinde *Papistrie* in these Countries, where now by the
contrarie, a man shall scarcely all his time here once of such things.
And yet were these vnlawfull artes farre rarer at that time: and neuer
were so much harde of, nor so rife as they are now.

PHI. What should be the cause of that?

EPI. The diuerse nature of our sinnes procures at the Iustice
of God, diuerse sortes of punishments answering thereunto. And
therefore as in the time of *Papistrie*, our fathers erring grosselie, &
through ignorance, that mist of errours ouershaddowed the Deuill
to walke the more familiarlie amongst them: And as it were by barnelie and affraying terroures, to mocke and accuse their barnelie erroures. By the contrarie, we now being sounde of Religion, and in
our life rebelling to our profession, God iustlie by that sinne of rebellion, as *Samuel* calleth it, accuseth our life so wilfullie fighting against
our profession.

PHI. Since yee are entred now to speake of the appearing of spirites: I would be glad to heare your opinion in that matter. For manie
denies that anie such spirites can appeare in these daies as I haue
said.

EPI. Doubtleslie who denyeth the power of the Deuill, woulde
likewise denie the power of God, if they could for shame. For since
the Deuill is the verie contrarie opposite to God, there can be no
better way to know God, then by the contrarie; as by the ones power
(though a creature) to admire the power of the great Creator: by the
falshood of the one to considder the trueth of the other, by the injus-

tice of the one, to considder the Iustice of the other: And by the cruelty of the one, to considder the mercifulnesse of the other: And so foorth in all the rest of the essence of God, and qualities of the Deuill. But I feare indeede, there be ouer many *Sadduces* in this worlde, that denies all kindes of spirites: For convicting of whose errour, there is cause inough if there were no more, that God should permit at sometimes spirits visiblie to kyith.

THE THIRDE BOOKE OF DÆMONOLGIE

ARGVMENT.

The description of all these kindes of
Spirites that troubles men or women.
The conclusion of the whole Dialogue.

CHAP. I. ARGV.

The diuision of spirites in foure principall kindes. The description
of the first kinde of them, called Spectra *&* vmbræ mortuorum.
What is the best way to be free of their trouble.

PHILOMATHES.

I Pray you now then go forward in telling what ye thinke fabulous, or may be trowed in that case.

EPI. That kinde of the Deuils conuersing in the earth, may be diuided in foure different kindes, whereby he affrayeth and troubleth the bodies of men: For of the abusing of the soule, I haue spoken alreadie. The first is, where spirites troubles some houses or solitarie places: The second, where spirites followes vpon certaine persones, and at diuers houres troubles them: The thirde, when they enter within them and possesse them: The fourth is these kinde of spirites that are called vulgarlie the Fayrie. Of the three former kindes, ye harde alreadie, how they may artificiallie be made by Witch-craft to trouble folke: Now it restes to speake of their naturall comming as it were, and not raysed by Witch-craft. But generally I must for-warne you of one thing before I enter in this purpose: that is, that although in my discourseing of them, I deuyde them in diuers kindes, yee must notwithstanding there of note my Phrase of speaking in that: For doubtleslie they are in effect, but all one kinde of spirites, who for abusing the more of mankinde, takes on these sundrie shapes, and vses diuerse formes of out-ward actiones, as if some were of nature better then other. Nowe I returne to my purpose: As to the first kinde of these spirites, that were called by the auncients by diuers names, according as their actions were. For if they were spirites that haunted some houses, by appearing in diuers and horrible formes, and making greate dinne: they were called *Lemures* or *Spectra*. If they appeared in likenesse of anie defunct to some friends of his, they wer called *vmbræ mortuorum*: And so innumerable stiles they got, according to their actiones, as I haue said alreadie. As we see by experience, how manie stiles they haue given them in our language in the like maner: Of the appearing of these spirites, wee are certified by the Scriptures, where the Prophet ESAY 13. and 34. cap. [marginal gloss: *Easy. 13 Iere.50*] threatning the destruction of *Babell* and *Edom*: declares, that it shal not onlie be wracked, but shall become so greate a solitude, as it shall be the habitackle of Howlettes, and of ZIIM and IIM, which are the proper Hebrewe names for these Spirites. The cause whie they haunte solitarie places, it is by reason, that they may affraie and brangle the more the faith of suche as them alone hauntes such places. For our nature is such, as in companies wee are not so soone mooued to anie such kinde of feare, as being solitare, which the Deuill knowing well inough, hee will not therefore assaile vs but when we are weake: And besides that, GOD will not permit him so to dishonour the societies and companies of Christians, as in publicke times and places to walke visiblie amongst them. On the other parte, when he troubles certaine houses that are dwelt in, it is a sure token either of grosse ignorance, or of some grosse and slanderous sinnes amongst the inhabitantes thereof: which God by that extraordinarie rod punishes.

PHI. But by what way or passage can these Spirites enter in these houses, seeing they alledge that they will enter, Doore and Window being steiked?

EPI. They will choose the passage for their entresse, according to the forme that they are in at that time. For if they haue assumed a deade bodie, whereinto they lodge themselues, they can easely inough open without dinne anie Doore or Window, and enter in thereat. And if they enter as a spirite onelie, anie place where the aire may come in at, is large inough an entrie for them: For as I said before, a spirite can occupie no quantitie.

PHI. And will God then permit these wicked spirites to trouble the reste of a dead bodie, before the resurrection thereof? Or if he will so, I thinke it should be of the reprobate onely.

EPI. What more is the reste troubled of a dead bodie, when the Deuill carryes it out of the Graue to serue his turne for a space, nor when the Witches takes it vp and joyntes it, or when as Swine wortes vppe the graues? The rest of them that the Scripture speakes of, is not meaned by a locall remaining continuallie in one place, but by their resting from their trauelles and miseries of this worlde, while their latter conjunction againe with the soule at that time to receaue full glorie in both. And that the Deuill may vse aswell the ministrie of the bodies of the faithfull in these cases, as of the vn-faithfull, there is no inconvenient; for his haunting with their bodies after they are deade, can no-waies defyle them: In respect of the soules absence. And for anie dishonour it can be vnto them, by what reason can it be greater, then the hanging, heading, or many such shameful deaths, that good men will suffer? for there is nothing in the bodies of the faithfull, more worthie of honour, or freer from corruption by nature, nor in these of the vnfaithful, while time they be purged and glorified in the latter daie, as is dailie seene by the vilde diseases and corruptions, that the bodies of the faythfull are subject vnto, as yee will see clearelie proued, when I speake of the possessed and Dæmoniacques.

PHI. Yet there are sundrie that affirmes to haue haunted such places, where these spirites are alleaged to be: And coulde neuer heare nor see anie thing.

EPI. I thinke well: For that is onelie reserued to the secreete knowledge of God, whom he wil permit to see such thinges, and whome not.

PHI. But where these spirites hauntes and troubles anie houses, what is the best waie to banishe them?

EPI. By two meanes may onelie the remeid of such things be procured: The one is ardent prayer to God, both of these persones that are troubled with them, and of that Church whereof they are. The other is the purging of themselues by amende ment of life from such sinnes, as haue procured that extraordinarie plague.

PHI. And what meanes then these kindes of spirites, when they appeare in the shaddow of a person newlie dead, or to die, to his friendes?

EPI. When they appeare vpon that occasion, they are called Wraithes in our language. Amongst the *Gentiles* the Deuill vsed that much, to make them beleeue that it was some good spirite that appeared to them then, ether to forewarne them of the death of their friend; or else to discouer vnto them, the will of the defunct, or what was the way of his slauchter, as is written in the booke of the histories Prodigious. And this way hee easelie decciued the *Gentiles*, because they knew not God: And to that same effect is it, that he now appeares in that maner to some ignorant Christians. For he dare not so illude anie that knoweth that, neither can the spirite of the defunct returne to his friend, or yet an Angell vse such formes.

PHI. And are not our war-woolfes one sorte of these spirits also, that hauntes and troubles some houses or dwelling places?

EPI. There bath indeede bene an old opinion of such like thinges; For by the *Greekes* they were called λυκανθρωποι which signifieth men-woolfes. But to tell you simplie my opinion in this, if anie such thing hath bene, I take it to haue proceeded but of a naturall super-abundance of Melancholie, which as wee reade, that it hath made some thinke themselues Pitchers, and some horses, and some one kinde of beast or other: So suppose I that it hath so viciat the imagination and memorie of some, as *per lucida interualla*, it hath so highlie occupyed them, that they haue thought themselues verrie Woolfes indeede at these times: and so haue counterfeited their actiones in goeing on their handes and feete, preassing to deuoure women and barnes, fighting and snatching with all the towne dogges, and in vsing such like other bruitish actiones, and so to become beastes by a strong apprehension, as *Nebucad-netzar* was seuen yeares: [marginal gloss: *Dan. 4.*] but as to their hauing and hyding of their hard & schellie sloughes, I take that to be but eiked, by vncertaine report, the author of all lyes.

CHAP. II. ARGV.

The description of the next two kindes of Spirites, whereof the one followes outwardlie, the other possesses inwardlie the persones that they trouble. That since all Prophecies and visiones are nowe ceased, all spirites that appeares in these formes are euill.

PHILOMATHES.

COme forward now to the reste of these kindes of spirites.

EPI. As to the next two kindes, that is, either these that outwardlie troubles and followes some persones, or else inwardlie possesses them: I will conjoyne them in one, because aswel the causes ar alike in the persons that they are permitted to trouble: as also the waies whereby they may be remedied and cured.

PHI. What kinde of persones are they that vses to be so troubled?

EPI. Two kindes in speciall: Either such as being guiltie of greeuous offences, God punishes by that horrible kinde of scourdge, or else being persones of the beste nature peraduenture, that yee shall finde in all the Countrie about them, GOD permittes them to be troubled in that sort, for the tryall of their patience, and wakening vp of their zeale, for admonishing of the beholders, not to truste

ouer much in themselues, since they are made of no better stuffe,
and peraduenture blotted with no smaller sinnes (as CHRIST saide,
speaking of them vppon whome the Towre in *Siloam* fell:) [marginal
gloss: *Luc.13.*] And for giuing likewise to the spectatators, matter to
prayse GOD, that they meriting no better, are yet spared from being
corrected in that fearefull forme.

PHI. These are good reasons for the parte of GOD, which appa-
rantlie mooues him so to permit the Deuill to trouble such persones.
But since the Deuil hath euer a contrarie respecte in all the actiones
that GOD employes him in: which is I pray you the end and mark he
shoots at in this turne?

EPI. It is to obtaine one of two thinges thereby, if he may: The
one is the tinsell of their life, by inducing them to such perrilous
places at such time as he either followes or possesses them, which
may procure the same: And such like, so farre as GOD will permit
him, by tormenting them to weaken their bodie, and caste them in
incurable diseases. The other thinge that hee preases to obteine by
troubling of them, is the tinsell of their Soule, by intising them to
mistruste and blaspheme God: Either for the intollerablenesse of
their tormentes, as he assayed to haue done with IOB; [marginal
gloss: *Iob.1.*] or else for his promising vnto them to leaue the troubling of them, incase they would so do, as is knowen by experience at this same time by the confession of a young one that was
so troubled.

PHI. Since ye haue spoken now of both these kindes of spirites comprehending them in one: I must nowe goe backe againe in
speering some questions of euerie one of these kindes in speciall.
And first for these that followes certaine persones, yee know that
there are two sortes of them: One sorte that troubles and tormentes
the persones that they haunt with: An other sort that are seruice-
able vnto them in all kinde of their necessaries, and omittes neuer to
forwarne them of anie suddaine perrell that they are to be in. And
so in this case, I would vnderstande whither both these sortes be but

wicked and damned spirites: Or if the last sorte be rather Angells, (as should appeare by their actiones) sent by God to assist such as he speciallie fauoures. For it is written in the Scriptures, that *God sendes Legions of Angells to guarde and watch ouer his elect.* [marginal gloss: *Gen.32. IKin.6 Psal.34.*]

EPI. I know well inough where fra that errour which ye alleage hath proceeded: For it was the ignorant *Gentiles* that were the fountaine thereof. Who for that they knew not God, they forged in their owne imaginationes, euery man to be still accompanied with two spirites, whereof they called the one *genius bonus*, the other *genius malus*: the Greekes called them ενδαιμονα & κακοδαιμονα: wherof the former they saide, perswaded him to all the good he did: the other entised him to all the euill. But praised be God we that are christians, & walks not amongst the *Cymmerian* conjectures of man, knowes well inough, that it is the good spirite of God onely, who is the fountain of all goodnes, that perswads vs to the thinking or doing of any good: and that it is our corrupted fleshe and Sathan, that intiseth vs to the contrarie. And yet the Deuill for confirming in the heades of ignoraunt Christians, that errour first mainteined among the Gentiles, he whiles among the first kinde of spirits that I speak of, appeared in time of *Papistrie* and blindnesse, and haunted diuers houses, without doing any euill, but doing as it were necessarie turnes vp and down the house: and this spirit they called *Brownie* in our language, who appeared like a rough-man: yea, some were so blinded, as to beleeue that their house was all the sonsier, as they called it, that such spirites resorted there.

PHI. But since the Deuils intention in all his actions, is euer to do euill, what euill was there in that forme of doing, since their actions outwardly were good.

EPI. Was it not euill inough to deceiue simple ignorantes, in making them to take him for an Angell of light, and so to account of Gods enemie, as of their particular friend: where by the contrarie, all we that are Christians, ought assuredly to know that since the comming of Christ in the flesh, and establishing of his Church by the Apostles, all miracles, visions, prophecies, & appearances of Angels or good spirites are ceased. Which serued onely for the first sowing of faith, & planting of the Church. Where now the Church being established, and the white Horse whereof I spake before, hauing made his conqueste, the Lawe and Prophets are thought sufficient to serue vs, or make vs inexcusable, as Christ saith in his parable [marginal gloss: *Luk.16.*] of *Lazarus* and the riche man.

CHAP. III. ARGV.

The description of a particular sort of that kind of following spirites, called Incubi *and* Succubi: *And what is the reason wherefore these kindes of spirites hauntes most the Northerne and barbarous partes of the world.*

PHILOMATHES.

THE next question that I would speere, is likewise concerning this first of these two kindes of spirites that ye haue conjoyned: and it is this; ye knowe how it is commonly written and reported, that amongst the rest of the sortes of spirites that followes certaine persons, there is one more monstrous nor al the rest: in respect as it is alleaged, they converse naturally with them whom they trouble and hauntes with: and therefore I would knowe in two thinges your opinion herein: First if suche a thing can be: and next if it be: whether there be a difference of sexes amongst these spirites or not.

EPI. That abhominable kinde of the Deuils abusing of men or women, was called of old, *Incubi* and *Succubi*, according to the difference of the sexes that they conuersed with. By two meanes this great kinde of abuse might possibly be performed: The one, when the Deuill onelie as a spirite, and stealing out the sperme of a dead bodie, abuses them that way, they not graithlie seeing anie shape or feeling anie thing, but that which he so conuayes in that part: As we reade of a Monasterie of Nunnes which were burnt for their being that way abused. The other meane is when he borrowes a dead bodie and so visiblie, and as it seemes vnto them naturallie as a man converses with them. But it is to be noted, that in whatsoeuer way he vseth it, that sperme seemes intollerably cold to the person abused. For if he steale out the nature of a quick person, it cannot be so quicklie carryed, but it will both tine the strength and heate by the way, which it could neuer haue had for lacke of agitation, which in the time of procreation is the procurer & wakener vp of these two natural qualities. And if he occupying the dead bodie as his lodging expell the same out thereof in the dewe time, it must likewise be colde by the participation with the qualities of the dead bodie whereout of it comes. And whereas yee inquire if these spirites be diuided in sexes or not, I thinke the rules of Philosophie may easelie resolue a man of the contrarie: For it is a sure principle of that arte, that nothing can be diuided in sexes, except such liuing bodies as must haue a naturall seede to genere by. But we know spirites hath no seede proper to themselues, nor yet can they gender one with an other.

PHI. How is it then that they say sundrie monsters haue bene gotten by that way.

EPI. These tales are nothing but *Aniles fabulæ*. For that they haue no nature of their owne, I haue shewed you alreadie. And that the cold nature of a dead bodie, can woorke nothing in generation, it is more nor plaine, as being already dead of it selfe as well as the rest of the bodie is, wanting the naturall heate, and such other naturall operation, as is necessarie for woorking that effect, and incase such a thing were possible (which were all utterly against all the rules of nature) it would bread no monster, but onely such a naturall of-spring, as would haue cummed betuixt that man or woman and that other abused person, in-case they both being aliue had had a doe with other. For the Deuilles parte therein, is but the naked carrying or expelling of that substance: And so it coulde not participate with no qualitie of the same. Indeede, it is possible to the craft of the Deuill to make a womans bellie to swel after he hath that way abused her, which he may do, either by steiring vp her own humor, or by herbes, as we see beggars daily doe. And when the time of her deliuery should come to make her thoil great doloures, like vnto that naturall course, and then subtillie to slippe in the Mid-wiues handes, stockes, stones, or some monstruous barne brought from some other place, but this is more reported and gessed at by others, nor beleeued by me.

PHI. But what is the cause that this kinde of abuse is thought to be most common in such wild partes of the worlde, as *Lap-land*, and *Fin-land*, or in our North Iles of *Orknay* and *Schet-land*.

EPI. Because where the Deuill findes greatest ignorance and barbaritie, there assayles he grosseliest, as I gaue you the reason wherefore there was moe Witches of women kinde nor men.

PHI. Can anie be so vnhappie as to giue their willing consent to the Deuilles vilde abusing them in this forme.

EPI. Yea, some of the Witches haue confessed, that he hath perswaded them to giue their willing consent thereunto, that he may thereby haue them feltred the sikarer in his snares; But as the other compelled sorte is to be pittied and prayed for, so is this most highlie to be punished and detested.

PHI. It is not the thing which we cal the *Mare*, which takes folkes sleeping in their bedds, a kinde of these spirites, whereof ye are speaking?

EPI. No, that is but a naturall sicknes, which the Mediciners hath giuen that name of *Incubus* vnto *ab incubando*, because it being a thicke fleume, falling into our breast vpon the harte, while we are sleeping, intercludes so our vitall spirites, and takes all power from vs, as maks vs think that there were some vnnaturall burden or spirite, lying vpon vs and holding vs downe.

CHAP. IIII. ARGV.

The description of the Dæmoniackes & possessed.
By what reason the Papistes may haue power to cure them.

PHILOMATHES.

WEL, I haue told you now all my doubts, and ye haue satisfied me therein, concerning the first of these two kindes of spirites that ye haue conjoyned. Now I am to inquire onely two thinges at you concerning the last kinde, I meane the Dæmoniackes. The first is, whereby shal these possessed folks be discerned fra them that ar trubled with a natural Phrensie or Manie. The next is, how can it be that they can be remedied by the *Papistes* Church, whome wee counting as Hereticques, it should appeare that one Deuil should not cast out an other, for then would *his kingdome be diuided in it selfe*, as CHRIST said. [marginal gloss: *Mat. 12 Mark. 3*]

EPI. As to your first question; there are diuers symptomes, whereby that heauie trouble may be discerned from a naturall sickenesse, and speciallie three, omitting the diuers vaine signes that the *Papistes* attributes vnto it: Such as the raging at holie water, their fleeing a back from the Croce, their not abiding the hearing of God named, and innumerable such like vaine thinges that were alike fashious and feckles to recite. But to come to these three symptomes then, whereof I spake, I account the one of them to be the incredible strength of the possessed creature, which will farre exceede the strength of six of the wightest and wodest of any other men that are not so troubled. The next is the boldning vp so far of the patients breast and bellie, with such an vnnaturall sturring and vehement agitation within them: And such an ironie hardnes of his sinnowes so stiffelie bended out, that it were not possible to prick out as it were the skinne of anie other person so far: so mightely works the Deuil in all the members and senses of his body, he being locallie within the same, suppose of his Soule and affectiones thereof, hee haue no

more power then of any other mans. The last is, the speaking of
sundrie languages, which the patient is knowen by them that were
acquainte with him neuer to haue learned, and that with an vncouth
and hollowe voice, and al the time of his speaking, a greater motion being in his breast then in his mouth. But fra this last symptome
is excepted such, as are altogether in the time of their possessing
bereft of al their senses being possessed with a dumme and blynde
spirite, whereof Christ releiued one, in the 12. Of *Mathew*. And as
to your next demande, it is first to be doubted if the *Papistes* or anie
not professing the the onelie true Religion, can relieue anie of that
trouble. And next, in-case they can, vpon what respectes it is possible vnto them. As to the former vpon two reasons, it is grounded:
first that it is knowen so manie of them to bee counterfite, which
wyle the Clergie inuentes for confirming of their rotten Religion.
The next is, that by experience we finde that few, who are possessed
indeede, are fullie cured by them: but rather the Deuill is content to
release the bodelie hurting of them, for a shorte space, thereby to
obteine the perpetual hurt of the soules of so many that by these
false miracles may be induced or confirmed in the profession of that
erroneous Religion: euen as I told you before that he doth in the
false cures, or casting off of diseases by Witches. As to the other part
of the argument in-case they can, which rather (with reuerence of
the learned thinking otherwaies) I am induced to beleeue, by reason
of the faithfull report that men sound of religion, haue made according to their sight thereof, I think if so be, I say these may be the
respectes, whereupon the *Papistes* may haue that power. CHRIST
gaue a commission and power to his Apostles to cast out Deuilles,
which they according thereunto put in execution: The rules he had
them obserue in that action, was fasting and praier: & the action it
selfe to be done in his name. This power of theirs proceeded not
then of anie vertue in them, but onely in him who directed them. As
was clearly proued by *Iudas* his hauing as greate power in that commission, as anie of the reste. It is easie then to be vnderstand that the

casting out of Deuilles, is by the vertue of fasting and prayer, and in-calling of the name of God, suppose manie imperfectiones be in the person that is the instrumente, as CHRIST him selfe teacheth vs [marginal gloss: *Mat. 7.*] of the power that false Prophets sall haue to caste out Devils. It is no wounder then, these respects of this action being considered, that it may be possible to the *Papistes*, though erring in sundrie points of Religion to accomplish this, if they vse the right forme prescribed by CHRIST herein. For what the worse is that action that they erre in other thinges, more then their Baptisme is the worse that they erre in the other Sacrament, and haue eiked many vaine freittes to the Baptisme it selfe.

PHI. Surelie it is no little wonder that God should permit the bodies of anie of the faithfull to be so dishonoured, as to be a dwelling place to that vncleane spirite.

EPI. There is it which I told right now, would prooue and strengthen my argument of the deuils entring in the dead bodies of the faithfull. For if he is permitted to enter in their liuing bodies, euen when they are ioyned with the soule: how much more will God permit him to enter in their dead carions, which is no more man, but the filthie and corruptible caise of man. For as CHRIST sayth, *It is not any thing that enters within man that defiles him, but onely that which proceedes and commeth out of him.* [marginal gloss: *Mark. 7.*]

CHAP. V. ARGV.

The description of the fourth kinde of Spirites called the Phairie: *What is possible therein, and what is but illusiones. How far this Dialogue entreates of all these thinges, and to what end.*

PHILOMATHES.

NOW I pray you come on to that fourth kinde of spirites.

EPI. That fourth kinde of spirites, which by the Gentiles was called *Diana*, and her wandring Court, and amongst vs was called the *Phairie* (as I tould you) or our good neighboures, was one of the sortes of illusiones that was rifest in the time of *Papistrie*: for although it was holden odious to Prophesie by the deuill, yet whome these kinde of Spirites carryed awaie, and informed, they were thought to be sonsiest and of best life. To speake of the many vaine trattles founded vpon that illusion: How there was a King and Queene of *Phairie*, of such a iolly court & train as they had, how they had a teynd, & dutie, as it were, of all goods: how they natu-rallie rode and went, eate and drank, and did all other actiones like naturall men and women: I thinke it liker VIRGILS *Campi Elysij*, nor anie thing that ought to be beleeued by Christians, except in gener-all, that as I spake sundrie times before, the deuil illuded the senses of sundry simple creatures, in making them beleeue that they saw and harde such thinges as were nothing so indeed.

PHI. But how can it be then, that sundrie Witches haue gone to death with that confession, that they haue ben transported with the *Phairie* to such a hill, which opening, they went in, and there saw a faire Queene, who being now lighter, gaue them a stone that had sundrie vertues, which at sundrie times hath bene produced in judgement?

EPI. I say that, euen as I said before of that imaginar rauishing of the spirite foorth of the bodie. For may not the deuil object to their fantasie, their senses being dulled, and as it were a sleepe, such hilles & houses within them, such glistering courts and traines, and what-soeuer such like wherewith he pleaseth to delude them. And in the meane time their bodies being senselesse, to conuay in their hande any stone or such like thing, which he makes them to imagine to haue receiued in such a place.

PHI. But what say ye to their fore-telling the death of sundrie persones, whome they alleage to haue seene in these places? That is, a sooth-dreame (as they say) since they see it walking.

EPI. I thinke that either they haue not bene sharply inough exam-ined, that gaue so blunt a reason for their Prophesie, or otherwaies,

I thinke it likewise as possible that the Deuill may prophesie to them when he deceiues their imaginationes in that sorte, as well as when he plainely speakes vnto them at other times for their prophesying, is but by a kinde of vision, as it were, wherein he commonly counterfeits God among the Ethnicks, as I told you before.

PHI. I would know now whether these kindes of spirites may only appeare to Witches, or if they may also appeare to anie other.

EPI. They may do to both, to the innocent sort, either to affraie them, or to seeme to be a better sorte of folkes nor vncleane spirites are, and to the Witches, to be a cullour of safetie for them, that ignorant Magistrates may not punish them for it, as I told euen now. But as the one sorte, for being perforce troubled with them ought to be pittied, so ought the other sorte (who may bee discerned by their taking vppon them to Prophesie by them,) That sorte I say, ought as seuerely to be punished as any other Witches, and rather the more, that that they goe dissemblingly to woorke.

PHI. And what makes the spirites haue so different names from others.

EPI. Euen the knauerie of that same deuil; who as hee illudes the *Necromancers* with innumerable feyned names for him and his angels, as in special, making *Sathan, Beelzebub, & Lucifer*, to be three sundry spirites, where we finde the two former, but diuers names giuen to the Prince of all the rebelling angels by the Scripture. As by CHRIST, the Prince of all the Deuilles is called, *Beelzebub* in that place, which I alleaged against the power of any hereticques to cast out Deuils. By IOHN in the Reuelation, the old tempter is called, *Sathan the Prince of all the euill angels*. And the last, to wit, *Lucifer*, is but by allegorie taken from *the day Starre* (so named in diuers places of the Scriptures) because of his excellencie (I meane the Prince of them) in his creation before his fall. Euen so I say he deceaues the Witches, by attributing to himselfe diuers names: as if euery diuers shape that he trans formes himselfe in, were a diuers kinde of spirit.

PHI. But I haue hard many moe strange tales of this *Phairie*, nor ye haue yet told me.

EPI. As well I do in that, as I did in all the rest of my discourse. For because the ground of this conference of ours, proceeded of your speering at me at our meeting, if there was such a thing as Witches or spirites: And if they had any power: I therefore haue framed my whole discours, only to proue that such things are and may be, by such number of examples as I show to be possible by reason: & keepes me from dipping any further in playing the part of a Dictionarie, to tell what euer I haue read or harde in that purpose, which both would exceede fayth, and rather would seeme to teach such vnlawfull artes, nor to disallow and condemne them, as it is the duetie of all Christians to do.

CHAP. VI. ARGV.

Of the tryall and punishment of Witches. What sorte of
accusation ought to be admitted against them. What is the cause
of the increasing so far of their number in this age.

PHILOMATHES.

THEN To make an ende of our conference, since I see it drawes late, what forme of punishment thinke ye merites these *Magicians* and Witches? For I see that ye account them to be all alike guiltie?

EPI. They ought to be put to death according to the Law of God, the ciuill and imperial law, and municipall law of all Christian nations.

PHI. But what kinde of death I pray you?

EPI. It is commonly vsed by fire, but that is an indifferent thing to be vsed in euery cuntrie, according to the Law or custome thereof.

PHI. But ought no sexe, age nor ranck to be exempted?

EPI. None at al (being so vsed by the lawful Magistrate) for it is the highest poynt of Idolatrie, wherein no exception is admitted by the law of God.

PHI. Then bairnes may not be spared?

EPI. Yea, not a haire the lesse of my conclusion. For they are not that capable of reason as to practise such thinges. And for any being in company and not reueiling thereof, their lesse and ignorant age will no doubt excuse them.

PHI. I see ye condemne them all that are of the counsell of such craftes.

EPI. No doubt, for as I said, speaking of *Magie*, the consulters, trusters in, ouer-seers, interteiners or sturrers vp of these craftes-folkes, are equallie guiltie with themselues that are the practisers.

PHI. Whether may the Prince then, or supreame Magistrate, spare or ouer-see any that are guiltie of that craft? vpon som great respects knowen to him?

EPI. The Prince or Magistrate for further tryals cause, may continue the punishing of them such a certaine space as he thinkes conuenient: But in the end to spare the life, and not to strike when God bids strike, and so seuerelie punish in so odious a fault & treason against God, it is not only vnlawful, but doubtlesse no lesse sinne in that Magistrate, nor it was in SAVLES sparing of AGAG [marginal gloss: *I. Sam. 15.*]. And so comparable to the sin of Witchcraft it selfe, as SAMVELL alleaged at that time.

PHI. Surely then, I think since this crime ought to be so seuerely punished. Iudges ought to beware to condemne any, but such as they are sure are guiltie, neither should the clattering reporte of a carling serue in so weightie a case.

EPI. Iudges ought indeede to beware whome they condemne: For it is as great a crime (as SALOMON sayeth,) *To condemne the innocent, as to let the guiltie escape free*; [marginal gloss: *Pro. 17.*] neither ought the report of any one infamous person, be admitted for a sufficient proofe, which can stand of no law.

PHI. And what may a number then of guilty persons confessions, woork against one that is accused?

EPI. The assise must serue for interpretour of our law in that respect. But in my opinion, since in a mater of treason against the Prince, barnes or wiues, or neuer so diffamed persons, may of our law serue for sufficient witnesses and proofes. I thinke surely that by a far greater reason, such witnesses may be sufficient in matters of high treason against God: For who but Witches can be prooues, and so witnesses of the doings of Witches.

PHI. Indeed, I trow they wil be loath to put any honest man vpon their counsell. But what if they accuse folke to haue bene present at their Imaginar conuentiones in the spirite, when their bodies lyes sencelesse, as ye haue said.

EPI. I think they are not a haire the lesse guiltie: For the Deuill durst neuer haue borrowed their shaddow or similitude to that turne, if their consent had not bene at it: And the consent in these turnes is death of the law.

PHI. Then SAMVEL was a Witch: For the Deuill resembled his shape, and played his person in giuing response to SAVLE.

EPI. SAMVEL was dead aswell before that; and so none coulde slander him with medling in that vnlawfull arte. For the cause why, as I take it, that God will not permit Sathan to vse the shapes or similitudes of any innocent persones at such vnlawful times, is that God wil not permit that any innocent persons shalbe slandered with that vile defection: for then the deuil would find waies anew, to calumniate the best. And this we haue in proofe by them that are carryed with the *Phairie*, who neuer see the shaddowes of any in that courte, but of them that thereafter are tryed to haue bene brethren and sisters of that craft. And this was likewise proued by the confession of a young Lasse, troubled with spirites, laide on her by Witchcraft. That although shee saw the shapes of diuerse men & women troubling her, and naming the persons whom these shaddowes represents: yet neuer one of them are found to be innocent, but al clearely tried to be most guilty, & the most part of them confessing the same. And besides that, I think it hath ben seldome harde tell of, that any whome persones guiltie of that crime accused, as hauing knowen them to be their marrowes by eye-sight, and not by hear-say, but such as were so accused of Witch-craft, could not be clearely tryed vpon them, were at the least publickly knowen to be of a very euil life & reputation: so iealous is God I say, of the fame of them that are innocent in such causes. And besides that, there are two other good helpes that may be vsed for their trial: the one is the finding of their marke, and the trying the insensiblenes thereof. The other is their fleeting on the water: for as in a secret murther, if the deade carcase be at any time thereafter handled by the murtherer, it wil gush out of bloud, as if the blud wer crying to the heauen for reuenge of the murtherer. God hauing appoynted that secret supernaturall signe, for tryall of that secrete vnnaturall crime, so it appeares that God hath appoynted (for a super-naturall signe of the monstruous impietie of the Witches) that the water shal refuse to receiue them in her bosom, that haue shaken off them the sacred Water of Baptisme, and wilfullie refused the benefite thereof: No not so much as their eyes are able to shed teares (thretten and torture them as ye please) while first they repent (God not permitting them to dissemble their obstinacie in so horrible a crime) albeit the women kinde especially, be able other-waies to shed teares at euery light occasion when they will, yea, although it were dissemblingly like the *Crocodiles*.

PHI. Well, wee haue made this conference to last as long as leasure would permit: And to conclude then, since I am to take my leaue of you, I pray God to purge this Cuntrie of these diuellishe practises: for they were neuer so rife in these partes, as they are now.

EPI. I pray God that so be to. But the causes ar ouer manifest, that makes them to be so rife. For the greate wickednesse of the people on the one parte, procures this horrible defection, whereby God justlie punisheth sinne, by a greater iniquitie. And on the other part, the consummation of the worlde, and our deliuerance drawing neare, makes Sathan to rage the more in his instruments, knowing his kingdome to be so neare an ende. [marginal gloss: *Reuel. 12.*] And so fare-well for this time.

FINIS.

Newes from Scotland.
Declaring the damnable life of Doctor Fian a notable Sorcerer, who was burned at Edenbrough in Ianuarie laſt.
1 5 9 1.

Which Doctor was regiſter to the deuill, that ſundrie times preached at North Baricke Kirke, to a number of notorious Witches.

With the true examinations of the ſaid Doctor and witches, as they vttered them in the preſence of the Scottiſh king.

Diſcouering how they pretended to bewitch and drowne his Maieſtie in the ſea comming from Denmarke, with ſuch other wonderfull matters as the like hath not bin heard at anie time.

Publiſhed accoʒding to the Scottiſh copie.

Pʒinted foʒ William Wʒight.

Figure 20

APPENDIX B
Original text of News from Scotland

Newes from Scotland,
Declaring the Damnable *life and death of Doctor* Fian
a notable Sorcerer, who was burned at Edenbrough in Ianuary last.
1591.

Which Doctor was regester to the Diuell,
that sundry times preached at North Barrick Kirke, to a number of
notorious Witches.

With the true examinations of the saide Doctor and Witches, as they
vttered them in the *presence of the Scottish King.*

Discouering how they pretended
to bewitch and drowne his Maiestie in the Sea
comming from Denmarke with such
other wonderfull matters as the like
hath not been heard of at
any time.

Published according to the Scottish Coppie.

AT LONDON
Printed for William
Wright.

TO THE READER

THE MANIFOLDE vntruthes which is spread abroade, concerning the detestable actions and apprehension of those Witches wherof this Historye following truely entreateth, hath caused me to publish the same in print: and the rather for that sundrie written Copies are lately dispersed therof, containing, that the said witches were first discouered, by meanes of a poore Pedler trauailing to the towne of Trenent, and that by a wonderfull manner he was in a moment conuayed at midnight, from Scotland to Burdeux in Fraunce (beeing places of no small distance between) into a Marchants Seller there, & after, being sent from Burdeux into Scotland by certaine Scottish Marchants to the Kinges Maiestie, that he discouered those Witches and was the cause of their apprehension: with a number of matters miracu / lous and incredible: All which in truthe are moste false. Neuertheles to satisfie a number of honest mindes, who are desirous to be enformed of the veritie and trueth of their confessions, which for certaintie is more stranger then the common reporte runneth, and yet with more trueth I haue vndertaken to publish this short Treatise, which declareth the true discourse of all that hath hapned, & aswell what was pretended by those wicked and detestable Witches against the Kinges Maiestie, as also by what meanes they wrought the same.

All which examinations (gentle Reader) I haue heere truelye published, as they were taken and vttered in the presence of the Kings Maiestie, praying thee to accept it for veritie, the same beeing so true as cannot be reproued.

A true discourse,
Of the apprehension of sundrye
Witches lately taken in Scotland: wherof
some are executed, and some are
yet imprisoned.

With a particuler recitall of their examinations,
taken in the presence of the Kinges Maiestie.

GOd by his omnipotent power, hath at al times and daily doth take such care, and is so vigillant, for the weale and preseruation of his owne, that thereby he disapointeth the wicked practises and euil intents of all such as by any meanes whatsoeuer, seeke indirectly to conspire any thing contrary to his holy will: yea and by the same power, he hath lately ouerthrown and hindered the intentions and wicked dealinges of a great number of vngodly creatures, no better then Diuels: who suffering themselues to be allured and inticed by the Diuell whom they serued, and to whome they were pritiatelye sworne: entered into ye detestable Art of witch-craft, which they studied and practised so long time, that in the end they had seduced by their sorcery a number of other to be as bad as themselues: dwelling in the boundes of *Lowthian*, which is a principall shire or parte of *Scotland*, where the Kings Maiestie vseth to make his cheefest residence or abode: and to the end that their detestable wickednes which they priuilye had pretended against the Kings Maiestie, the Commonweale of that Country, with the Nobilitie and subiects of the same, should come to light: God of his vnspeakeable goodnes did reueale and lay it open in very strange sorte, therby to make knowne vnto the worlde, that there actions were contrarye to the lawe of God, and the naturall affection which we ought generallye to beare one to another: the manner of the reuealing wherof was as followeth.

Within the towne of *Trenent* in the Kingdome of *Scotland*, there dwelleth one *Dauid Seaton*, who being deputie Bailiffe in the saide Towne, had a maide seruant called *Geillis Duncane*, who vsed secretly to be absent and to lye foorth of her Maisters house euery other night: this *Geillis Duncane* took in hand to help all such as were troubled or greeued with any kinde of sicknes or infirmitie: and in short space did perfourme manye matters most miraculous, which thinges forasmuch as she began to doe them vpon a sodaine, hauing neuer doon the like before, made her Maister and others to be in great admiracion, and wondred thereat: by meanes wherof the saide *Dauid Seaton* had his maide in some great suspition, that she did not those things by naturall and lawfull wayes, but rather supposed it to be doone by some extraordinary and vnlawfull meanes.

Whervpon, her Maister began to growe very inquisitiue, and examined her which way and by what meanes she were able to perfourme matters of so great importance: whereat she gaue him no answere, neuerthelesse, her Maister to the intent that he might the better trye and finde out the trueth of the same, did with the helpe of others, torment her with the torture of the Pilliwinckes vpon her fingers, which is a greeuous torture, and binding or wrinching her head with a corde or roape, which is a most cruell torment also, yet would she not confesse any thing, whereupon they suspecting that she had beene marked by the Diuell (as commonly witches are) made dilligent search about her, and found the enemies marke to be in her fore crag or foreparte of her throate: which being found, she confessed that all her dooings was doone by the wicked allurements and inticements of the Diuell, and that she did them by witchcraft.

After this her confession, she was committed to prison, where she continued for a season, where immediatly she accused these persons following to be notorious witches, and caused them foorthwith to be apprehended one after an other, vidz. *Agnis Sampson* the eldest Witch of them al, dwelling in Haddington, *Agnes Tompson* of Edenbrough, *Doctor Fian, alias Iohn Cunningham,* maister of the Schoole at Saltpans in Lowthian, of whose life and strange actes, you shall heare more largely in the ende of this discourse: these were by the saide *Geillis Duncane* accused, as also *George Motts* wife dwelling in Saltpans, *Robert Griersonn* skipper, and *Iennit Bandilandis,* with the

Porters wife of Seaton, the Smith at the brigge Hallis with innumerable others in that partes, and dwelling in those bounds aforesaide: of whom some are alreadye executed, the rest remaine in prison, to receiue the doome of Iudgement at the Kings maiesties will and pleasure.

The said *Geillis Duncane* also caused *Ewphame Meealrean* to be apprehended, who conspired and perfourmed the death of her Godfather, and who vsed her art vpon a gentleman being one of the Lords and Iustices of the Session, for bearing good will to her Daughter: she also caused to be apprehended one *Barbara Naper*, for bewitching to death *Archibalde*, last Earle of Angus, who languished to death by witchcraft and yet the same was not suspected, but that he died of so strange a disease, as the Phisition knew not how to cure or remedy the same: but of all other the saide witches, these two last before recited, were reputed for as ciuill honest women as any that dwelled within the Citie of Edenbrough, before they were apprehended. Many other besides were taken dwelling in Lieth, who are detayned in prison, vntill his Maiesties further will and pleasure be known: of whose wicked dooings you shall particularly heare, which was as followeth.

This aforeaside *Agnis Sampson* which was the elder Witch, was taken and brought to Haliciud house before the Kings Maiestie and sundry other of the nobility of Scotland, where she was straitly examined, but all the perswasions which the Kings maiestie vsed to her with ye rest of his counsell, might not prouoke or induce her to confesse any thing, but stood stiffely in the deniall of all that was laide to her charge: whervpon they caused her to be conueied awaye to prison, there to receiue such torture as hath been lately prouided for witches in that country: and forasmuch as by due examination of witchcraft and witches in Scotland, it hath latelye beene found that the Deuill dooth generallye marke them with a priuie marke, by reason the Witches haue confessed themselues, that the Diuell dooth lick them with his tung in some priuy part of their bodie, before hee dooth receiue them to be his seruants, which marke commonly is giuen them vnder the haire in some part of their bodye, wherby it may not easily be found out or seene, although they be searched: and generally so long as the marke is not seene to those which search them, so long the parties that hath the marke will neuer confesse any thing. Therfore by special commaundement this *Agnis Sampson* had all her haire shauen of, in each parte of her bodie, and her head thrawen with a rope according to the custome of that Countrye, beeing a paine most greeuous, which she continued almost an hower, during which time she would not confesse any thing vntill the Diuels marke was found vpon her priuities, then she immediatlye confessed whatsoeuer was demaunded of her, and iustifying those persons aforesaid to be notorious witches.

Item, the saide *Agnis Tompson* was after brought againe before the Kings Maiestie and his Counsell, and being examined of the meetings and detestable dealings of those witches, she confessed that vpon the night of *Allhollon* Euen last, she was accompanied aswell with the persons aforesaide, as also with a great many other witches, to the number of two hundreth: and that all they together went by Sea each one in a Riddle or Ciue, and went in the same very substantially with Flaggons of wine making merrie and drinking by the waye in the same Riddles or Ciues, to the Kerke of North Barrick in Lowthian, and that after they had landed, tooke handes on the land and daunced this reill or short daunce, singing all with one voice.

Commer goe ye before, commer goe ye,
Gif ye will not goe before, commer let me.

At which time she confessed, that this *Geilles Duncane* did goe before them playing this reill or daunce vpon a small Trump, called a Iewes Trump, vntill they entred into the Kerk of north Barrick.

These confessions made the King in a woderful admiration and sent for ye said *Geillis Duncane*, who vpon the like Trump did playe the said daunce before the Kings Maiestie, who in respect of the strangenes of these matters, tooke great delight to bee present at their examinations.

Item, the said *Agnis Tompson* confessed that the Diuell being then at North Barrick Kerke attending their comming in the habit or likenes of a man, and seeing that they tarried ouer long, he at their comming enioyned them all to a pennance, which was, that they should kisse his Buttockes, in signe of duetye to him: which being put ouer the Pulpit barre, euerye one did as he had enioyned them: and hauing made his vngodly exhortations, wherein he did great-lye enveighe against the King of Scotland, he receiued their oathes for their good and true seruice towards him, and departed: which doone, they returned to Sea, and so home againe.

At which time the witches demaunded of the Diuel why he did beare such hatred to the King, who answered, by reason the King is the greatest enemy he hath in the worlde: all which their onfessions and depositions are still extant vpon record.

Item, the saide *Agnis Sampson* confessed before the Kings Maies-tie sundrye thinges which were so miraculous and strange, as that his Maiestie saide they were all extreame lyars, wherat she answered, she would not wishe his Maiestie to suppose her woords to be false, but rather to beleeue them, in that she would discouer such matter vnto him as his maiestie should not any way doubt off.

And therupon taking his Maiestie a little aside, she declared vnto him the verye woordes which passed betweene the Kings Maiestie and his Queene at Vpslo in Norway the first night of their mariage, with their answere eache to other: whereat the Kinges Maiestie won-dered greatlye, and swore by the liuing God, that he beleeued that all the Diuels in hell could not haue discouered the same: acknowl-edging her woords to be most true, and therefore gaue the more credit to the rest which is before declared.

Touching this *Agnis Tompson*, she is the onlye woman, who by the Diuels perswasion should haue entended and put in execution the Kings Maiesties death in this manner.

She confessed that she tooke a blacke Toade, and did hang the same vp by the heeles, three daies, and collected and gathered the venome as it dropped and fell from it in an Oister shell, and kept the same venome close couered, vntill she should obtaine any parte or peece of foule linnen cloth, that had appertained to the Kings Maiestie, as shirt, handkercher, napkin or any other thing which she practised to obtaine by meanes of one *Iohn Kers*, who being attendant in his Maiesties Chamber, desired him for olde acquaintance betweene them, to helpe her to one or a peece of such a cloth as is aforesaide, which thing the said *Iohn Kers* denyed to helpe her too, saying he could not help her too it.

And the said *Agnis Tompson* by her depositions since her apprehension saith, that if she had obtained any one peece of linnen cloth which the King had worne and fouled, she had bewitched him to death, and put him to such extraordinary paines, as if he had beene lying vpon sharp thornes and endes of Needles.

Moreouer she confessed that at the time when his Maiestie was in Denmarke, she being accompanied with the parties before specially named, tooke a Cat and christened it, and afterward bound to each parte of that Cat, the cheefest partes of a dead man, and seuerall ioynts of his bodie, and that in the night following the saide Cat was conueied into the midst of the sea by all these witches sayling in their riddles or Cities as is aforesaide, and so left the saide Cat right before the Towne of Lieth in Scotland: this doone, there did arise such a tempest in the Sea, as a greater hath not beene scene: which tempest was the cause of the perrishing of a Boate or vessell comming ouer from the towne of Brunt Iland to the towne of Lieth, wherein was sundrye Iewelles and riche giftes, which should haue been presented to the now Queen of Scotland, at her Maiesties comming to Lieth.

Againe it is confessed, that the said christened Cat was the cause that the Kinges Maiesties Ship at his comming foorth of Denmarke, had a contrary winde to the rest of his Ships, then being in his companye, which thing was most strange and true, as the Kings Maiestie acknowledgeth, for when the rest of the Shippes had a faire and good winde, then was the winde contrarye and altogither against his Maiestie: and further the saide witche declared, that his Maiestie had neuer come safelye from the Sea, if his faith had not preuailed aboue their ententions.

Moreouer the said Witches being demaunded how the Dwell would vse them when he was in their company, they confessed that when the Diuell did receiue them for his seruants, and that they had vowed themselues vnto him, then he would Carnallye vse them, albeit to their little pleasure, in respect of his colde nature: and would doo the like at sundry other times.

As touching the aforesaide Doctor *Fian, alias Iohn Cunningham*, the examination of his actes since his apprehension, declareth the great subtiltye of the diuell, and therfore maketh thinges to appeere the more miraculous: for being apprehended by the accusation of the saide *Geillis Duncane* aforesaide, who confessed he was their Regester, and that there was not one man suffered to come to the Diuels readinges but onlye he: the saide Doctor was taken and imprisoned, and vsed with the accustomed paine, prouided for those offences, inflicted vpon the rest as is aforesaide.

First by thrawing of his head with a roape, wherat he would confesse nothing.

Secondly, he was perswaded by faire means to confesse his follies, but that would preuaile as little.

Lastly he was put to the most seuere and cruell paine in the world, called the bootes, who after he had receiued three strokes, being enquired if he would confesse his damnable acts and wicked life, his tung would not serue him to speak, in respect wherof the rest of the witches willed to search his tung, vnder which was found two pinnes thrust vp into the head, whereupon the VVitches did laye, *Now is the Charme stinted*, and shewed that those charmed Pinnes were the cause he could not confesse any thing: then was he immediatly released of the bootes, brought before the King, his confession was taken, and his owne hand willingly set ther-vnto, which contained as followeth.

First, that at the generall meetinges of those witches, hee was alwayes preasent: that he was Clarke to all those that were in subiection to the Diuels seruice, bearing the name of witches, that alwaye he did take their othes for their true seruice to the Diuell, and that he wrot for them such matters as the Diuell still pleased to commaund him.

Item, he confessed that by his witchcrafte he did bewitch a Gentleman dwelling neere to the Saltpans, where the said Doctor kept Schoole, onely for being enamoured of a Gentlewoman whome he loued himselfe: by meanes of which his Sorcerye, witchcraft and diuelish practises, he caused the said Gentleman that once in xxiiij. howres he fell into a lunacie and madnes, and so cotinued one whole hower together, and for the veritie of the same, he caused the Gentleman to be brought before the Kinges Maiestie, which was vpon the xxiiij. day of December last, and being in his Maiesties Chamber, suddenly he gaue a great scritch and fell into a madnes, sometime bending himselfe, and sometime capring so directly vp, that his head did touch the seeling of the Chamber, to the great admiration of his Maiestie and others then present: so that all the Gentlemen in the Chamber were not able to holde him, vntill they called in more helpe, who together bound him hand and foot: and suffering the said gentleman to lye still vntill his furye were past, he within an hower came againe to himselfe, when being demaunded of the Kings Maiestie what he saw or did all that while, answered that he had been in a sound sleepe.

Item the said Doctor did also confesse that he had vsed means sundry times to obtain his purpose and wicked intent of the same Gentlewoman, and seeing himselfe disapointed of his intention, he determined by all waies he might to obtaine the same, trusting by coniuring, witchcraft and Sorcery to obtaine it in this manner.

It happened this gentlewoman being vnmaried, had a brother who went to schoole with the said Doctor, and calling his Scholler to him, demaunded if he did lye with his sister, who answered he did, by meanes wherof he thought to obtaine his purpose, and therefore secretlye promised to teach him w'tout stripes, so he would obtain for him three haires of his sisters priuities. at such time as he should spye best occasion for it: which the youth promised faithfullye to perfourme, and vowed speedily to put it in practise, taking a peece of coniured paper of his maister to lappe them in when he had gotten them: and therevpon the boye practised nightlye to obtaine his maisters purpose, especially when his sister was a sleepe.

But God who knoweth the secrets of all harts, and reuealeth all wicked and vngodlye practises, would not suffer the intents of this diuilish Doctor to come to that purpose which he supposed it would, and therefore to declare that he was heauilye offended with his wicked entent, did so woorke by the Gentlewomans owne meanes, that in the ende the same was discouered and brought to light: for she being one night a sleepe, and her brother in bed with her, suddenlye cryed out to her mother, declaring that her Brother would not suffer her to sleepe, wherevpon her mother hauing a quick capacitie, did vehemently suspect Doctor *Fians* entention, by reason she was a witche of her selfe, and therefore presently arose, and was very inquisitiue of the boy to vnderstand his intent, and the better to know ye same, did beat him with sundry stripes, wherby he discouered the trueth vnto her.

The Mother therefore being well practised in witchcrafte, did thinke it most conuenient to meete with the Doctor in his owne Arte, and therevpon tooke the paper from the boy, wherein hee should haue put the same haires, and went to a young Heyfer which neuer had borne Calfe nor gone to the Bull, and with a paire of sheeres, clipped off three haires from the vdder of the Cow, and wrapt them in the same paper, which she againe deliuered to the boy, then willing him to giue the same to his saide Maister, which he immediatly did.

The Schoolemaister so soone as he had receiued them, thinking them indeede to bee the Maides haires, went straight and wrought his arte vpon them: But the Doctor had no sooner doone his intent to them, but presentlye the Hayfer or Cow whose haires they were indeed, came vnto the doore of the Church wherein the Schoole-maister was, into the which the Hayfer went, and made towards the Schoolemaister, leaping and dauncing vpon him, and following him foorth of the church and to what place so euer he went, to the great admiration of all the townes men of Saltpans, and many other who did beholde the same.

The reporte whereof made all men imagine that hee did woorke it by the Dwell, without whom it could neuer haue beene so sufficientlye effected: and thervpon, the name of the said Doctor *Fien* (who was but a very yong man) began to grow so common among the people of Scotland, that he was secretlye nominated for a notable Cuniurer.

All which although in the beginning he denied, and would not confesse, yet hauing felt the pain of the bootes (and the charme stinted, as aforesayd) be confessed all the aforesaid to be most true, without producing anie witnesses to iustifie the same, & thervpon before the kings maiesty he subscribed the sayd confessions with his owne hande, which for truth remaineth vpon record in *Scotland*.

After that the depositions and examinations of the sayd doctor *Fian Alias Cuningham* was taken, as alreadie is declared, with his owne hand willingly set therevnto, hee was by the master of the prison committed to ward, and appointed to a chamber by himselfe, where forsaking his wicked wayes, acknowledging his most vngodly lyfe, shewing that he had too much folowed the allurements and entisements of sathan, and fondly practised his conclusions by coniuring, witchcraft, inchantment, sorcerie, and such like, hee renounced the deuill and all his wicked workes, vowed to leade the life of a Christian, and seemed newly connected towards God.

The morrow after vpon conference had with him, he granted that the deuill had appeared vnto him in the night before, appareled all in blacke, with a white wand in his hande, and that the deuill demaunded of him if hee would continue his faithfull seruice, according to his first oath and promise made to that effect. Whome (as hee then sayd) he vtterly renounced to his face, and sayde vnto him in this manner, *Auoide Satan, auoide,* for I haue listned too much vnto thee, and by the same thou hast vndone mee, in respect whereof I vtterly forsake thee. To whome the deuill answered, *That once ere thou die thou shalt bee mine.* And with that (as he sayde) the deuill brake the white wande, and immediatly vanished foorth of his sight.

Thus all the daie this Doctor *Fian* continued verie solitarie, and seemed to haue care of his owne soule, and would call vppon God, shewing himselfe penitent for his wicked life, neuerthelesse the same night hee founde such meanes, that hee stole the key of the prison doore and chamber in the which he was, which in the night hee opened and fled awaie to the Salt pans, where hee was always resident, and first apprehended. Of whose sodaine departure when the Kings maiestie had intelligence, hee presently commanded diligent inquirie to bee made for his apprehension, and for the better effecting thereof, hee sent publike proclamations into all partes of his lande to the same effect. By meanes of whose hot and harde pursuite, he was agayn taken and brought to prison, and then being called before the kings highnes, hee was reexamined as well touching his departure, as also touching all that had before happened.

But this Doctor, notwithstanding that his owne confession appeareth remaining in recorde vnder his owne hande writing, and the same therevnto fixed in the presence of the Kings maiestie and sundrie of his Councell, yet did hee vtterly denie the same.

Wherevpon the kinges maiestie perceiuing his stubbourne wilfulnesse, conceiued and imagined that in the time of his absence hee had entered into newe conference and league with the deuill his master, and that hee had beene agayne newly marked, for the which hee was narrowly searched, but it coulde not in anie wise bee founde, yet for more tryall of him to make him confesse, hee was commaunded to haue a most straunge torment which was done in this manner following.

His nailes vpon all his fingers were riuen and pulled off with an instrument called in Scottish a *Turkas*, which in England wee call a payre of pincers, and vnder euerie nayle there was thrust in two needels ouer euen up to the heads. At all which tormentes notwithstanding the Doctor neuer shronke anie whit, neither woulde he then confesse it the sooner for all the tortures inflicted vpon him.

Then was hee with all conuenient speed, by commandement, conuaied againe to the torment of the bootes, wherein hee continued a long time, and did abide so many blowes in them, that his legges were crushte and beaten togeather as small as might bee, and the bones and flesh so brused, that the bloud and marrowe spouted forth in great abundance, whereby they were made unseruiceable for euer. And notwithstanding al these grieuous paines and cruell torments hee would not confesse anie thing, so deeply had the deuill entered into his heart, that hee vtterly denied all that which he had before auouched, and woulde saie nothing therevnto but this, that what hee had done and sayde before, was onely done and sayde for feare of paynes which he had endured.

Upon great consideration therefore taken by the Kings maiestie and his Councell, as well for the due execution of iustice vppon such detestable malefactors, as also for example sake, to remayne a terrour to all others heereafter, that shall attempt to deale in the lyke wicked and vngodlye actions, as witchcraft, sorcery, cuniuration, &such lyke, the sayde Doctor *Fian* was soone after araigned, condemned, and adiudged by the law to die, and then to bee burned according to the lawe of that lande, prouided in that behalfe. Wherevpon hee was put into a carte, and beeing first strangled, hee was immediatly put into a great fire, being readie prouided for that purpose, and there burned in the Castle hill of *Edenbrough* on a saterdaie in the ende of Ianuarie last past. 1591.

The rest of the witches which are not yet executed, remayne in prison till farther triall, and knowledge of his maiesties pleasure.

This strange discourse before recited, may perhaps giue some occasion of doubt to such as shall happen to reade the same, and thereby coniecture that the Kings maiestie would not hazarde himselfe in the presence of such notorious witches, least therby might haue insued great danger to his person and the generall state of the land, which thing in truth might wel haue bene feared. But to answer generally to such, let this suffice: that first it is well knowen that the King is the child & seruant of God, and they but seruants to the deuil, hee is the Lords annointed, and they but vesselles of Gods wrath: he is a true Christian, and trusteth in God, they worse than Infidels, for they onely trust in the deuill, who daily serue them, till he haue brought them to vtter destruction. But heereby it seemeth that his Highnesse caried a magnanimious and vndanted mind, not feared with their inchantmentes, but resolute in this, that so long as God is with him, hee feareth not who is against him. And trulie the whole scope of this treatise dooth so plainely laie open the wonderfull prouidence of the Almightie, that if he had not bene defended by his omnipotencie and power, his Highnes had neuer returned aliue in his voiage frõ Denmarke, so that there is no doubt but God woulde as well defend him on the land as on the sea, where they pretended their damnable practise.

FINIS.

APPENDIX C

*Witchcraft Act and Tolbooth Speech
of James the First*

THE WITCHCRAFT ACT OF 1604

One of the first things James did upon being crowned king of England was to set about repealing the Witchcraft Act of 1563 that had been in force for most of the reign of Queen Elizabeth. The history of the civil witchcraft laws in England began with the statute of 1542, passed under the reign of King Henry VIII. This statute was found to be unenforceable and was repealed in 1547. In 1563 Elizabeth brought the witchcraft laws back onto the books in a form somewhat more severe than had existed so briefly under the rule of her father. However, they were not severe enough for James, who, if he had been allowed free action in drafting the new statute, would probably have made every act of magic or witchcraft punishable by death.

The text below is faithful to the original text of the statute. Only the spelling and some of the punctuation have been modernized to make comprehension easier.

*An Act against conjuration, witchcraft and dealing with
evil and wicked Spirits.*
s. Eliz.c16. Be it enacted by the king our sovereign lord of the Lords Spiritual and Temporal and the Commons in this present Parliament

assembled, and by the authority of the same, That the Statute made in the fifth year of the Reign of our late Sovereign lady of the most famous and happy memory Queen Elizabeth, entitled An Act against Conjurations, Enchantments and witchcrafts, be from the Feast of St. Michael the Archangel next coming, for and concerning all Offenses to be committed after the same Feast, utterly repealed.

II. And for the better restraining of said offenses, and more severe punishing the same, be it further enacted by the authority aforesaid, That if any person or persons, after the said feast of Saint Michael the Archangel next coming shall use, practice, or exercise any Invocation, or Conjuration of any evil and wicked spirits, or shall consult, covenant with, entertain, employ, feed or reward any evil and wicked spirit to or for any intent or purpose, or take up any dead man, woman or child out of his or her or their grave, or any other place where the dead body resteth, or the skin, bone, or any other part of any dead person, to be employed or used in any manner of witchcraft, sorcery, charm, or Enchantment; or shall use, practice, or exercise any witchcraft, Enchantment, charm, or sorcery whereby any person shall be killed, destroyed, wasted, consumed, pined, or lamed in his or her body, or any part thereof; then that every such Offender or Offenders, their Aiders and Abettors and Counselors, being of any the said Offenses duly and lawfully convicted and attainted, shall suffer pains of death as a Felon or Felons, and shall lose the privilege and benefit of Clergy and Sanctuary.

III. And further, to the intent that all manner of practice, use, or exercise of Witchcraft, Enchantment, Charm, or Sorcery should be from henceforth utterly avoided, abolished, and taken away, Be it enacted by the authority of this Present Parliament, that if any Person or Persons shall, from and after the said feast of Saint Michael the Archangel next coming, take upon him or them by Witchcraft, Enchantment, Charm, or Sorcery to tell or declare in what place any treasure of Gold or silver should or might be found or had in the earth or other secret places, or where Goods or Things lost or stolen should be found or be come; or to the intent to Provoke any person to unlawful love; or whereby any chattel or Goods of any Person shall be destroyed, wasted, or impaired; or to hurt or destroy any Person in his or her body, although the same be not effected and done: that then all and every such Person and Persons so offending, and being thereof lawfully convicted, shall for the said Offense suffer Imprisonment by the space of one whole year, without bail or mainprize [surety], and once in every quarter of the said year, shall in some market town, upon the market day, or at such time as any Fair shall be kept there, stand openly upon the pillory by the space of six hours, and there shall openly confess his or her error and offense. And if any person or persons being once convicted of the same offenses as is aforesaid, do eftsoons perpetrate and commit the like offense, that then every such Offender, being of the said offenses the second time lawfully and duly convicted and attained as is aforesaid, shall suffer pains of death as a Felon or felons, and shall lose the benefit and privilege of Clergy and Sanctuary: saving to the wife of such person as shall offend in anything contrary to this Act, her title of dower; and also to the heir and Successor of every such person, his or their titles of inheritance, succession, and other Rights, as though no such Attainder of the Ancestor or Predecessor had been made; provided always that if the Offender in any cases aforesaid shall happen to be a Peer of this realm, then his Trial there is to be had by his Peers, as is used in cases of Felony or Treason and not others.

1603–4 in the year of his majesty James Stuart of England and Scotland VI

The Tolbooth Speech of 1591

The original Tolbooth was constructed in Edinburgh in 1501 to house the parliament and courts of justice. A new building replaced it in 1563. It later served as a prison, and was finally torn down in 1817. It was located in what is presently the lower High Street, just a few blocks east of Castle Hill where many of the North Berwick witches were burned.

It was here that James confronted the jury that acquitted Barbara Napier of witchcraft on June 7, 1591. James was furious at the acquittal, which seemed to him to fly in the face of the evidence that he had heard given out of the very mouths of the witches; he also regarded it as an affront to his authority since he had made plain his interest in seeing all the North Berwick witches condemned. He charged the members of the jury with "willful error on assize, acquitting a witch" and later had them all tried on this account.

June 1591 King James' speech to accused jurors:
"For witchcraft, which is a thing grown very common amongst us, I know it to be a most abominable sin, and I have been occupied these three quarters of this year for the sifting out of them that are guilty herein. We are taught by the laws both of God and men that this sin is most odious, and by God's law punishable by death. By man's law it is called *maleficium* or *veneficium,* an ill deed or a poisonable deed, and punishable likewise by death. Now if it be death being practiced against any of the people, I must needs think it to be—at least — the like if it be against the King . . . As for them who think these witchcrafts to be but fantasies, I remit them to be catechized and instructed in these most evident pointes. . . . because I see the pride of these witches and their friends, which cannot be prevented but by mine own presence. And for these witches, whatsoever hath been gotten from them hath been done by me myself; not because I was more wise then others, but because I was not partial, and believed that such a vice did reign and ought to be repressed.

"The thing that moved [the men of the assize] to find as they did, was because they had no testimony but of witches; which they thought not sufficient. By the civil law I know that such infamous persons are not received for witnesses, but in matters of heresy and *lesae majestatis.* For in other matters it is not thought meet, yet in these matters of witchcraft good reason that such be admitted. First none honest man can know these matters; secondly, because they will not accuse themselves; thirdly, because no act which is done by them can be seen.

"Further, I call them witches which do renounce God and yield themselves wholly to the Devil; but when they have recanted and repented, as these have done, then I account them not as witches, and so their testimony sufficient. In this I refer myself to the ministers. Besides, the inquest is to judge of the quality of the testimony and circumstances concerning the same. Also it may be observed that never any of good life were charged with that crime."

BIBLIOGRAPHY

Adler, Margot. *Drawing Down the Moon: Witches, Druids, Goddess-Worshippers and Other Pagans in America Today*. New York: The Viking Press, 1979.

Agrippa, Henry Cornelius. *Three Books of Occult Philosophy* [1533]. Edited and annotated by Donald Tyson. St. Paul, MN: Llewellyn Publications, 1993.

Ahmed, Rollo. *The Black Art* [1936]. Introduction by Dennis Wheatley. London: Arrow Books, 1966.

Anonymous. *Henry Cornelius Agrippa, His Fourth Book of Occult Philosophy*. Translated into English by Robert Turner [1655]. Facsimile edition. Contains *Fourth Book of Occult Philosophy*, *Of Geomancy*, *Magical Elements of Peter de Abano*, *Astronomical Geomancy*, *The Nature of Spirits*, and the *Arbatel of Magick*. London: Askin Publishers, 1978.

Ankarloo, Bengt, and Clark, Stuart. *Witchcraft and Magic in Europe: Ancient Greece and Rome*. Philadelphia, PA: University of Pennsylvania Press, 1999.

Barnstone, Willis (editor). *The Other Bible*. New York: HarperCollins Publishers, 1984.

Barrett, Francis. *The Magus or Celestial Intelligencer, Being A Complete System of Occult Philosophy* [1801]. Facsimile limited edition. New York: Samuel Weiser, no date.

Betz, Hans Dieter (editor). *The Greek Magical Papyri in Translation, Including the Demotic Spells*. Second edition. Volume one: texts. Chicago and London: University of Chicago Press, 1992.

Bores, George. *The Damnable Life and Death of Stubbe Peeter*. London: Edward Venge, 1590.

Carus, Paul. *The History of the Devil and the Idea of Evil* [1900]. New York: Gramercy Books, 1996.

Couliano, Ioan P. *Eros and Magic in the Renaissance* [1984]. Translated by Margaret Cook, foreword by Mircea Eliade. Chicago and London: University of Chicago Press, 1987.

de Givry, Grillot. *Witchcraft, Magic and Alchemy*. Translated by J. Courtenay Locke [1931]. New York: Dover Publications, 1971.

Elworthy, Frederick. *The Evil Eye* [1895]. New York: Collier Books, 1970.

Evans-Wentz, Walter Yeeling. *The Fairy-Faith in Celtic Countries* [1911]. New York: University Books, 1966.

Farrar, Stewart and Janet. *A Witches' Bible: The Complete Witch Handbook*. Contains *Eight Sabbats for Witches* [1981] and *The Witches' Way* [1984] bound together under one cover. Custer, Washington: Phoenix Publishing, 1996.

Frazer, Sir James George. *The Golden Bough: A Study in Magic and Religion*. Abridged edition [1922]. New York: The Macmillan Company, 1951.

Gardner, Gerald B. *The Meaning of Witchcraft* [1959]. Foreword by Leo Louis Martello. New York: Magickal Childe, 1982.

———. *Witchcraft Today* [1954]. Forward by Margaret Murray, preface by Raymond Buckland. New York: Magickal Childe, 1982.

Gesenius, Friedrich Heinrich Wilhelm. *Hebrew and Chaldee Lexicon to the Old Testament Scriptures* [1810–12]. Translated and edited by Samuel Prideaux Tregelles [1846]. New York: John Wiley and Sons, 1890.

Gifford, George. *A Dialogue Concerning Witches and Witchcraftes* [1593]. Shakespeare Association Facsimilies No. 1. London: Oxford University Press, 1931.

Godwin, Joscelyn. *Mystery Religions in the Ancient World*. San Francisco: Harper and Row, 1981.

Graves, Robert. *The White Goddess* [1948]. Amended and enlarged edition. New York: Farrar, Straus and Giroux, 1966.

Guazzo, Francesco Maria. *Compendium Maleficarum* [1608]. Translated by E. A. Ashwin, edited by Montague Summers [1929]. New York: Dover Publications, 1988.

Hansen, Chadwick. *Witchcraft at Salem*. Toronto: Signet Books, 1970.

Hansen, Harold A. *The Witch's Garden* [1976]. Translated from the Danish by Muriel Crofts. Yorke Beach, ME: Samuel Weiser, 1983.

Harrison, G. B. (editor). *King James the First Daemonologie* [1597]. London: John Lane the Bodley Head, 1924.

Keightley, Thomas. *The Fairy Mythology* [1880]. Reprinted under the title *The World Guide to Gnomes, Fairies, Elves and Other Little People*. New York: Avenel Books, 1978.

Kieckhefer, Richard. *Forbidden Rites: A Necromancer's Manual of the Fifteenth Century*. University Park, PA: Pennsylvania State University Press, 1997.

Knox, Ronald. *The Holy Bible* [Old Testament: 1945, New Testament: 1949]. London: Burns and Oates, 1961.

Kramer, Heinrich, and Sprenger, James. *The Malleus Maleficarum* [1486]. Edited and translated by Montague Summers [1928]. New York: Dover Publications, 1971.

Leland, Charles G. *Aradia, or the Gospel of the Witches* [1890]. Custer, Washington: Phoenix Publishing, 1990.

———. *Gypsy Sorcery and Fortune Telling* [1891]. New York: University Books, 1963.

Lethbridge, T. C. *Witches* [1962]. New York: Citadel Press, 1968.

Mackay, Charles. *Extraordinary Popular Delusions and the Madness of Crowds* [1841]. Ware, Hertfordshire: Wordsworth Editions, 1995.

Mannix, Daniel P. *The History of Torture.* New York: Dell Publishing, 1964.

Marwick, Max (editor). *Witchcraft and Sorcery: Selected Readings.* Harmondsworth, Middlesex: Penguin Books, 1970.

Masters, R. E. L. *Eros and Evil: The Sexual Phychopathology of Witchcraft* [1962]. Contains the full text in English translation of *Demoniality* by Ludovico Maria Sinistrari. Baltimore, MD: Penguin Books, 1974.

Mather, Cotton. *Cotton Mather On Witchcraft: Being The Wonders of the Invisible World* [1692]. New York: Bell Publishing Company, no date.

Mathers, Samuel Liddell MacGregor. *The Goetia: The Lesser Key of Solomon the King.* Edited by Aleister Crowley [1904]. Illustrated second edition. York Beach, Maine: Samuel Weiser, 1995.

———. *The Key of Solomon the King* [1888]. Foreword by Richard Cavendish. York Beach, Maine: Samuel Weiser, 1989.

Meyer, Marvin, and Smith, Richard. *Ancient Christian Magic: Coptic Texts of Ritual Power.* New York: Harper Collins Publishers, 1994.

Murray, Margaret A. *The God of the Witches* [1931]. London: Oxford University Press, 1970.

———. *The Witch-cult in Western Europe* [1921]. Oxford: Clarendon Press, 1962.

Oesterreich, Traugott K. *Possession: Demoniacal & Other* [1921]. Translated by D. Ibberson. Reprinted under the title *Possession and Exorcism.* New York: Causeway Books, 1974.

Ovid. *The Fasti, Tristia, Pontic Epistles, Ibis, and Halieuticon of Ovid.* Translated by Henry T. Riley. London: George Bell and Sons, 1881.

Parrinder, Geoffrey. *Witchcraft, European and African* [1958]. London: Faber and Faber, 1965.

Peel, Edgar, and Southern, Pat. *The Trials of the Lancashire Witches: A Study of Seventeenth-Century Witchcraft*. Newton Abbot, Devon: David and Charles, Publishers, 1972.

Philostratus. *The Life of Apollonius of Tyana*. Translated by F. C. Conybeare. Two volumes. Cambridge, MA: Harvard University Press, 1912.

Remy, Nicolas. *Demonolatry* [1595]. Translated by E. A. Ashwin, edited by Montague Summers. London: John Rodker, 1930.

Robbins, Rossell Hope. *The Encyclopedia of Witchcraft and Demonology*. London: Spring Books, 1959.

Scot, Reginald. *The Discoverie of Witchcraft* [1584]. Introduction by Montague Summers [1930]. New York: Dover Publications, 1972.

Scott, George Ryley. *The History of Capital Punishment*. London: Ben's Books, 1950.

Scott, Sir Walter. *Demonology and Witchcraft: Letters Addressed to J. G. Lockhart, Esq.* Second edition [1830]. New York: Bell Publishing Company, 1970.

Seligmann, Kurt. *The History of Magic*. Originally published under the title *The Mirror of Magic*. New York: Pantheon Books, 1948.

Skeat, Walter W. *An Etymological Dictionary of the English Language*. Oxford: Clarendon Press, 1882.

Smith, Charlotte Fell. *John Dee: 1527–1608*. London: Counstable and Company, 1909.

Spottiswoode, John. *History of the Church and State of Scotland* [1655]. Two volumes. Edinburgh, 1851.

Starkey, Marion L. *The Devil In Massachusetts: A Modern Enquiry Into the Salem Witch Trials* [1949]. New York: Doubleday & Company (Anchor Books edition), 1969.

Summers, Montague. *A Popular History of Witchcraft* [1937]. New York: Causeway Books, 1973.

———. *Geography of Witchcraft* [1926]. Secaucus, NJ: The Citadel Press, 1973.

———. *The History of Witchcraft and Demonology* [1926]. Castle Books, 1992.

———. *The Werewolf* [1933]. New York: Bell Publishing Company, 1966.

———. *Witchcraft and Black Magic* [1945]. New York: Causeway Books, 1974.

Tyson, Donald. *Tetragrammaton*. St. Paul, MN: Llewellyn Publications, 1995.

Wedeck, Harry E. *A Treasury of Witchcraft*. New York: Philosophical Library, 1961.

Weyer, Johann. *On Witchcraft: an abridged translation of Johann Weyer's De praestigiis daemonum*. Edited by Benjamin G. Kohl and H. C. Erik Midelfort, from the Latin edition of 1583. Asheville, NC: Pegasus Press, 1998.

INDEX

ILLUSTRATION SOURCES

The modernized texts are based on my copy of the 1924 Bodley Head edition of King James the First Daemonologie, to which the tract Newes From Scotland, declaring the Damnable Life and death of Doctor Fian is appended. According to its editor, G. B. Harrison, these works are "reprinted line for line and page for page" from the original 16th century texts. The Bodley Head edition was published jointly by John Lane the Bodley Head Ltd., London, and by E. P. Dutton and Company, New York.

All of the woodcuts used to illustrate this book were selected from the same historical period during which the book was written, as nearly as this was possible. Where necessary for clarity I have cleaned and enhanced the images, but their contents have not been altered.

Illustrations 1, 14, 15, 16, 17, and 18 are to be found in the 1924 Bodley Head edition of King James the First Daemonologie, published by John Lane the Bodley Head Ltd., London, and E. P. Dutton, New York, in 1924.

Illustrations 3, 5, 6, 7, 8, 9, 10, 11 and 13 are to be found in Picture Book of Devils, Demons and Witchcraft by Ernst and Johanna Lehner, published by Dover Publications in 1971.

Illustration 2 is to be found in the first volume (p. 597) of Heinrich Cornelius Agrippa's two volume collection of works, Opera omnia, which bears no date but was first published around the year 1600. This Latin work was reproduced in facsimile in two volumes by Georg Olms Verlag of Hildesheim and New York in 1970.

Illustration 4 is found on p. 244 of the Discoverie of Witchcraft by Reginald Scot, first published 1584. The 1972 Dover Publications edition is a reprint of the 1930 edition of John Rodker, London.

Illustration 12 is from Olaus Magnus's Historia de gentibus septentrionalibus, 1555. It is reproduced on the second unnumbered plate following page 200 of A Treasury of Witchcraft by Harry E. Wedeck, published in 1961 by Philosophical Library, New York.

Illustration 19 is found on page 131 of the second volume of Charles Mackay's Memoirs of Extraordinary Popular Delusions and the Madness of Crowds, published in its Third Edition in 1856 by G. Routledge & Co., London. Mackay derived it from page 26 of the first volume of the Pictorial Edition of the Works of Shakspere by Charles Knight, published in 8 volumes in 1839. Knight's version is a redrawing of a woodcut in the Praxis criminis persequendi by Millaeus, published at Paris in 1541. This woodcut appears as the fifth plate following page 128 of Daniel P. Mannix's The History of Torture, published in 1964 by Dell Publishing Company, New York.

Illustration 20 forms the title page of the first edition of Newes from Scotland, published in 1592 (not 1591 even though this date appears on the page). It is to be found on the Internet at the Web site of Edward H. Thompson (http://homepages.tesco. net/~eandcthomp/newes.htm), and on several other Internet sites.

TO WRITE TO THE AUTHOR

If you wish to contact the author or would like more information about this book, please write to the author in care of Llewellyn Worldwide Ltd. and we will forward your request. Both the author and publisher appreciate hearing from you and learning of your enjoyment of this book and how it has helped you. Llewellyn Worldwide Ltd. cannot guarantee that every letter written to the author can be answered, but all will be forwarded. Please write to:

Donald Tyson
⁒ Llewellyn Worldwide
2143 Wooddale Drive
Woodbury, MN 55125-2989

Please enclose a self-addressed stamped envelope for reply,
or $1.00 to cover costs. If outside the U.S.A., enclose
an international postal reply coupon.

Many of Llewellyn's authors have websites with additional information and resources. For more information, please visit our website at http://www.llewellyn.com.